Nothing
Makes
You
Free

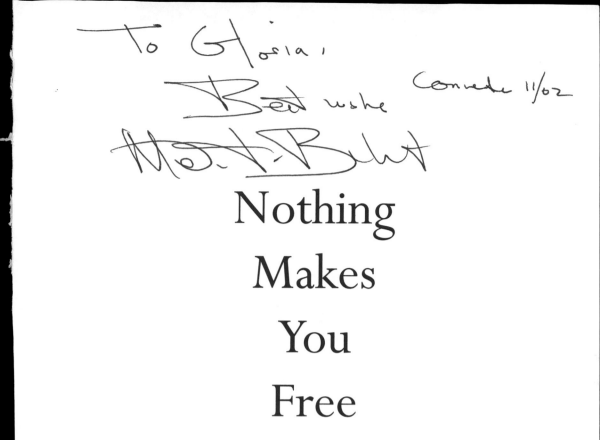

To Gloria,
Best wishe Comrade 11/02
M.J. Bukiet

Nothing

Makes

You

Free

Writings by Descendants of Jewish Holocaust Survivors

Edited by Melvin Jules Bukiet

W. W. Norton & Company

New York London

Since this page cannot legibly accommodate all the copyright notices, pages 391–94 constitute an extension of the copyright page.

The text of this book is composed in Perpetua with the display set in Perpetua
Composition by Molly Heron
Manufacturing by Maple-Vail Book Manufacturing Group
Book design by Chris Welch
Production manager: Julia Druskin

Library of Congress Cataloging-in-Publication Data
Nothing makes you free : writings by descendants of Jewish Holocaust survivors / edited by Melvin Jules Bukiet.
p. cm.
ISBN 0-393-05046-7
1. Children of Holocaust survivors, Writings of. 2. Holocaust, Jewish (1939–1945)—Fiction. 3. Holocaust survivors—Biography. 4. Holocaust, Jewish (1939–1945)—Influence—Fiction. 5. Children of Holocaust survivors—Biography. 6. Jewish fiction—Translations into English. I. Bukiet, Melvin Jules.

PN6071.H713 N68 2002
808.8'0358—dc21   2001055863

W. W. Norton & Company, Inc., 500 Fifth Avenue, New York, N.Y. 10110
www.wwnorton.com

W. W. Norton & Company Ltd., Castle House, 75/76 Wells Street, London W1T 3QT

1 2 3 4 5 6 7 8 9 0

To: Madelaine, Louisa, and Miles,
also known as Mindel, Chaya Leah, and Meier

Contents

Part II

Part III

Introduction

A rock drops into the center of a pond. Ripples spread. Make that a flaming comet crashing into a boiling tar pit. A tidal wave ensues. Consider the Holocaust as that first event. Call the pit "Europe."

The Jews, poor schnooks, believed that Europe was a temporary residence they occupied while awaiting return to the true Holy Land. Until that day of redemption arrived, however, they lived quietly: working, studying, making sure their chickens were kosher. Most engaged in daily worship to the God who drove them from Zion into Babylonia, Rome, Spain, medieval Mittel-Europa and, finally, the fertile Polish countryside. Even the few city sophisticates who read and wrote for newspapers breathed exile. So occasionally a drunken peasant cudgeled a Jewish tot, who died. So there were blood libels. Pogroms. What did you expect? This was Eastern Europe where—despite Marx, Rothschild, and Freud; Kafka, Chagall, and Schoenberg—not much had changed since the Middle Ages. Life was precarious, yet it went on as it had in ages past. How could these people dream that here, in their own time, centuries of fruitfulness and multiplication would come to nothing?

A friend of my family grew up in Oswiecim, a village thirty miles west of Cracow which, due to the German tongue's inability to pronounce the Slavic syllables, came to be known as Auschwitz. He played there with the other children amidst the groves of birch trees where a world of Jews would utter their last prayers before a bullet . . . before a knife . . . before a brick . . . before a doctor, a butcher, a baker . . . before the gas.

Then came D-Day, the Red Army, German surrender. Concentration camps were "liberated," and approximately one hundred thousand Jews were released from Hell. Many more emerged from years of hiding in terror.

What a strange world they inhabited. Their homes were burnt, their culture destroyed, their God silent. It was a world without very young or very old people, because most of those who survived were between twenty and thirty and had been deemed fit for work, temporarily. Perhaps most bizarrely, the survivors' was a world without parents, a world of orphans.

Like their literal mothers, their mameloshen, Yiddish, was now as dead as Sanskrit. That was appropriate, because the survivors were ghosts floating across the devastated landscape. Much congratulatory celebration is made these days of their vigor, their character, and their mere existence, but let's keep one terrible truth on the table. In fact, Hitler won. The Jews lost, badly. The continent is morally, culturally, essentially Judenrein. Thus, the survivors were expected to remain unobtrusive supernatural phenomena, not disturbing the living with the clanking of their chains and their alarming stories. In return, a guilty world tried to salvage its conscience by granting passports to the United States and other nations to those whose entry they barred a decade earlier.

For the most part, the survivors obliged. They pretended to live normal lives, to find work, pay rent, eat dinner. A few like Elie Wiesel and Primo Levi chronicled their individual and communal catastrophe in print, but most lived as privately abroad as they had in their destroyed homes. This was the 1950s and the Holocaust had not entered the public consciousness as it would thirty years later. But the survivors could not wait to be discovered, so the tailor in Borough Park, the builder in New Jersey, the housewife in Miami, and their co-equals in Tel Aviv and London and Melbourne told their stories to each other over games of gin. They also told them to the only others who had no choice but to listen: their children.

Despite every possible attempt to obliterate them from the face of the earth, these phantoms had returned to the land of the living, and that meant meeting and mating and bearing squawling infants who wouldn't have stood a chance one single decade earlier. Whether they remained in Europe as eighteenth-generation Germans or were born in the United States as first-generation Americans, within Holocaust circles the children are known as the Second Generation.

In a way, life has been even stranger—though infinitely less perilous—for the chidren than the parents. If a chasm opened in the lives of the First Generation, they could nonetheless sigh on the far side and recall the life Before, but for the Second Generation there is no Before. In the beginning was Auschwitz. On the most literal level, their fathers would not have met their mothers if not for the huge dislocations that thrust the few remnants of European Jewry into contact with spouses they would never have otherwise encountered except for DP camps or in the twentieth-century Diaspora. The Second Generation's very existence is dependent on the whirlwind their parents barely escaped.

No one who hasn't grown up in such a household can conceive it, while every 2G has something in common. Every one of these happy or unhappy families knows a variation of the same unhappy story. Of course, some survivors spoke incessantly of the Holocaust while others never mentioned it. Of those who didn't speak, some were traumatized while others hoped to protect their offspring from knowledge of the tree of evil.

The Second Generation will never know what the First Generation does in its bones, but what the Second Generation knows better than anyone else is the First Generation. Other kids' parents didn't have numbers on their arms. Other kids' parents didn't talk about massacres as easily as baseball. Other kids' parents had parents.

Other kids' parents loved them, but never gazed at their offspring as miracles in the flesh. Most of us weren't born in mangers, but we might as well have been. Other kids weren't considered a retroactive victory over tyranny and genocide.

So what do you do with this cosmic responsibility? You were born in the fifties so you smoked dope and screwed around like everyone else. But your rebellion was pretty halfhearted, because how could you rebel against these people who endured such loss? Compared to them, what did you have to complain about?

How do you deal with it? As adults, many 2G's took up the "helping" occupations and became shrinks or social workers while others became involved with Jewish charities. And if you were a writer, you wrote.

Lord knows, you weren't alone, because along with your personal maturity the Holocaust has ripened, and the floodgates to exploration of this awful era opened. Why it didn't happen immediately after the war, I don't know. Understandably, people didn't want to think about it, but a delayed-action fuse eventually ignites and we are witnessing the explosion right now.

The comet hits at six million miles per hour and the waves spread. From the primary sources of the First Generation to the Second Generation it has swelled to include other Jews (Saul Bellow's *Mr. Sammler's Planet,* Cynthia Ozick's *The Shawl*) and then non-Jews (John Hersey's *The Wall* and William Styron's putative Holocaust book, *Sophie's Choice,* followed by Pat Conroy's *Beach Music* and Carribean writer Caryl Phillips's *The Nature of Blood*). Over the last few years, I've noticed that virtually every book I've read—an Australian novel about a millennial cult in the outback, a Brazilian novel about gangsters and gem dealers, a gay cross-dressing fantasia, a noirish portrayal of the movie business, a semi-memoir of a young black poet in an L.A. slum—to greater or lesser extent involve the Holocaust. Some are good books, some are bad, but that's not the point. What's important is that the Holocaust has become a talismanic touchstone that every writer must genuflect toward. Try an experiment. Take every tenth book of fiction off the shelves of your local bookstore. A few will actually be about the Holocaust, but count how many others mention, just mention, in passing, as a metaphor, the H word as a kind of seal of literary seriousness. My guess is seven out of ten.

The weird thing is that, contravening all physical laws, the waves do not diminish. They build upon each other, getting larger rather than smaller as history itself recedes. No other event of our time has attained this emblematic significance. The only thing one can compare it to in terms of its lasting effect may be the French Revolution and subsequent ascendance of Napoleon. Fifty years after Waterloo, Raskolnikov tacks a lithograph of the emperor onto his garret wall in St. Petersburg and the world understands why; that image represents the heights and the depths of human experience far beyond its native grounds.

To the extent that the two greatest and most basic subjects for writing have always been life and death—what it feels like to be alive and what it feels like to fear death—the Holocaust offers the greatest opportunity of our era. Indeed, hardly a week goes by without some other aspect of the Holocaust in the news. It's transcended the domain of history and become mythic. And no particular myth, either. It's a historic Rorschach blot: people see in it what they wish. If you're depressive, you can justify despair. If you're hopeful, you can find redemption. If you're stupid, you can discern the triumph of the spirit.

For a writer, it's irresistible. So irresistible that it recently led to the grotesque fraud of "Benjamin Wilkomirski," whose book *Fragments* purported to be a memoir of his childhood in a concentration camp, but turned out to be a fiction by a man who appears genuinely to believe in his self-adopted identity. This is victim envy, survivor-wannabeness at its grossest. Yet the Wilkomirski case reflects something larger than one disturbed consciousness. People can't keep their fingers off the Holocaust.

In the midst of this festive free-for-all, the 2G's occupy a special place. Whatever wisdom others bring to it comes from the heart and head, but for us it's genetic. To be shabbily proprietary, we own it. Our parents owned it, and they gave it to us. Just as John Quincy Adams and Ken Griffey Jr. followed in their parents' footsteps, we go into Shoah business. I'd like to tell everyone from the Bellows and the Ozicks to the Styrons and the Wilkomirskis, "Bug off. Find your own bad news," but no one can legislate artistic imperative, and perhaps no one should. Yet if the history really is ours, then the mythos is public domain. Still, even here, we retain primacy. We have been given an obscene gift, a subject of predetermined value that no one can deny. It's our job to tell the story, to cry, "Never Forget!" despite the fact that we can't remember a thing.

"Memory" is the mantra of all the institutions that reckon with the Holocaust, but memory is an inaccurate term. For anyone who wasn't *there,* on either side of the barbed wire, Jew or German, thinking about the Holocaust is really an act of the imagination. All we know is how little we know.

Nonetheless you've got this . . . event, the Holocaust, always capitalized. Actually, I don't like the word. "Holocaust" was an uncommon common noun until the 1940s, but since then it became unique and almost immediately thereafter debased by overuse. For most of those fifty years it referred to events in Europe, and yet, because of its potency, it's been wrongly adopted for other localities, Rwanda, Cambodia, the Balkans, the slums. Because of this, I prefer a more singular term. "Shoah" means essentially the same thing as "Holocaust" in Hebrew, but that seems wrong, too, because it comes from a different culture. So from here on I'll say,

"Khurbn," the Yiddish for disaster, which, branded with "the," can refer to no other khurbn.

The first thing you learn is not to try to explain it. Asking why makes you crazy. Of course, there was a sequence of historical causes and effects, World War I, the depression, the rise of and reaction to communism, church anti-Semitism. But those are insufficient. The only reason the Germans killed the Jews was because they wanted to. Why? Because. Because they were poor or because they were rich. Because they were clannish and isolated or because they wore top hats and attended the opera. Because their tailors and seamstresses were spiritual, unworldly wraiths or because their bankers and journalists insidiously plotted to dominate the world from within the corridors of power. Because they did not believe in the common deity or because they did believe in their own tribal God. Because they drank the blood of Christian children. Because, like Everest, they were there. Because.

The Khurbn is a black hole that devours light. The more illumination cast upon it, the less you see.

Thus, the second thing you learn is that you can't realistically render it. The one picture I have of my grandparents is a formal family portrait taken in the mid-1920s and sent to relatives in America. In it, a stiff man in a wide-brimmed black hat stares uncomfortably at the camera while an attractive young woman sits with a baby on her lap. The baby, my father, is blurry. Other children and other relatives fill out the frame. I've heard stories about these people's lives; I will not turn their deaths into fiction.

Still, one yearns to attribute meaning to the blurry baby, as if his motion at the moment of the shutter's opening will keep him moving twenty years later and keep him alive to bear me to describe his motion. In this direction, however, lies vile theodicy.

But if you can't place yourself in the mass grave, you can't quite drag yourself out of it, either. You're left with the existential dilemma described by the French thinker Alain Finkielkraut in *The Imaginary Jew*. He says: "I inherited a suffering to which I had not been subjected, for without having to endure oppression, the identity of the victim was mine. . . . The allotment was inescapable: for them, utter abandonment and anonymous death, and for their spokesperson, sympathy and honor . . . I owed to the bond of blood this intoxicating power to confuse myself with the martyrs . . . no trace of them remains, except perhaps my taste for poppy seed bread, scorching hot tea, and the way I hold sugar in my teeth rather than let it dissolve."

In other words, how do you cope when the most important events of your life occurred before you were born? What does this do to your sense of time? Of authenticity? As they were ghosts in history, you're a ghost in your own safe little suburban bedroom with cowboy lampshades. All you know is that you've received a tainted inheritance, secondhand knowledge of the worst event in history. In fact, you see only the most benign effects of the Khurbn, because, by definition, this is as good as it gets. The manifold imaginary offspring of the six million actual dead do not have the Second Generation's opportunities. Perhaps their books are buried on the shelves in some library of the deceased, but we don't have a card to that library.

The library we know by heart is our parents. Maybe some don't fit this image, but I think of all the men as short, round, bald, and tough as spikes and the women as plump with dyed hair, tough as spikes. I remember one "gathering" many years ago where then Vice President George H. Bush was addressing about five thousand survivors and their offspring in front of the Washington Monument. I left, because of my politics, and sat in the first of several dozen waiting buses. One elderly woman had preceded me, and a few others followed us. For them, leaving the Mall was a matter of practicality; the first bus filled would be the first to depart.

Unfortunately, there was a problem. The first bus had been reserved for VIPs. As soon as the speech ended and a multitude of survivors swarmed toward the buses, an officious young woman told us we had to vacate the vehicle. We who had been so clever would be consigned to the back of the line. The elderly woman in front of me started bitching. She was saying things like, "Hitler didn't beat us, and you won't," and I egged her on. We were ready to link arms and go limp. I could see the bad press take shape in twenty-point type in my mind: "Survivors Arrested in Protest at Washington Monument."

Eventually, authority caved in and told us we could have our damn bus, but the elderly woman was still muttering and cursing, "How dare they?" As the bus looped around the Mall, I leaned forward and said, "But we had fun, didn't we?" and she gave me a smile as bright as sunshine. We had never met before, but we knew each other.

Later that night, I spoke to the woman in New York I'd eventually marry. Not a child of survivors, she assumed we'd be wearing sackcloth and ashes and delicately asked how things were going. I think I shocked her when I crowed, "We're having a great time." Knowledge of death imparts appreciation for life.

Knowledge of death also imparts an unusual kind of resignation. In the forthcoming *Encyclopedia of Holocaust Literature,* there are 167 entries. Three quarters of the people represented are still alive, but of the forty dead, at least half a dozen were suicides. Larry Amsel, a psychiatrist who studies suicide, says that the probability of this percentage of suicides occurring out of a random sampling may exceed a billion. The natural supposition is that the reason Jean Amery, Tadeusz Borowski, Paul Celan, Jerzy Kosinski, Piotr Rawicz, and, perhaps, Primo Levi killed themselves was because of severe depression traceable to the war; but I prefer to think otherwise. It's simply that when life becomes unbearable because of debilitating disease or scandal or whatever, then death is not fearsome. These people are so intimate with mortality that at a certain point they can shrug and say, "It's time."

When friends he loves die, my father calls me and says, "Let's go to the funeral," and we do. That's it. No fuss, no bother. His tear ducts have been cauterized. When three presidents of the Cracow Society died in the space of a year and my uncle was asked to assume the post, he said, "It's a dangerous job." Life is a dangerous job.

That same uncle tells about a moment during the liquidation of the Cracow ghetto. Two groups of about fifty men each stood side by side, the first deemed *Arbeiter* or workers, the second, including my uncle, *Menschen*. He didn't know why, but my uncle just felt that it would be better to be a worker, so he moved from one group to the other, a matter of a few feet.

Just then Kommandant Amon Goeth arrived. He asked the German in charge what the two groups were, listened, pointed to the menschen, and said, "Weg mit dieser scheisse." This means, "Get rid of this shit." The men were marched into an alley and shot.

But Goeth must have noticed a Bukiet family blur and turned to my uncle and said, "Weren't you with the other group?"

"No," my uncle replied.

"What sort of worker are you?"

"Um . . . a mechanic."

"Where do you work?"

My uncle remembered a mechanic's shop nearby and named it. Still suspicious, Goeth looked at my uncle and said, "If you're lying to me, I'll hang you tomorrow."

So my uncle thought—and here's the punch line—"I'd rather be hung tomorrow than shot today."

Were the novelists and poets and dramatists and cartoonists of the Second Generation born writers or were we compelled to write by our proximity to extremity? I don't know. I only know that these are the stories I heard at the dinner table. Thus, rendering life with people who are capable of saying, "I'd rather be hung tomorrow than shot today. Pass the salt," becomes one's most enduring subject.

Throughout history, there have been two parallel, millennia-long strands of Jewish responses to catastrophe. First, there is a tone of mournful lamentation that echoes from the psalms of the Bible through medieval poetry through the somber, sober reflections of Elie Wiesel and his kin. Yet off on the side, there was always an unpleasant, hectoring voice of shrieking hysteria that came from the prophets, God-haunted maniacs on hilltops, and segued into the

Hasidic messianists who tossed away their worldly possessions every time another fraud promised redemption. Opposed to wishful-thinking realpolitik Zionists who aspired to salvation on earth, they were so doubtful of their era's ability to bring forth deliverance that they could only believe in redemption in connection with the End of Days.

Fifty some years ago, the End of Days arrived for one third of the Jews on earth. Nonetheless, the literature of the Khurbn, with few exceptions until now—notably Jerzy Kosinski's *The Painted Bird* and the ferocious *This Way for the Gas, Ladies and Gentlemen,* by Tadeusz Borowski, a gentile—has not been written in the voice of lunacy and apocalyptic frenzy. That voice explodes with renewed vigor in the Second Generation, whose fury at what they have been denied—history, deity, grandparents—comes out on the page.

Two traits distinguish the Second Generation from the canonical Elie Wiesels and Primo Levis of the Khurbn syllabus. The first difference is stylistic. Wiesel and the (mostly) men who have written about the war emerged from a tradition of rabbinical tale telling; their works, compelled by the enormity of their experience, reflect that older, more traditional mode, whereas the Second Generation for the most part came of cultural age by reading Joyce, Proust, and the great shapers of modern literature. Their work thereby has a manifestly contemporary texture that could not exist in any other era.

Also, a matter of genre, even when the First Generation claim they're writing fiction, their pages usually bestride memoir. They have no need to imagine; we have no option but to imagine.

In imagining, a particular tone bleeds through in all but the mildest of Second Generation writers. Though often literarily exuberant and sometimes "experimental," they are viciously unredemptive, scoured of weakness as they look atrocity straight in the face with barely contained rage. Despite today's insipid fetish for "healing," frequently engaged in by the social workers of the Second Generation, the writers heal nothing and comfort no one with their work. Healing is another word for forgetting. Healing is what movies like *Life Is Beautiful* and *Schindler's List* seek—the former with gratuitous vulgarity, the latter with insidious skill—as they concoct a spurious ray of light to falsely illumine the night. Instead of closure, the writers prefer the open wound. And should that wound threaten to close, they rip out the stitches. As a young German Jewish writer provocatively titled an essay about tourism and voyeurism, "See Auschwitz and Die."

Sorrow comes from recollection, outrage from reflection. Then, recollecting fury, it grows. The Second Generation's work is angrier than the First's. Not for them the celebration of European Yiddishkeit. Not for them the God of their fathers. God? Who's that? Never met Him. Or worse, if God reveals Himself at moments of vastness—what Arthur A. Cohen called "Tremendum"—what more aptly qualifies than Auschwitz, 1944? If God appeared, He was wearing a brown shirt.

"If." There are a lot of if's in this essay. That's because the only thing the Second Generation knows is the imponderable, which means that we don't know anything and distrust anyone with an answer. The wonderfully equalizing thing about the Khurbn is that it denies all wisdom, throws everyone it touches into the abyss of ignorance.

On the other hand, the only tenderness in the writing of the Second Generation is reserved for those we do know, our parents. Yet even they are portrayed without sentimentality, but that's a testament to their humanity. Some may be noble; most aren't. It doesn't make a difference. If you are a minor person, shabby, greedy, or vulgar, it still doesn't mean that the Germans should slaughter your mother.

No one—not a German and not a Jew—who isn't a child of survivors can begin to understand the bottomless depths of rage inside those born into the Khurbn. No one can understand how we can hold collectively guilty not only the octogenarian perpetrators but the rest of the nation that saw nothing for the twelve-year reign of the Thousand Year Reich, and their children and their children's children and the yet unborn tainted by their German blood. This is, I know, by any moral standards and by any sane logic, wrong. But because the pure flame of undying hatred is wrong doesn't mean that it isn't true, and if this reflects a deep flaw in my soul, so be it. They put it there. Remember, no particular moral stature adheres to suffering and less so to being born of those who suffered. Jews are different since 1945. Not that the Chosen People were especially saintly Before. We had our share of horse thieves as well as rabbis—generally I prefer the company of the former—but there was a sense of passive acquiescence to circumstance that is no longer. Now, we are strident. Now, we rub the world's nose in our misery. Go to our museums. Go see our movies. Go read our books. Look at what you did. Behold.

P.S. 108016 is the secret personal identification number for my bank account. 108016 is also the code to enter my computer and answering machine at work. Whenever I need a number in this age that compels them, I use 108016. A few years ago, I presented a novel I wrote to German Chancellor Kohl, and signed it "108016." Herr Kohl looked baffled; he probably thought it was my phone number. Indeed, it would be if I could make the arrangement. After a journalist chronicled the encounter, Herr Kohl might have called me, but the only number he had was the only number I had: 108016.

It would be disingenuous for me to claim that those six digits were the first I knew. Presumably I could count, but the artless aniline blue of 108016 tattooed on my father's forearm was an abiding sign of the past in our present. It was his alone and then, as much as such a thing can ever be, it became mine, and now it's yours; we can *share*.

A Note on Method and Category

"Writings by Descendants of Jewish Holocaust Survivors"—almost every word in the subtitle to this book requires an explanation.

Writings: For reasons of space and textual coherence, writings here means prose, primarily fiction and memoir. At first, I wanted to include just about any representation of the Holocaust and its aftermath from fields as far apart as daily journalism and high theoretical literary criticism. For example, as editorial page director of the *New York Post,* the late Eric Breindel's columns passionately defended a strong right-wing Israeli position; this must have had some basis in Mr. Breindel and his family's personal history. Likewise, Bella Brodzki's essays on the idea of exile must have emerged from the fact that Ms. Brodzki grew up with her parents who grew up during World War II. I also considered a sweet essay about the grandfather he never knew by Menachem Rosensaft, founding chairman of the

International Network of Children of Jewish Holocaust Survivors, and I wanted straight-out nonfiction on the assumption that, for example, Daniel Jonah Goldhagen's *Hitler's Willing Executioners* and Leon Wieseltier's *Kaddish,* which present themselves as objective examinations of, respectively, funereal history and funerary ritual, were impelled by their authors' lives and experiences. I don't psychologize, but there must be a reason why intellectually minded children of survivors choose to spend their professional lives writing about German anti-Semitism or Jewish death customs. And yet those writers and many others in just about any realm of endeavor, be it history, psychology, anthropology, or whatever, are not here, because the implicit question that this book asks—and aspires to reveal some answer to—is how atrocity gets filtered through imagination.

Yet even within that more limited realm, I couldn't approach comprehensiveness. I originally conceived of including reproductions of visual art (Melissa Gould, Meir Appelfeld), or snippets of film scripts (Abraham Ravett, Chantal Akerman), or even architectural blueprints (Daniel Liebeskind) or musical notations (Yehuda Poliker and Yakov Gilad). Lastly, and well within my chosen boundaries, I thought of poetry (Joel Lewis, Regina Weinreich) and theater (Lisa Lipkin, Deb Filler), but didn't include those either because editing is not a neutral pursuit; it inevitably reflects its editor's nature. I am a novelist and did not feel adequate to making value judgments about either theater or poetry. I respect and appreciate them, but they're just not mine. Those forms of response to this history remain to be collected by someone else.

Descendants: Although I've made free use of the term "Second Generation" in the Introduction because it's become a term of art, it's not strictly accurate any more. As time passes, the stories and sensibility created by the Khurbn are passed down through further generations. In most cases it is diluted, but in others it remains strong, so there is at least one writer here whose grandparents were survivors, as well as one who is, astonishingly, *fourth* generation.

A thornier question has to do with one's date of birth. Imagine a writer born on May 7, 1945, the day before World War II officially ended in Europe. Not that so many women were pregnant in the winter of 1944, but imagine one. Is that hypothetical child a survivor or a child of survivors? Strictly speaking, he or she would be both, but the essence of this book is to explore the inherited rather than the experienced. Obviously such a child would have no recollection of one day under German occupation, but in that direction lay a slippery slope. I'm not a developmental psychologist and did not want to have to assert that if you were two years old you were innocently ignorant, but if you were three you might retain a tinge of memory. The Yugoslav writer, Danilo Kis, for example, was born in 1937 and clearly shares the survivor's mentality, but Austrian writer Robert Schindel, born in 1944, is not included either, and neither, most egregiously since he was born in early 1945, is Joseph Berger, whose book *Displaced Persons* chronicles his upbringing among survivors on the Upper West Side. I drew the line at the day the war ended.

Jewish: Again, a question, this time a tormenting, theological one: Who is a Jew? For millennia, a Jew was considered to be someone born of a Jewish mother or someone who converted. Only in our time have some Jews begun to accept patrilineal descent, and so do I. One of the writers in this book had a gentile mother and a Jewish father who was in Auschwitz. This question was easy for me to answer. If your ancestors were Jewish enough for Hitler, you are Jewish enough for me.

Holocaust: Oddly, this most potent word needs no elucidation. Although I've mentioned my ambivalence to the term in the Introduction, it has taken on a specific historical reality that can never be doubted.

Survivors: This may be the most complicated word here. We live in an age in which victimization carries a special weight and is therefore deliberately adopted. So who is a survivor? Obviously, anyone who spent any time in a German extermination, concentration, or labor camp qualifies. Also obviously, anyone in hiding for their lives in the woods in Poland or in an attic in Amsterdam qualifies. But what if you fled eastward, into Russia? Is there a line on the map at, say, the Volga River that, when crossed, makes you a refugee rather than a survivor? I believe so. Certainly such people survived the catastrophe of war, but they were fortunate enough to avoid the catastrophe of the Khurbn.

Of course, this leads to awkward distinctions. I know of two writers, David Lehman and David Curzon, whose parents fled Vienna in 1939. Both of them lost grandparents and both of them identify with this cohort, yet they're not here either, on the assumption that in some way the experience their parents passed down to them was one of escape rather than entrapment. I know this leads to curiosities and inequities, because some who suffered horribly do not fit my definitions while others whose personal experiences were not—on this awful scale—so terrible happen to fit. Nonetheless, again for clarity, and solely for the purposes of this book, I've tried to include only writers with at least one surviving ancestor who spent at least one day between September 1, 1939, and May 8, 1945, under the flag of the twisted cross.

What proof do I have that all these criteria hold true for all of the writers included here? None. Could one of them have changed a date of birth to a later date for reasons of vanity? Yes. Or worse, is it possible that there is a Second Generation Wilkomirski in the table of contents? Yes. I did not ask for photographs of the writers' fathers' forearms. I took people at their word and made literary judgments about their work. In fact, it strikes me that if there is a fraud here, that would be interesting. And yet if it was discovered, I'd excise that person from the next edition, and, if my publisher let me, I'd leave empty pages where the work first appeared.

Lastly, I thank the many people who helped guide me toward writers I might not have otherwise encountered, particularly the non-Americans. I may have forgotten some, for which I apologize, but among those I spoke to are: Marjorie Agosin, Amiel Akaly, Mark Anderson, Uli Baer, Henryk Broder, Elizabeth Bronfen, Janet

Burstein, Alessandro Carrera, Bryan Cheyette, Henry Dasko, Julia Epstein, Sidra deKoven Ezrachi, Moris Farhi, Charles Fenyesi, Eva Forgacz, Monica Garbowska, Konstanty Gebert, Sander Gilman, David Grossman, Henryk Gruenberg, Michael Henry Heim, Elena Lappin, Adam Makkai, Olga Mannheimer, Diane Matza, Tomek Mirkowiecz, Leslie Morris, Anthony Polonsky, Ellen Presser, David Roskies, Judith Serafini-Sauli, Morton Shein, Michael Steinloaf, Susan Suleiman, Laura Susign, Mikos Vija, Andrew Wachtel, James Young, and Froma Zeitlin, as well as some of the translators and writers in this book who led me to others.

There are Jews in every country on earth, and I tried to find and include as many as possible. If I missed any writers whose work is significant, the fault is mine and the book weaker for their absence, as the world is weaker for the absence of the six million. If it's also stronger because of those whose work you are about to read, that's good.

Part I

from *Nightfather*

BY CARL FRIEDMAN

Translated from the Dutch by Arnold and Erica Pomerans

Camp

He never mentions it by name. It might have been Trebibor or Majdawitz, Soblinka or Birkenhausen. He talks about "the camp," as if there had been just one.

"After the war," he says, "I saw a film about the camp. With prisoners frying an egg for breakfast." He slaps his forehead with the palm of his hand. "An egg!" he says shrilly. "In the camp!"

So camp is somewhere where no one fries eggs.

⌁

CAMP IS NOT so much a place as a condition. "I've had camp," he says. That makes him different from us. We've had chicken pox and German measles. And after Simon fell out of a tree, he got a concussion and had to stay in bed for weeks.

But we've never had camp.

~~

MOST OF THE TIME he drops the past participle for convenience. Then he says, "I have camp," as if the situation hadn't changed. And it's true, it hasn't. He still has camp, especially in his face. Not so much in his nose or his ears, although they're big enough, but in his eyes.

~~

I SAW A WOLF in the zoo once, with eyes like that. He was pacing back and forth in his cage, up and down and up and down, to the front and back again. I spent a long time staring at him through the bars.

Full of worry, I went to look for Max and Simon. They were hanging over the railings around the monkey rock, laughing at a baboon throwing pebbles.

"Please, come and look at the wolf," I said, but they weren't interested. Only when I started to cry did Max reluctantly turn away and follow me.

"Well?" he said in a bored voice when we were standing in front of the wolf's cage. "What's the matter with him?"

"He has camp!" I sobbed. Max glanced through the bars.

"Impossible," he said. "Wolves don't get camp."

Then he pulled me by the hand. I had to go back to the monkeys with him.

When we got home and my mother saw my tear-stained cheeks, she asked what had made me unhappy. Max shrugged.

"She isn't big enough yet for the zoo."

Nice

Max is drinking from a puddle. He's lying flat in the mud, sucking the brown water up through a straw.

"What does it taste like?" we ask impatiently. But he shuts his eyes contemptuously and goes on sucking.

"You little pig!" my mother calls from afar. "You'll make yourself sick!"

We have to go inside, even Simon and I, although we haven't had our turn at tasting yet.

During the night, Max complains about feeling sick. He clutches his stomach and groans, "I must have swallowed worms. I can feel them wriggling!"

YOU DON'T GET camp from drinking muddy water. You don't get camp from playing outside without your coat on or from never washing your hands. I don't know how or why my father got camp. Maybe he got it because he's different from most of the people I know. Because he's different, my mother is different, too. And because the two of them are different, Max, Simon, and I are different from ordinary children. At home you don't notice it, but at school you do.

"A MAN FLYING through the air!" The teacher smiles as she bends over my drawing.

"He isn't flying," I tell her, "he's hanging. See, he's dead, his tongue is blue. And these prisoners have to look at him as a punishment. My father is there, too. Here, he's the one with the big ears."

"That's nice," says the teacher.

"It's not," I say. "They're starving and now they have to wait a long time for their soup." But she's already moved on to the next desk.

"Two pixies on a toadstool," she calls out, clapping her hands. "That's really nice!"

In a rage I make great scrawls across my drawing and turn the paper over. What's so nice about a couple of pixies? I draw a whole lot more than two: five in the snow and one on top of the watchtower.

Roll Call

He doesn't have camp only in his face but in his fingers, too. They often drum nervously on the edge of the table or on the arms of his chair.

And he has camp in his feet. In the middle of the night his feet slide out of bed, carrying him down the stairs and through the hallway. We can hear him far away, opening and closing doors without ever finding the peace he's looking for behind any of them.

"Were you on the prowl again last night?" my mother asks when we are at breakfast. He nods. She puts her hand over his. "Ephraim," she says, "Ephraim."

SOMETIMES HIS PROWLING wakes us up. Then we go downstairs in our pajamas to keep him company. He walks around in circles while we watch him from the sofa. When my mother comes in, he stops.

"I'm keeping you all up," he mumbles. She rubs her eyes and sighs.

"Never mind," she says. "You're alive, that's what counts. You can dance on the roof all night as far as I'm concerned."

He bends over her. She nudges her forehead into the hollow at the bridge of his nose. Their faces fit together like a jigsaw puzzle.

ONE NIGHT SIMON and I are woken up by loud thumps. Together we go to see what's happening. The landing light is on. We stand on the cold linoleum, blinking in its glare. The door to the main bedroom is open. My father is lying on the floor inside. His eyebrow is bleeding. Max and my mother are kneeling beside him.

"You take his other arm," my mother says, "otherwise he'll fall against the closet again."

They pull him to his feet. As soon as he's up, he jumps to attention and brings his hand to his head.

"Caps off," he whispers in German. He lets his arm drop to his side, then jerks it up again. "Caps on."There's blood on his fingers.

"No, Ephraim." My mother takes him by the shoulders. Max skips around the two of them like a puppy.

"The bell for roll call has rung," says my father in a voice I don't recognize.

"There isn't any bell here," my mother says, pushing him toward the bed. "You're home, with me."

When he's sitting on the edge of the bed, she turns around without letting him go and says, "It's all right, go back to bed now."

⌒

DEEP DOWN UNDER the covers I start to cry.

"Don't be frightened," says Simon. "It isn't real. Papa's been dreaming everything, the bell and the roll call."

"And the blood?" I ask him from under the blankets. "Did he dream that, too?"

There is no reply.

Bon Appetit

"That's your third helping," my mother says to Max. "Make sure you leave room for the cherries." He nods.

"I could easily eat a whole pound of cherries, I'm so hungry."

"You, hungry?" My father laughs. "You don't even know the meaning of the word."

"Yes, I do," says Max indignantly. "It's when your stomach growls."

My father shakes his head.

"When you're really hungry, it doesn't growl, it gnaws. You're completely empty inside and as limp as a punctured balloon." His eyes grow distant. "You can't even begin to understand," he says. "We had to work for twelve hours a day or more, and all we got to eat was beetroot soup and a lump of bread. The beetroot soup was a sort of cloudy water which had never even seen a beetroot. Now and then something would float up to the top, but no one had any idea what it was.

"The soup was doled out by Sigismund the Flogger. Sigi was a Pole and much stronger than we were. He never lost a single ounce of weight in the camp. Every day he held back some of our soup and then swapped it for cigarettes. With the cigarettes he bought bread, goulash, blankets. He even had wool underwear.

"There was an enormous steel ladle hanging from his belt which he used for pouring the soup into our bowls. If anyone new dared to complain about the quality of the soup, he got his brains bashed in with that ladle. Then Sigi would point to the mess and say, 'Be grateful! Now you can have meat in your soup, too!'"

"And how much bread did you get?" Simon asks.

My father holds out his hand over the plates and the empty bowls and pinches the air. There's a narrow space between his forefinger and his thumb.

"That much," he says, "and even less later on. It was made out of flour mixed with straw and sawdust."

"Sawdust?" Simon makes a face. "Like Jonah's?"

Jonah is our hamster. Every week Max sprinkles fresh sawdust over the bottom of his cage.

"You don't understand," my father says.

He gets up, but the bread ration continues to hover over the table like a ghost. I look at it helplessly and feel a sudden disgust for the cherries my mother is serving.

How very lucky we are.

Little Red Riding Hood

It's a muggy summer evening. We're sitting in the garden making angels-on-horseback in the dark, turning our sticks patiently above the glowing embers of a dying fire. Thin slices of dough are folded around the end of each stick. When they are done, we eat them with butter and sugar. Max makes the most beautiful angels, mine are all crumpled.

"Tell us a story," says Simon.

My father doesn't need time to think.

"Right next to the place where we built that factory," he says, "there were woods. I'd keep sneaking looks there during the day, and at night, on my bunk, I'd plan the most amazing escapes. If I could only reach the woods without being seen, I kept telling myself, I'd get away for sure.

"Not long afterward I found out that the woods that were going to be my salvation were no more than thirty yards deep. And immediately behind them was the *Hundezwinger,* where they trained their dogs. Imagine if I had been able to get away. I would have run straight into the jaws of those bloodthirsty beasts!

"And beasts they were, believe me. I saw them tear prisoners to pieces more than once. Being so weak ourselves, we didn't stand a chance against them. They also got better food than we did, a kind of biscuit made out of crushed bones and blood. It wasn't very solid and tended to crumble when it was being transported. The scraps were emptied from the trucks into a dump at the edge of the woods.

"We went crazy over this stuff. While a few of us would distract the SS guard, by dropping a load of stones, for instance, others would crawl to the dump on their bellies to swipe some of the dog meal. That was dangerous for all concerned. Anyone dropping stones could count on a vicious beating. And stealing meant the gallows. We took turns with the risks.

"We hid the stolen dog food in the empty soup kettles that went back to the camp with us at the end of the day. We would chuck twigs, pine cones, and acorns into them, too, anything that would burn and get the stove in the barracks going.

"When we were marched back at night, the kettles were full to the brim. We made sure that the strongest prisoners, meaning those who had lost the least weight, conserved their energy on the way. Just before entering the camp they would take over the heavy kettles, because only they were able to swing them so nonchalantly, as if they were empty. They swung them to the festive accompaniment of the camp orchestra at the gate that welcomed us home like prodigal sons every night.

"Once in the barracks, we quickly lit the little stove and mixed the dog food with water. It was absolutely foul, covered with thick gobs of mold. When the brew came to the boil, the stink could drive you out of the barracks.

"Everyone was given a portion in his mess tin. I would hold mine at arm's length between mouthfuls to stop myself from throwing up. And I'd wonder then why I had risked my life for such vile slop."

"That isn't a story," Simon grumbles with disappointment. "That really happened."

"Do you want a story then? Okay, have it your way!" says my father. "Little Red Riding Hood is walking with her basket through the woods. Suddenly a vicious dog jumps out of the *Hundezwinger*. 'Hello, Little Red Riding Hood, where are you going?' 'I'm going to see my grandmother,' says Little Red Riding Hood. 'She's in the hospital block with typhus.'"

"No," says Simon, "that's not how it goes."

Willi

Whenever Nellie goes to the toilet, she looks down between her legs. She's sure there's a crocodile lurking in the water just waiting to bite her. I'm not scared of crocodiles. I'm scared of vermin. What I'm most scared of is Willi Hammer.

~

"WILLI WAS A *Kapo*, a work boss," says my father. "With a criminal record long enough to paper this room at least twice over. A German criminal who specialized in the raping of minors, but an expert at common assault and murder, too. He must have been about fifty. Bald head, low forehead, and a squint. A squinting caveman. He carried a chain with a lead ball the size of a biggish Ping-Pong ball at one end. He'd use it suddenly to lay into some prisoner chosen at random, and he wouldn't stop until the man was dead. Everyone shivered in his shoes when he was around.

"Some people—and there will always be this sort of person—sucked up to him. He would make them steal for him and sleep with him. When he got tired of them, their hours were numbered. I remember a Russian boy who worked in the vegetable garden and who stole tomatoes for him. He was in favor for a whole month, and Willi even called him Sweetie. One night we heard the boy screaming, panic-stricken, 'Please don't send me to the gas chamber!'

"'What do you take me for?' Willi replied. 'The gas chamber is far too impersonal. I think so much of you, Sweetie, I'm going to finish you off with my bare hands!'

"That man was one of the lowest forms of life, on a level with a stinkhorn. Only scum like that could get ahead in the camp. We were completely at the mercy of vermin like him. Willi made us pay for every last thing that had ever been done to him, for all his mistakes, all his humiliations, all his failures. No one had it in for us like Willi Hammer.

"He always picked on me. 'I take a special interest in you,' is how he put it.

"In practice what it amounted to was this. Every night after work he would take me aside and beat me up. He'd leave the lead ball in his pocket and use his bare fists. Coming from him, that was as good as a compliment, a mark of affection.

"Though he clubbed other prisoners and sent them off to meet their Maker without a second thought, when he laid hands on me he raised beating to a fine art. He'd take careful aim and hit my most vulnerable spots every time. After he'd knocked me to the ground, he'd take a break. Sometimes he'd smoke a cigarette or file his nails, while I picked myself up and stood at attention. I never uttered a sound. I knew instinctively that if I did, he'd lose interest in me and go on beating me until he'd laid me out for good.

"At first I would bite my lips until they bled to keep control of myself. Later on, it was easy. I despised him. True, he could hurt me, but even pain has a limit. I was superior to him. That's why he hated me, that's why he beat me up, and that's why he was attached to me. Where would he have been without me? I gave him a purpose in life, he was as dependent on me as I was on him."

My father looks at his hands and shakes his head slowly.

"He succeeded in the end, too."

"How?" I ask anxiously.

"How?" asks Simon. But we get no reply.

"Vermin," says my father, "lousy vermin."

Underpants

"You often see pictures of prisoners in striped pajamas," my father says, "but during the last years of the war only the camp hotshots had clothes like that. Some block leaders were the proud owners of a striped jacket. We wore rags considered too shabby even for the Winter Relief.

"We had no shoes. In the beginning we walked around on bits of wood. Later on we went barefoot. They ought to have fitted us with horseshoes, that would have been more practical. For a while I was in the *Kabelkommando,* the outside work party that extracted copper from old electricity cables so it could be used again. The stuff was easy to steal. Back in the barracks you could go on picking at it until you were left with thin strands of wire. If you could lay your hands on a few scraps of cloth somewhere, then you could join them together with the copper wire. It meant you didn't need a needle. It took a lot of patience, but that's how we made ourselves socks, or something that looked like socks from a distance.

"There wasn't any underwear. When I arrived in the camp I still had my own underpants. I wore them backwards and inside out until they were stiff with filth. Now and then I managed to wash them with snow. They fell apart eventually."

"Did you go around with a bare behind then, like a ballet dancer?" Simon asks.

"Ballet dancers don't have bare behinds!" cries Max. "They wear tights!" Simon bursts into tears.

"Once," my father continues, "there was a rumor that we were about to get new underwear. I didn't believe a word of it, but I was evidently mistaken, because after roll call one morning we were marched off to the *Bekleidungskammer,* the clothing stores, where we were issued one pair of underpants each. And what pants! They were brown paper bags with two holes for the legs. At the top they had a piece of string for tying them around your middle. Useless trash, which we had to throw away after a few hours, since all of us had diarrhea and were up to our ears in shit the whole time."

Simon wipes his tear-stained cheeks.

"How can you go on living if you don't have underpants?" he says mournfully. My mother strokes his hair. She gives my father a quizzical look. He jumps up and walks around the room.

"Wait a moment," he says, "I've forgotten something! Everyone got those underpants except me. When it was my turn, they were all gone. That's right, I remember now. While the others put on their paper underpants in the snow, I was left empty-handed. Just then the assistant camp commandant, the *Lagerführer* himself, came by. He shook his head and said, 'Impossible! This poor devil's entitled to a pair of underpants, and a pair of underpants he'll have, damn it, even if I have to turn the whole camp upside down to find them!'

"'But the box is empty!' said the man running the *Bekleidungskammer*.

"'What!' the *Lagerführer* shouted. 'Are you trying to tell me that the Third Reich is short of a pair of underpants?'

"His hand disappeared into the box, groped about inside, and, as if by magic, came up holding a pair of underpants. These underpants differed in every respect from the paper ones. They were made of blue velvet and came down to your knees. The fly had ivory buttons, each in the shape of a small German eagle."

"Really and truly?" Simon asks. My father nods.

"Those pants were indestructible. Top quality. And that's not all. Within a week they started to talk! I think it was just after I'd been detailed to a forest work party. In any case, it happened in the woods. We had to dig pits, the ground was frozen solid, and the handle of my shovel snapped in half. When the guards saw that, they nearly kicked me to death. As if that was any help I went on working with a broken shovel, and then those underpants suddenly addressed me."

"What did they say?" I ask.

"They spoke in German," says my father. "I don't feel like translating all of it right now, but one of the things they told me was that they answered to the name of Heinrich and that they had once belonged to Adolf Hitler. They'd been looking up Adolf's asshole for years and had learned the most confidential state secrets that way.

Then, one day, they were arrested and sent to the camp because they knew too much."

"Talking underpants? But that can't be true!" says Simon. My father raises his hands helplessly.

"Heinrich couldn't believe it himself! He had never tried to speak before, the thought had never even occurred to him. But once he found he could talk, there was no stopping him. And what a lot of talking we did, Heinrich and I! The Nazis were bastards. But their underpants? I won't hear a word said against them!"

"What happened to Heinrich?" we ask.

"By the end of the war I had grown so skinny the underpants didn't fit anymore. They kept falling down around my ankles. One day they were picked up by the wind and carried away high, high up into the air.

"'Heinrich!' I shouted. 'Come back!'

"'No,' Heinrich called down, 'the view from up here is much too beautiful!'

"'What can you see?' I asked.

"'Everything, everything,' Heinrich replied. 'All of Europe. I can even see the future. I can see bread on the table and I can see that girl with the black braids you've been telling me about. And children, I can see children, too.'

"'How many?' I yelled up, but I couldn't hear Heinrich anymore, he had grown as small as a kite that's broken its string."

⌐

SIMON STILL FINDS it hard to believe.

"Clothes can't talk," he says while we're getting undressed. Max, who doesn't have to go to bed for a long time, leans against the closet.

"Why not?" he says. "Crazier things happened in the camp, people were gassed there." Simon shrugs his shoulders.

"Of course people were gassed there," he says. "That's what a camp is for, isn't it?"

Animal

"In nineteen forty-four, the factory was bombed," he tells us. "There was a small passageway under the concrete floor, at most three feet wide, where the gas mains ran. You could get into it at the base of the outside wall, through a manhole, which was usually closed with an iron lid. As soon as the first bomb dropped, the SS pulled the cover off and lined us up against the wall. 'Down, you bastards!' It didn't matter to them how we got down: most of us never got a chance to get hold of the narrow ladder, and fell down backwards or headfirst. But we didn't fall fast enough, so they aimed the fire hoses at us and literally washed us underground.

"We stood there packed like sardines, soaked to the skin and teeth chattering, the whole time the air raid went on. The earth shook and we rocked backwards and forwards, passageway and all. Because that made the gas pipe behind us creak ominously, we weren't too cheerful either. The SS kept us shut up in there for thirty-six hours. When we were finally allowed up again, the air was so full of smoke we couldn't tell if it was day or night. That could also have been because our eyes had sunk so deep into their sockets with fear that they were somewhere at the back of our heads.

"We walked around in a daze. I fled the smoke and found myself in a part of the factory that was still burning. Suddenly there I was, face to face with Willi Hammer. His sleeve had caught on fire. He was beating the flames out with his cap. How he'd ended up there, I didn't know. What I did know was that he'd never get away from there again.

"As soon as he saw me, he reached into his pants pocket. Scarcely had he brought out the chain with the lead ball than I was sitting on top of him with the chain tight around his neck."

"Did he die?" Max asks. "Did he die?" My father nods.

"I strangled him." He spreads his fingers and looks at them as if they weren't his. "That's something I will never forgive those brutes. They did everything they could to turn me into an animal. A new chapter of the Creation," he laughs grimly. "'Come, let us make man after our likeness!' And they succeeded. I became their image. I can no longer look in a mirror without coming face to face with a murderer." He bows his head and whispers, "I would do anything to bring Willi back to life, anything! I'd pray for weeks to make that happen. I'd descend to hell to bring him back, even if the road there was paved with splinters of glass and I had to crawl all the way on my belly."

Max goes behind my father's chair and places a hand on his shoulder.

"Then you aren't an animal," he consoles him, "because animals can't feel sorry for what they've done."

"Sorry?" My father curls his upper lip and bares his teeth menacingly. "Sorry? The only reason I want to bring him back to life is so I can murder him all over again. I did it much too quickly the first time. This time I'd take it nice and easy. I'd wring his neck at my leisure, little by little. Now and then I'd give him just enough breath to squirm or scream. The only thing I regret is that I didn't make him suffer in mortal fear long enough."

None of us speaks now. Simon sips his milk but doesn't dare swallow. Now we know why my father keeps strangling his blankets at night. He's practicing for the day when he'll haul Willi back out of hell. He wants to make sure he's still got the right touch.

"Paradise"
from *Lost in Translation*

BY EVA HOFFMAN

It is a beautiful, sunny day in Cracow, and I'm holding my mother's hand as we stroll toward our favorite park—Park Krakowski. But in the middle of this relaxed saunter, the tone of her voice changes as if she wanted to tell me something very important. "You're grown up enough now to understand this," she says. "It's time you stopped crossing yourself in front of churches. We're Jewish and Jews don't do that." It doesn't come as that much of a surprise, really. Of course, I've known we're Jewish as long as I can remember. That's why everyone died in the war. But the knowledge has been vague, hazy; I didn't understand its implications. I feel almost relieved at having it officially confirmed.

The sense of being Jewish permeates our apartment like the heavy, sweet odor of the dough that rises in our kitchen in preparation for making hallah. The Jewishness lives in that bread, which other people don't seem to make; it's one of the markers of our

difference. But until I'm seven years old, I cross such markers regularly; I keep the distinctions blurry. Indeed, insofar as I acquire any
explicit religious education, it's Catholic. It's hard not to. Catholi-
cism is everywhere: it's the atmosphere I breathe. "Jesus, Joseph, and
Sainted Maria," my mother says in a humorous tone, when she's
exasperated, or when things get out of hand. On the street, we often
see nuns in their cowls and priests in graceful long soutanes, and I
know by the respectful looks people give them that they're special,
exempt from ordinary rules. My friends, with whom I play on the
street or at the tiny local playground, are much concerned with the
question of sainthood. Danuta Dombarska, an earthy, blond girl who
lives in the next building to us and is one of my best friends, informs
me earnestly one day, while we are waiting our turn at the swing,
that she wants to be a saint when she grows up. St. Veronica, maybe,
or St. Teresa. Her eyes grow dreamy; this is clearly a pleasurable,
romantic fantasy. "I don't want to be any sort of saint," I tell her
firmly by the time we're on the swing. I don't know whence this
conviction comes, but it's very strong. Being a saint means lying
down in a white dress, perhaps on a cross. I don't like this supine
position. I want to roam the world and have adventures. Or maybe
it's that I don't believe in saints, as I don't "believe" in what goes on
when we attend church on Sunday. Yes, I go to church with Danuta
and other kids quite often; my parents, until that official announce-
ment, don't stop me. They're not, after all, believers themselves, and
they don't want to make my young life unnecessarily difficult. Let
her go and play with the others is their implicit message—and that's
how the whole thing feels. It's a kind of charade, made more satisfy-
ing by all the trappings of seriousness—as if one got to play house on
a very grand scale. I like the gray-stone, curvy Baroque facade of our
neighborhood church, and its incense-smelling interior. I kneel
down with the others, and I sing the beautiful anthems; I get a particular thrill when some clear, strong voice emerges from the unison
crowd. And once, as we kneel in a row to receive the priestly bene-
diction, the priest puts his hand on my head and, looking worriedly

into my face, tells me that if I want to ask him anything, I should come in and talk. I guess he knows I don't belong.

I guess I know it too. For all these Sunday forays, and the fun of going to church at Easter, dressed up in a nice dress and carrying a basket filled with candied bunnies, I assume that in spite of the gratifyingly earnest looks I and the other children put on for such occasions, everyone knows this isn't really real. So it comes as a surprise to me when one day Danuta talks to me about God—his goodness, his intolerance of sin, his forgiveness—and her face again takes on the dreamy, deeply earnest look. Then I realize she means it. God is as real to her as her neighbors; I look at her with some awe—perhaps, after all, she knows something I don't?—but I have no images of God that are mine, that I've been taught to visualize or love.

Our maids make more concerted efforts to infuse me with some Christian feeling. The first of these is a fresh country girl, shy and fawnlike, but after being with us awhile, she starts coming into my room when my parents are out for the evening, and, curling up beside me on my bed, tells me stories of saints' lives and of Jesus Christ. During one of these sessions, she informs me that she wants to save my soul and give it to Jesus. I guess I'm impressed enough by this, or perhaps a little scared—will she really change me somehow?—that I tell my parents about it, and after that the stories stop.

Another maid takes me to Cracow's great churches, particularly St. Mary's, a forbidding edifice in the middle of the city with a Gothic spire and famous medieval sculptures inside—angular, wooden, anguished figures of Christ in a coffin, surrounded by St. Mary and the apostles, which impress me with their contorted postures of deep suffering. Maybe it's this maid who tells me that I should cross myself in front of a church, which from then on I conscientiously do, even when we pass one on the tramway. Most of the other riders cross themselves too—a small, surreptitious gesture across the chest, repeated throughout the car and accompanied by quick, conspiratorial glances.

In the house, we have a Christmas tree every year, and I get gifts on St. Nicholas's Day; my parents do this not as a gesture of assimilation but so my sister and I won't feel left out of the surrounding festivities. I don't see any incongruity between this and the Passover dinner—the only Jewish ritual we observe at home. They are both exceptional occasions, both holidays. Even after my mother unchristens me, the Christmas tree continues. But it's easy enough for me to stop the other rites. The confirmation of Jewishness straightens things out. So being Jewish is something definite; it is something that I am. Though Jewishness, until now, has been filled with my mother's tears and whispers in a half-understood tongue, when she finally speaks of it directly, she conveys that it is something to be proud of—something to stand up for with all one's strength. "They'll tell you that you are worse than them," she says, "but you must know that you are not. You're smart, talented—you're the equal of anybody."

The subject of anti-Semitism now comes up frequently, but when my parents—mostly my mother—speak of it, there is anger rather than shame in their voices. "After all we've gone through they still hate us," my mother says bitterly. "Can you imagine something so primitive? It's something they drink in with their mother's milk." "Primitive" is a much more damning term than "immoral" or "evil." Primitive means "vulgar, unenlightened"—something nobody would want to be. Anti-Semitism is a darkness of the mind, a prejudice—rather than a deviation from moral principles. Altogether, such principles don't seem to have much of a hold over Polish imaginations. Poland is a Francophile culture, and people around me judge each other by their intelligence and style (to say that someone is "stupid" is the most definitive and frequent dismissal one can issue), by how elegant, or charming, or clumsy, or witless they are, rather than by their rectitude or lack of it.

Anti-Semitism comes under the heading of barbarian stupidity, and that makes me feel immediately superior to it. The signs of such stupidity, however, are everywhere. My father comes home one day reporting on a fistfight he got into when someone on the street said to him that "the best thing Hitler did was to eliminate the Jews"—that classic line so conveniently brought out whenever a Pole quickly wants to express a truly venomous hatred. On another occasion, my mother comes home incensed; Pani Orlovska, the mother of my friend Krysia, and a "better" person—she is educated and a doctor's wife—wanted to know, in the intimate confidence of their friendship, whether really, really, it was true that Jews mixed in some Christian blood with their matzo for Passover. "And this is an intelligent person?" my mother says furiously. But somehow the anger does not become wholesale enough for my mother to stop seeing Pani Orlovska, or even liking her. There are other parts to Pani Orlovska, after all, as there are to all the people who have drunk anti-Semitism with their mother's milk, but among whom we live in friendship and even intimacy, and with all the complexities of affection and impatience that those bring.

I gradually come to understand that it is a matter of honor to affirm my Jewishness and to do so with my head held high. That's what it means to be a Jew—a defiance of those dark and barbaric feelings. Through that defiance, one upholds human dignity. This is no Sartrean, conscious conclusion on my part, of course, but an outgrowth of some basic pride that is as strong in me as it is in most children. It seems a simple affirmation of justice, of rightness, of reason that Jews are human the way other people are human. After all, I see that with my own two eyes, and I'm too young yet to believe that the emperor is wearing clothes. Besides, maybe I don't want to be riven from my non-Jewish friends—not yet. I don't want to suspect the worst of them, don't want to look out for how they'll hurt me, to be on guard. My mother warns me: there's an anti-Semite in every Pole; be careful; even the most educated among them are superstitious about Jews; even the best will betray you. But this is where I stop heeding her. I sense that if I want to keep my dignity, I cannot act suspicious, cannot wait for slights as if I knew they were going to come. Besides, I do not feel they will come. I cannot believe that the friends with whom I play so happily look on me as a dark stranger.

Still, there are incidents. One day, Julita, who's almost a friend, though not quite—she is too haughty, too beautiful, too earnest—passes me a note in class. "Is it true that you are of Hebraic faith?" she writes me. "I'm a Jew," I answer on a piece of paper, confused by her strange locution. But from that day on, I hate her, and cherish dreams of revenge. Someday I'll be more beautiful, more famous than she. Then she'll see.

My pride receives a more serious wound—because it's more intentionally inflicted—in an incident involving Yola, a spoiled, timid little girl who counts as a friend among a small group of companions I hang around with, but whom we tease quite mercilessly and with considerable inventiveness. We concoct whole gothic stories for her benefit, complete with notes hidden in the ground, boxes with odd objects, and suggestions of ominous dangers. I don't know whence these fantasies spring, or why Yola—perhaps it's because she is so credulous and easily frightened—becomes the object of such imperious cruelty. After a while, though, she can help herself no longer; she tells her father. Our little cabal is summoned to her house. We stand in front of Yola's father, heads hung down in some form of remorse—but it is me he singles out. "It was you who thought this up, right?" he says, while I shake my head no. "I know you," he continues nevertheless, looking at me with utter disdain. "You are the leader of this. You little Jew." It's the gleam of malicious satisfaction in his eyes—as if he were tightening the right screw—that registers like a cold touch and that I can never forgive. From then on, Yola and I ignore each other with the consistency and pretended indifference of seasoned diplomats—a difficult feat, since we live in the same neighborhood and see each other frequently.

In 1957, prayers and religion classes begin to be instituted in Polish schools. This signals a shift in the political balance of power; in the constant tug-of-war between church and state, the church, for the moment, has won a substantial victory. So now, after the morning roll call, the class stands up and, led by the teacher, recites the Lord's Prayer—the Polish version of it, which includes a special plea for the Virgin Mary's intercession. Then we betake ourselves to the schoolwide assembly, where every day we sing the *Internationale,* whose stirring melody never fails to fill me with the requisite inspirational feeling.

I'm too young to appreciate the delicious political comedy of this juxtaposition. Indeed, it's with a not altogether unpleasant sense of righteousness and heroism that I stand silently while others recite the Lord's Prayer. This is what I have been instructed to do by my parents: show respect by standing up, but do not compromise yourself by actually saying the words. I feel a great self-assurance about this gesture. I'm upholding human dignity through it. And because I know I'm in the right, I'm doubly surprised when one day a group of kids I don't know very well runs after me and starts pummeling me and shouting, "Out with the Yids!" In the melee, several of my friends quickly come to my aid, dispersing the assault, and it is to them that my feelings turn. Of course, I would be defended. The others are just stupid, primitive. My sense of trust is undiminished. Justice is justice. Truth is truth. At eleven, this is what every fiber in my body wants to believe.

Soon after these watershed events begin, Marek is accused of stealing by his schoolmates and gets into a ferocious scrape with them—a scrape in which he too is called ugly, anti-Semitic names. There are low-voiced discussions between his parents and mine, and they warn us that things may get bad. But we should know that we're as good as anybody—maybe better. I don't like these speeches, in which I hear a false, sententious tone, but the introduction of religion in schools, greeted by most Poles with joy as an anti-Soviet triumph, is taken by many Jews as an official mandate for anti-Semitism, and people are worried.

My own fledgling ideas of Jewishness, however, receive a more comical test. It is about this time that my parents go for a longish trip to Russia, leaving my sister and me in the hands of a maid, neighbors, and friends. And it is during their absence that Alinka begins to attend religion classes after school. She's only seven, and remembering my parents' tolerance of my own childhood Catholic foibles, I decide that she might as well go. Until, that is, I find her, one evening, kneeling in front of the light switch, hands clasped, eyes turned piously upward, reciting an evening prayer. What are you doing? I inquire. Well, the priest told the class to pray in front of holy pictures, she explains. Such pictures are a feature of every Polish home I know—usually cheap imitations of Raphael's *Madonna and Child,* or some other variation on the subject—and people use them as icons in front of which to kneel in prayer. The light switch is the closest thing to such pictures that my sister could find in our bare-walled apartment. I don't know why her very pragmatic solution strikes me as a sacrilege, as going too far. Passive participation is one thing, but she seems to be falling for the whole thing; she's taking it seriously.

I know it's up to me to provide firm guidance here, but I'm baffled as to what it should be, so I decide to take the very adult action of calling Marek's mother to solicit her advice. I feel very grown up indeed as I ask our downstairs neighbors if I can use their telephone, and dial it myself for the first time ever. I explain the situation to Pani Ruta breathlessly and ask her what I should do. "Leave her alone," she says in her husky, humorous voice. "What harm is it doing her? She can't understand these things yet."

Well, I should have known. Pani Ruta's tolerance on the subject of Jewish observance is even more extensive than my parents'. Her family was assimilated enough so that they could "pass," using "Aryan papers" during the war and living through it in relative comfort in their Cracow apartment. And she's not only irreligious but naughtily irreverent. My parents, for all their conscious disbelief, fast on Yom Kippur; they observe the dietary prohibitions of Passover. They do so partly out of respect for the dead—but partly because these central injunctions, for all their postwar secularism, still have the powerful force of taboos. But violating taboos is precisely what Pani Ruta likes to do, and one time during Yom Kippur, when everyone else is praying at the synagogue, she takes me to a restaurant and does the most shocking thing possible—she orders pork cutlets for herself and me. "You're an intelligent girl," she says. "You don't have to go along with these superstitions." I'm flattered, of course, and I eat my pork cutlet with a tingling sense of my own sophistication. Yes, I'm the kind of person who will defy superstition and convention. Of course. But I feel a bit uneasy too; the defiance seems too deliberate, as if it were calculated to betray. I don't think my parents would be happy about it, and I don't tell them of the incident until much later.

My family goes to the synagogue only once a year, on the High Holidays. The day on which this happens is a disruption of everything ordinary, a small journey into a hermetic otherness. The morning begins in a solemn mood; we all put on our best clothes, and my parents kiss my sister and me formally—not in affection, but as if they were stamping on our foreheads the seal of an impersonal legacy. For this day, we cease being their children and become something both larger and smaller. Then we begin the long walk to the synagogue—a walk that takes us gradually farther away from the familiar streets and into a sleepy, becalmed realm, the Jewish Quarter. Here the houses are white and low, the streets narrow and winding, and almost nothing stirs, except sometimes through the first-story windows we see a figure of a bearded man.

The synagogue itself has a Moorish facade with tiled mosaics and a portico with toylike, miniature arches. There's a courtyard adjoining it, where people who haven't seen each other all year exchange greetings with commiserating nods and talk in grave, sad voices. These meetings are commemorations of all their dead, as well as religious rituals, and everyone respects the mood.

Once the service starts, the children are left to their own devices outside, but from time to time, I go in to see my parents. I enter through a low-ceilinged, musty, long, damp corridor; on one side, there are hundreds and hundreds of candles, flickering dimly. They've been placed here to honor the dead, and I feel how many of them there are: an endless procession, and someone is always adding more. Then the interior, so dark that the men—they are all men downstairs—become spectral silhouettes, marked by the swaying movement of the white tallithim. An irregular arrhythmic hum, so unlike the music of the Catholic Church—this is more rapt and more private—rises and falls in the darkness. Peering, I make out my father's figure, and I approach him eagerly. I want a little attention from him. But he barely notices me; he takes my hand without interrupting his chant, and I feel painfully that he has become inaccessible to me. Then I go upstairs to where the women are praying and sit next to my mother; she at least smiles at me, but she also soon returns to her book.

Across the lawn from the main temple, there's a tiny white building, no bigger than the space of a large room. I never know what its uses are, so when it's opened one day, I'm almost fearful to go in. When I do, I stand still with wonder, for what I see is a circle of men, dressed in long, black coats, moving round and round in a drunken, ecstatic dance. They're paying no attention to the few spectators who have gathered around them; their eyes are raised toward the Torah, which they pass on from hand to hand as tenderly as if it were a baby. "Hasidim," somebody tells me. I don't know what that means, but I feel I've come upon something even more mysterious than the main synagogue.

One day, as I sit quietly under the one tree in this gnostic garden, a bee stings me on the back of my neck. At first, it seems like just an ordinary sting, but then my limbs swell alarmingly, I break out in a rash, and I can hardly breathe. My parents, terrified, rush me to a doctor, who offers a diagnosis: I'm heavily allergic to bee sting. Such an allergy gets worse with every injection of the venom. If I get stung again and don't get help immediately, I may well die.

I don't know why, but this sting under the leafy branches of the synagogue tree becomes my private transaction with Mystery. I've been injected with a bit of my own mortality; I've received a strange sign.

My Little Pledge of Us

BY VICTORIA REDEL

W e were Russia.

We weren't only Russia. We were Bessarabia, which meant we included those small cities and towns, Galatz and Reni, just across the River Prut in Romania. Our grandfather was Egypt. Our mother's papers said Persia. There were months in Constantinople, our great-grandfather Soltanitzky the composer to the sultan. There were certain Belgians. A Polish Mexican arrived and said he was our uncle.

So much of this happened in another language.

In the easy suburban evening, our parents waited for our American disaster. We were schooled in the talk of fires. We knew what should be grabbed. We were taught to recognize the men who would one day walk up our front walk to take candlesticks, a bribe. We knew the smell of gypsies, who would come to take the youngest child.

In our house, everything ran too hot or too cold.

But don't get me wrong. We girls were girls who could ride bikes. We girls ate franks, drank colas, had TV dinners on Sunday nights.

So, of course, please, don't worry, come in.

Come in out of the barbecue evening; step over the potsys marking the hopscotch game, out of range of the bells of the Good Humor truck. Come in through the red curtain to here, where it smells of cooked beets and sour cream, of sorrel and koulibiak. Come in where the vodka is in cups. Don't be shy. We have no time, only generations. Raise a finger, a voice. Chime in. Everyone is speaking, all at once, all in different languages.

Please to the table; of course you will eat.

A spinach pie.

A blintz.

A cabbage soup.

Sha sha.

Speak up. Have more. Have more. Have a spoon or three of the caviar Mattus has smuggled in the bellies of painted nesting dolls. Squish in, among the dead and the living and the children.

⌇

INTRODUCTIONS?

That can all come later.

Now it is enough to know that they came with our faces on them. Out of waters, off of boats, onto wharf and land, they came with our long and with our skinny faces, only longer and skinnier, and when they spoke through our bulbed lips, and did not speak our tongue, we shook our heads to say we understood.

Such tales.

So it is said that our great-grandfather knelt on one knee and played a melody so sweet that the sultan leaned over and kissed his head.

So it is said that our mother learned to dance her tarantella from a strumming band of wine-soaked merchants.

So it is said.

It is said, and it is said, and we girls said, *Cithagan yithagou ithagundithagerstithagand mithagee?*

Natured, nurtured, everyone at this table has a fantastic, tortured story.

How will it be told? With a needle and a spoon, it will be told. And it will be told, too, with a mother's waltz and a father's worry coin and with a treasure box where the youngest child has hidden buttons and feathers, the woolly scraps that help her to sleep, the soup spoon and bread crust she will need when the gypsies steal her and she must find her way back home. It will be told secretly, camouflaged, in a mended language made newly of the old, frayed words. It will be spoken in tarnished silver, in a beaten egg and a whisper, and in the shouting all-at-once voices of all the relatives, each claiming the other is dreaming, has it wrong, and that his story, her story, this story is the only story, the one to ward off disaster, the only one that is right.

Ah, gypsies.

Ah, Galatz.

Have a little more herring, no?

BEHIND OUR HOUSE were the woods we called the River Prut, where we girls ran to hide, drifting on layers of damp, rotting leaves, floating over to the edge of the woods to see whether our house was in flames yet, or if the milkman had dragged our mother off in his metal truck.

Was there ever a disaster? Was there ever a time that we were actually called to the front, we three girls, their young recruits, we three girls, already defectors, armed and trained to shoot to kill? If we had killed, what would we have killed? A cossack? A postman? The slow boy who lived down the block? Our mother? Our father?

In the woody River Prut, we stashed away rations that we claimed would hold us for a week. We worked our way through a box of crackers in an afternoon and buried the empty carton. My sister said we would learn to survive on air. She gave each one of us one of Mama's cigarettes. We foraged for acorns. We chewed sticks. We made plans for a rendezvous at the mouth, where the River Prut meets the Danube.

We were, always, finally, their only disaster.

Our mother standing at the back door screaming our names.

Bloody noses.

A stitched eye.

Our papa waiting up for us when we tottered in, smoky, from parties we swore were chaperoned.

We were always teetering, on the verge of looking too much like whatever was out there.

"You are not American," our father said when we marched with the school band.

"You are not American," our father said when a sister came downstairs frosted-lipped, wearing a black armband.

"What do you think you are?" our father asked.

For enough of the time, we girls were like everybody else—kids hanging from trees, kids with forks and stiff-legged dolls, kids looking for other kids we could tease for being different or dumb, some kid my sister tricked into eating soap powder, the slow boy we bribed to strip almost naked, anyone we could master or make stick out so that we did not stick out quite as much.

From the banks of the River Prut, we watched our house. We saw how our family must look to the others on our street. What was inside looked suspicious, our uncle in shirtsleeves, waving a wooden spoon, our mother and father rushing at each other, playing bullfight with a table spread. We could hear our father shouting, "Do you think I am the tsar!" as he went through rooms. It was not what our father said but how he said it, his rhythms all wrong, and the way he switched midsentence into another of his languages or stopped at a window and stared out as if he were seeing our street for the first time.

Mostly though, even in daytime, the shades of our house were drawn. They were foreign inside, shadows stretched funny by light, and we could not recognize exactly who was who or what lived inside of that house.

We could see our mother, the strained look on her face when she called, "Girls." She stood in the doorway in a sheer wrap skirt and tights. "Girls," she repeated, getting softer with a fear we could watch overtake her body, so that soon she was not so much walking through our yard as creeping through it, whispering our names.

"Don't go back!" our sister said.

"Girls," our mother trembled close to us.

Our oldest sister grabbed our wrists.

"Don't even breathe," our sister said.

We thought about the air we had eaten. It should hold us.

We pretended our mother was not our mother.

It burned where our sister's nails dug into our skin.

"Please," our mother whispered, bargaining with the soldiers we knew she believed had come for us.

It looked terrible—our mother hunching through the yard in her chiffon skirt. She stumbled and muttered. The ground was muddy with spring. We could have touched her, come out to her or brought her into our hideout on the banks of the River Prut. We let her stay out there, wheeling and crawling through the yard, calling out for her children until doors opened. Other parents cradling babies—hands protectively on the necks of the older ones—came out for a look.

Our mother ran in for our father.

Our oldest sister said she deserved the worry, the way our mother dressed in slippers that laced at her ankles. Our sister asked, did we see any other mother who drove through town in leotards, a camel hair jacket draped over her shoulders?

Our oldest sister started singing. "Oh beautiful," she sang. She walked up to the front door, singing.

We followed.

"For purple mountains," we sang together.

Our parents came to the door. Our father said something to our mother in a language we did not understand. She pulled in, standing close to him. They looked past us to the other neighbors watching our family from their front steps.

"Are you through?" our father asked, though it sounded like *true*.

The wind was thick behind us, racketing in over the woody River Prut.

"Come in, girls," our mother said, flaring her nostrils once.

We went in.

The bowls of kasha were still burning hot.

—

Now is the time.

It might as well be the time, I think, to relax, get cozy, take off the shoes if you have not already, and make our introductions. Mama, the mother; Papa, the father, Nana Gusta with her sisters and her brothers, and her husband, our grandfather, and his father, and perhaps, too, the drunk sultan himself with his thirst for music, and Uncle Marie with his good head of hair and his sour wives and their curdled offspring, and even here, too, is Fokine, nephew of the famous Mr. Fokine, and Madame Swoboda, and Esperanza, one of the flamenco twins from Seville, and Irina Fedovata, and the Polish uncle from Mexico that we called Monsieur Max.

Shake hands.

Kiss cheeks—both cheeks.

Do not worry that you cannot remember the one from the other. Stay a little while; have a bowl of Fokine's bouillabaisse, and you will start to simmer in dialects of languages that you have never learned. There are, of course, others—a cousin who arrived by mail, floated in when my parents forgot themselves and left a door slightly ajar. There were cakes named for aunts who never showed up, and there was an extra sister we believed our mother kept in the old bassinet just in case the youngest child never found her way back home.

Us girls? We are the daughters one, two, and four, the third our mother's fifth-month loss. We are called for always all at once. We come downstairs together, a flock, all flutter and hem, hand-me-downs handed down twice. We are the Anderson sisters, shoulder to shoulder to shoulder, singing, "Daisy, Daisy, answer my question true. . . ." Myrna, Louise, Greta, Bette, and Marilyn, we name ourselves straight out of Hollywood. Our names change with the marquee each week.

Seen but not heard, napkins bunchy with bread and lox, we are off to resupply our stash on the River Prut.

We will be back.

In the meantime, try the pirogi.

OUR MOTHER RODE through town in her tights and chiffon wrap skirt, a camel hair jacket draped over her shoulders, the pink slippers ribboned to her feet. Rumor was she had danced with the Bolshoi and for a season with the Ballet Russe de Monte Carlo.

"That girl—not one, but three left feet." Mama laughed and flicked her lit cigarettes onto trim lawns.

The town police waited for our mother. They liked to pull her over, stand at the window and ask her to step outside, "For just a moment, please." Our mother went Frenchie on us for the town police, everything Z-ish and high-rolling R's, her chiffon dance skirt melting in the headlights. She had a kick to her, up on tiptoes, arched and ready for a cancan. We watched the policeman light a cigarette for our mother. She dipped, swayed, gave a little curtsey. We saw the taut line between her shoulders, her readiness to take off and run. They took their time each time—warnings, radio checks, rules explained so slowly that when our mother got back in the car, she said, "All the same, those guards, les idiots. Take me home, girls." And she would pull off, smoking out just a bit too fast.

The Russians had nothing good to say about one another. They were always fighting, our mother and Fokine, about shrimp or

Fokine's famous uncle, Mr. Fokine, or our electric stove, which Fokine said was impossible and made true bouillabaisse impossible, or our mother saying what did an old Russian know from bouillabaisse, having never been anywhere closer to Marseille than a bowl of borscht.

The house smelled fishy.

Bass heads glanced up out of pots. There were legs on the counter. Grunt and eel leaned, scaled and clean, on the cutting board.

And there were always other Russians in our kitchen, saying other no-good things to one another. There were sudden bursts of silence. They watched one another with slandering eyes.

The kitchen reeked of garlic.

In our house, there was no grace. There were split shells on the table. There was wine. There was Fokine polishing over our polish. There were more fights among the Russians. There was a mazurka and a polonaise. There was rum. There were cries of Bolshevik. There were stains on the linen. There was an aria from Monsieur Max, who fell in love with Esperanza, the elder flamenco twin from Seville. There was the youngest child napping in our papa's lap, waking up enough to say, "I am not sleepy." There were dishes in the sink and dishes on the table and an open bottle of cognac and our papa carrying us one by one up to our beds to tuck us—God willing—in for the night.

Outside, at intersections, with their oaths and eager badges, they waited.

They would wait all night if they had to.

They would pledge themselves ready for what they knew had already crossed the border, had infiltrated, assimilated, weakened the dollar.

They would wait in the dark till it came.

They would flip a switch, pin it in spotlight.

They would cruise the streets of our town, listening to the electric wires.

They would get out the dogs.

They would make it walk the yellow line.

They would watch for lapses, look it in the eye, warn it, ticket it.

They would dismantle it.

They would make it hoist the flag.

They would keep it out.

They would wait all night to keep it out.

They would maintain the order.

Inside, in our house, the sultan—glutted, exhausted, arbitrary as ever—kissed each of our traveled foreheads, closed his one good eye, and, for at least this night, kept the assassins out.

~

MONSIEUR MAX SAT outside on a plastic lawn chaise and waited for the Mexican wind that he said passed through our woods.

"That's my Oaxaca, girls," said our uncle, closing his eyes.

We sat behind him at the edge of the woods. Monsieur Max said that out of the woods was coming the Mexican wind, and up the street were coming the armies of Europe.

It was gummy in our yard, the road filmy with heat.

"Oh, yes," said Max. "Here it comes, girls."

We closed our eyes most of the way, kept him a flickery thing, a bulge and sag in the grass.

We could hear kids down the street. They were a motley after-dinner band, brothers straggling behind brothers, sisters, any kid who wasn't inside or off anywhere better, wandering to the corner, looking for other kids who had wandered out, stringing together chase or war or red rover red rover, or just sitting on the curb waiting for another kid who might have a better idea or just any idea at all.

Monsieur Max said there were bandits in these woods and, fierce and cruel as a Mexican bandit was, we should hide under their wool serapes when the armies of Europe landed on our street.

"Among enemies," our uncle said, "choose your friends."

We could hear them down the street. We could hear that the teams were uneven.

It blued with shadow by the woods where we sat behind Monsieur Max.

"Under their serapes, there is always something—a tortilla, a chipped knife, a bottle to fill with wind for when they flee their country," he said.

He stood up to turn his chair and sat back down.

"Remember, a bandit," our uncle said, "is not so different—like a Polish soldier—that same hollow knock."

He stood up to turn his chair and sat back down.

The game was growing; we could hear it, a mailbox base for safety, someone screaming, "That's not fair," screaming, "Yes," screaming and screaming and screaming until that was, we knew, the game—kids screaming out of bushes, through flower beds, tagging and bombing, tagged and bombed, and now we could hear the mothers out screaming, "Right now!" and "Your father!" and "I mean it!" until they were all alone and the street was so quiet with quiet and dark with the first dark of night.

Monsieur Max said, "There it is, my Valladolid."

We thought we felt it then, the wind, whatever, something in that heat that came through us. We shut our eyes and waited for more.

*

"You are not American," our father said.

He said it, it seemed to us, the way we heard other fathers tell their children not to run out into the street. He said it to us as if the worst had already happened, the way we knew those other fathers knew that there is always a child lurching off a curb, lunging after a stray ball and getting hit.

*

Papa called us in from evening street games to look at our books.

"All wrong," he said.

It was, we said, the way they wanted it done.

There was, Papa said, the problem of the numbers. There was the problem of the straightness of rows. There was, our father said, the entire problem of American teachers, who were, he said, hardly teaching anything but a poorness of all habit that might prove to be needed.

We loved them one and all, our teachers with their crisp blouses and blue grade books. Oh, to her blond flip, and after Christmas the diamond ring that Miss Skilken held up to the light. We loved the nurse's cot, where we rolled the thermometer under our tongues. Oh, to color-coded readers, stories of girls and boys out on picnics, the mother with her pleated skirt at the open door. We loved the shop teacher with his jigsaw and belt sander and Mrs. Herman, who read us the news and cried for the hungry children on the other side of the world.

"It will be needed," Papa said. Our father paced the floor, his money belt strapped under his shirt. "And what is all this?" he asked, waving our compositions.

Oh, too, to the under-desk minutes where we practiced waiting for the Russian bomb.

Our father said the teachers listened—a giveaway vowel, a lapse into any language.

We were the Russias. Any explosion was ours. We were tongue-tied, students of the way our teachers spoke, a Boston R we brought home, announcing at the table, "Miss Brenner says that's not true."

Papa turned with his sharp look. "I'll show you true."

"All too much," he said, "and too much against America." He blew into the backs of his fingers. "So much opinion? Who are you, the president?" He jiggled his belt, feeling for coins that would pay his way across borders, buy us new names.

We rewrote our compositions while he blew hard onto his fingers again to keep—despite his squandered, lost children—what little he had hoarded of luck.

⌒

But too much talk without nothing! Not so much this as a blintz or a kugel. Not a nothing little sweet? Not a little burek stuffed with spinach and sweet cheese? Not even a tea, the leaves at the bottom forever spelling out *doom?*

Come, come with us. We will sneak away from the table, down the stairs to the basement, where the costumes Nana sews for Mama's ballet are kept.

There were Chinese courtesans, snowflakes, brocade dresses for Cinderella's nasty sisters, bolts of toile and crepe, sequins tacked and stacks of crowns, garlands, the Sugarplum Fairy's tutu, a tutu for each season hung upside down on hangers from the pipes in our basement, where we girls went to light matches and smoke our mother's cigarettes.

Our hands were our mother's hands, her cigarettes put to our mouths, or held ashy at a distance until the ashes dropped. The ashes always dropped. Our legs were ashy and seared where we tested one another, burning the faint hairs down to skin. Our skin was our mother's skin, traversed, foreign, each of us girls a country she crept through to come to bring us forth.

We could hear them through the ceiling, rattling in the pipes, our father counting his stacks of coins, making money belts for each of us, planning and replanning routes out of town, towns to go to, countries where someone else was already living with our name. We could hear Mother opening the back door, asking Father, "Where are the girls?"

We were right there below them, lighting books of matches.

They were never out of sound, the scuffle of feet above us mapping their worries. Their feet seemed slow to us. These were the easy feet to catch, walking predictable turns through rooms, heavy feet, easy to catch up with or run from. We were getting ready to make the run. We stuck matches together, watched them fuse and burn out. We burned our nails and the soles of our feet. We put on the wolf's costume and consumed the swan. We put on the swan's costume and never became the prince's bride. We blew smoke rings in the crotch of Sleeping Beauty. We woke as Sleeping Beauty, torched the castle, and went back to sleep. We woke into the fifteenth century in the burning city of Bern, filled our wooden buckets, and prayed.

We woke in our basement, in our house, on our same street, to the smell of tart apple and brandy and brown sugar in the skillet. We woke tired and weak of foot.

There was crème fraîche on the table.

Spoons in every bowl.

We hurried to eat more than our share.

<hr />

THE RIVER PRUT flooded. Leaves covered our yard.

Our father said, "Look at us."

We looked almost like every other American family out for Saturday chores—raking, piling leaves to burn. We were all out, even Fokine in his gray suit, picking up leaves one by one. Mother called out orders. We were to get under the rosebushes and up on the rosebushes, where leaves had spun up and stuck on the thorns. The thorns made our hands bleedy and we wiped the blood on the legs of our pants. Monsieur Max stood up from his plastic lawn chair and called out to the brutal winds of Chiapas that he said tore through our woods. It was, declared Monsieur Max, like the love he loved for Esperanza, something to make a man sing. We heard our father singing songs in languages with notes we could not imitate.

"Only in America," said our father.

The piles of leaves toppled and fell, and we girls fell, too, our parents scattering, falling after us, trying to save us from drowning in the River Prut.

WE OFFER OUR youngest sister for a look at the slow boy scrawl-
ing her name with his dick piss. We will double with the Dutch for
titty for his father's cigarettes, and more, too, about where our parents have buried arms, and the thing we swear to him we have seen a
bandit do to a boy with a bandit's teeth. We could, it feels, keep talking, and we do, telling the boy how to say *fuck* in Pogo Pogo, how we
have seen a man charm a snake down his throat, how our uncle has
killed a soldier just with words. The eldest is our talker, walking
around the slow boy in fast circles until, grinding and turning after
her, he trips against the road curb. We take him roughly. We speak in
Crocodile and Bulgarian. She tells the slow boy that there are places
for a boy like him. "Just look!" She points at his wadded pants.
"You're dead." We leave him, scraped, road pebbles stuck bloody to
his knees. We leave him, pants down.

We walk home.

We are spies and counterspies.

We are starlets hiding bombs in the spangle of dresses.

They are hiding out in that house, waiting for the soldier and the
milkman with his metal truck.

We are running.

Here we come.

LISTEN. . . . YOU CAN HEAR the sultan's dreams when he takes
his night sleep by day at our dinner table. The sultan always sleeps by
day, fighting Turks in his empire. He tosses, wipes tears from his one
good eye on our tablecloth, rises crusty-eyed and hungry when we
are called to eat.

Watch. . . . He will not eat from his own plate, not with a fork or
with his hands, not until we are all done and the plates are bones and
chewed stems and the cabbage we girls spread to the china's far rim.
Not until then and then some. The sultan starts with our mother's

plate, sucking at the blued empty shells she has stacked, using an end of bread to sop up juice of spinach and garlic from our father's plate, and, over our plates, he winks at us, his mouth stuffed full of all that we girls have wasted.

We were always, the sultan said, in his dreams, wielding great swords. We were true armsmen, beheading without a second thought when the sultan cried out for a head. The sultan said we showed our family's refined taste, catching with a free, gloved hand and never letting a severed head just drop.

But to listen into his dreams, we let his empires fall.

What burned by whose hand where? What woods are these? The scorched pot? The soup all gone? Where stirred the wind? The Prut, we girls knew, the Danube turned and running inland? A bag of shells? A cigarette? The polished gleam off Fokine's shoes? The tutus aflame? The flames flared out the window like a red flag? What did they see—the slow boy standing on Monsieur Max's lawn chair, screaming *fuck* in Pogo Pogo, the fathers in a huddle behind him? Did they come in the night or by day, the milkman in his metal truck? Did they ride off with the pretty sister whooping, "Take me!"? Or with the prettier sisters, did they kiss and steal into the woods? Whose woods? I think I know. Every house became a secret language. Everything on fire. But nothing burned.

The sultan sighed in his sleep. He called out for us in the names he had for us, and you could hear in the pause between his cries that we girls, his darlings, were traitors, ministering to him so tenderly from a poisoned cup.

WE HAD NO ACCENT.

Every language they spoke in that house was a secret language, a code we were always on the verge of breaking.

We spoke English.

We have walked into rooms into far cities and felt at home in the cluck and warble of what we could not understand.

We understand so little. What we do not understand pulses, clots familiarly inside. A worried thread we pull. The frayed woolly edge of a child's blanket.

We have had our children.

We have wandered into Russian beauty shops and, under the facialist's puffy hands and gossip's tongue, fallen fast asleep. We wake to the fighting of Romanian cocks. We feel a wind and hear its Mexican heat.

Our sister sleeps in a pinstripe suit.

Our sister has the messy scrawl of a poet.

Our sister is a mother.

We wake into the disaster of another calm day.

We wake again.

She wakes from a dream of her father, who is not sleeping. He walks in her dream through the halls, stopping at doorways, counting heads. She takes her money belt down to the market and buys her future long. She finds her daughter squatting over a mirror, trying to see up to her heart.

Today is July Fourth.

Please come to our houses. We will feed you a little something, a glass of pale wine. Our doors, we leave them open. We douse charcoal with lighter fluid. We light matches. We have no accents. We eat burgers with catsup, dogs with mustard.

We hear of fleeing, the ones who come on boats.

What a pack of liars is this Russia!

Do you think our father saved a single one? The *patria*. The *patria*.

We gather with the others to watch fireworks.

One sister writes, "It is the Fourth of July." One sister holds a son in her lap.

He says, "Boom."

One sister watches for interest rates to plunge.

They are gone, Monsieur Max and our mother's chiffon skirt.

The money belts are tied up in treasury bills and bonds.

It is America. We are America.

The house is a house that looks like every other house, the River Prut a straggly tangle of trees, our mama, our papa—a mother and father we watch age into the common fretting of the old.

Cithagan yithagou ithagundithagerstithagand mithagee?

My sisters say I have it all wrong. I leave out what is important.

We speak such good English.

I leave out Amelia Wanderling and Paul Logaurcia, who danced the part of the prince. I have not said enough about Uncle Marie's good head of hair. Have I said *containment?* Have I said how we held our hands to our hearts and pledged ourselves, how we are sisters who let nothing burn?

There are seconds on burgers, if you are still hungry.

We live, all of us, in the same city, on the same bus line, close to the freeway. We read with a tribal heart about cities in ruin.

They say there are no gypsies.

I have not said Akerman.

The band starts to play. The crowd cheers.

The sultan closes his one good eye when the band starts to play. He listens. The sultan drifts, with a wheeze and a God bless America, into dreamless sleep.

My sisters say there is no sultan.

Drink up. It is the Fourth of July. This is my America.

I have got it all wrong.

The Fate of Great Love

BY TAMMIE BOB

When she was eleven Ruthie discovered romantic love, not as a participant but as an inflamed, yearning spectator. The affair featured her cousin Elisabeth, home for Thanksgiving from her first year at Brandeis University. Thanksgiving was at the home of Elisabeth's parents, Uncle Sol and Aunt Leonora, because of all the family, only they already owned a house with enough room to seat everyone, all the aunts and near-aunts. In America doctors made money quickly, Mommy and Daddy remarked more than once, even not very good doctors like Uncle Sol, who was unsure from one moment to the next whether he was in Poland or Germany or Cleveland, whether he was hiding from Nazis or searching his closet for a tie.

As a result, he had to be a doctor in the Hough area, where the Negroes lived, which Ruthie thought was too bad for them. But what could you do, Daddy would shrug, shaking his head as if it were sad for him to once again have to explain to Ruthie an example of the world's harshness. Most doctors wouldn't practice in that neighborhood, and even a doctor like Sol was better for those people than no doctor at all.

And, Mommy would add, lowering her eyelashes to cast a tragic shadow over her cheekbones, another sad fact was that in America learning was not respected as it was in Europe. That was why it took a long time for a professor like Daddy to earn enough money for a house, especially since they'd started out with nothing, which was what everyone had brought from Europe, *nichts,* because Hitler had stolen everything except their lives, which, of course, were all that mattered, finally. (A sour note in Mommy's voice suggested that now, with life long out of jeopardy, she again longed for what was taken.) But when Daddy got tenure, soon, Mommy said, their family would have a house, although probably not as big as Uncle Sol's and certainly not as grand as the ones lost in Europe.

Everybody was eager to see Elisabeth during her first visit home from Brandeis, such a first-class school, comparable to Heidelberg, the Sorbonne, Oxford, or Harvard here in America—but for Jews, named for a Jew, a Judge Brandeis. Their European accents pronounced it "Brendt-Ice," making Ruthie, who understood German, picture burning ice, a frozen pond aflame. (It was the pond in Boston Commons, portrayed in a postcard Elisabeth had sent her. The blaze consumed ice skaters and swan boats; it leaped snowdrifts to scorch and blacken ivied buildings, the Jewish Supreme Court judge, and, most horribly, Elisabeth, as if her attendance at this important college were connected to the family's suffering in Europe at the hands of the Nazis twenty years earlier.)

She was bringing a boy home with her, already . . . one aunt telephoned another, spreading the news. What could that mean, after such a short time? Ach, what happens when children leave home: shock and heartache! Why did Sol and Leonora allow her to study so far away, knowing their days would bloat, listless and flabby, with Elisabeth gone? Uncle Sol had announced that his daughter would study at the best place for her chosen field, psychology, just as he had gone from Poland to Germany as a young man to study medicine. He admitted, teeth glinting gold beneath his mustache, that he had made a little money in America, could afford to send his daughter to any college she wished . . . it was not the nineteenth century anymore, when girls had to stay home until they married.

Who would think Sol capable of such new ideas, the way he constantly reentered his terrible past, twisting every emblem into a swastika, ranting about the evil world that tolerated and even encouraged atrocities, invoking the words and deeds of his murdered parents, brothers, sisters, friends, as if he had seen them just yesterday or expected them to drop by tomorrow. Yet he did see that Elisabeth was not part of that world, even though she had been born in the refugee camp Bergen-Belsen, a tulip poking through foul refuse, a diamond swept from the poisonous cinders of the former death camp.

Of course boys adored Elisabeth, the family knew any boy would want to pursue her . . . but to bring him here right away? Could it be serious already? Aunt Leonora didn't say, or didn't know; she had always refrained from interfering too much in Elisabeth's activities, raising her daughter "the way it's done in America," as if those words were an antidote against the poisons that had polluted her own life. In contrast, Mommy, who had determined to leave Europe's awfulness behind (perhaps because her wartime life of pretense and hiding had taught her to adapt), believed she should have a hand in every aspect of her children's lives. Why shouldn't they benefit from her great experience? For example, she often advised Ruthie that with careful grooming and a sweet smile she would not feel so inferior to her older cousin.

"You shouldn't be jealous of Elisabeth's blond hair, or all her prizes: debating, writing, cheerleading. You're as smart as she is— what you should watch is how she combines her brains with sweetness, with humor to convince people that she's the most beautiful, the most talented. Femininity can be learned. Do what she does. Then when you're older you'll have many boyfriends, too."

Ruthie knew this was untrue; she could no more become like Elisabeth by observing her than she could acquire the delicacy of a hummingbird by observing it. (She was proud of this particularly elegant metaphor, but wasn't ready to say it aloud yet . . . it was possible that Mommy would laugh.) Anyhow, she wasn't jealous of her cousin, any more than she was jealous of a Mozart symphony—for envy there had to be some basis of comparison, and between herself and Elisabeth she could find none. Like the rest of the world, she idolized and treasured her cousin. Still, she could see how Mommy, so lovely and clever, would expect to have a daughter like Elisabeth instead of pudgy, stringy-haired Ruthie, whose dour face, whose aura of gravity, could easily be imagined belonging to a daughter of Aunt Leonora.

Ruthie thought that if she were Elisabeth, she, too, would want to go to college as far away as possible to escape her gloomy parents, although her cousin had never expressed or implied such a wish, even during the intimate times when she'd invited Ruthie into her room, allowing her younger cousin to examine her fascinating possessions: teen magazines, yearbooks, mascara, garter belts, letter jackets boys had given her to wear.

(What must that boy's family think, him going home with a girl his first break from Brandeis! Upsetting, too, that his name was Antonio Vitarelli. Aunt Leonora let that slip out so everyone would be prepared, an Italian. With so many Jews at Brandeis, you didn't expect such a thing. But Elisabeth had always shown wisdom and logic in her choices, so one mustn't jump to conclusions.)

—

THANKSGIVING, ELISABETH AND Antonio Vitarelli were stationed at the front doorway, so everyone could meet him right away. He was entirely American, you could tell by his relaxed shoulders, the swing of his arms (so gorgeous in his nubby white sweater). "Please don't call me Tony," he said, manfully shaking Daddy's hand. "It just doesn't suit me."

"It's the same with me," Elisabeth added. "I could never be a Liz or a Betty." She gazed at Antonio as if it were this absence of nicknames that bound them together. Ruthie, suddenly shy, did not quite recognize Elisabeth, although there was no specific change in her appearance. She barely acknowledged Ruthie, and neither did anyone else, understandably; the aunts and uncles who usually fussed over Ruthie's grades and growth spurts now were buzzing about their Elisabeth, beautiful, more than ever, like a movie star, and look at him, what do you think, the Italian, such nice manners, even Elisabeth might lose her head over a boy who looked like that. (Eyes like that can make trouble for a girl.)

"Sure, he's a nice boy, why shouldn't he be a nice boy?" Leonora squared off against the curious multitude helping in her kitchen. "Elisabeth always has nice friends." But would a mere "friend" come home with her for a holiday? Didn't his own family want him?

Antonio and Elisabeth organized a hunt for marshmallow-roasting sticks for the younger children: Ruthie's brother Marvin and two small boys from a distant cousin they rarely saw. Ruthie hesitated to join this group because she was eleven, although she wanted to be with Elisabeth, and Antonio too, even though she felt strange around him. Soon they gathered in front of the fireplace, boxes of graham crackers and bars of chocolate nearby. She would have liked an invitation to Elisabeth's bedroom to hear about her new life, but there was no chance of that today.

"You want a stick—Ruthie?" He knew her name! Antonio was holding a stick out to her! She took it, growing warm as she got close to him. Somehow she couldn't look straight at him, as if she had forgotten how you look at someone, maybe because he was so tall. She didn't know what to say, the whole time letting her marshmallow char away in the fire while the little boys jabbered about Sky King and cowboys. Antonio and Elisabeth were laughing, encouraging the stupid talk about television while Ruthie couldn't think of a thing to say. Her face was burning, all of her was, maybe from facing the fireplace while she roasted her marshmallows. A few times she

found herself watching him, the way his hair curled over his ears, the way he sucked some marshmallow off his fingers.

The entire activity was too exotic for the various aunts and uncles who had never been American Scouts. So much dirt in the house, sticks and sticky fingers! Parents fussed at their children, warning them not to get too close to the fire, not to burn themselves.

Later, after stripping the turkey, which was undeniably dry, having absorbed the flavor of the paper bag in which it had been cooked, the dozen or so grown-ups gathered in the living room to assist Huntley-Brinkley with the news and to sample runny liqueur-filled chocolates. They compared what their doctors had to say about their sinuses, their digestive systems, their circulations. The little boys went outside to run around. Ruthie foraged for a deck of cards in Uncle Sol's study, ignoring his collection of stuffed birds, rabbits, squirrels, raccoons. He chose his specimens from roads and fields, already dead but not mutilated, and had them preserved precisely in their moment of death. Normally Ruthie preferred not to be alone in this room, but she needed a deck of cards so she could entice Elisabeth and Antonio into a game of 500 rummy, just the three of them.

But when she went to convey this invitation, it turned out that Elisabeth and Antonio were locked together in a corner of the dining room, kissing. Perhaps they were pretending that the slatted door opening out from the kitchen sheltered a private nook. Ruthie watched because she had never seen kissing like this before, this kissing entirely different from the pursed-lip pecks of her own experience, and also different from the loving but tired kisses that Mommy and Daddy had, and still different from, but related to, long romantic movie kisses that involved a couple rotating their heads first one way and then the other. Neither Antonio's dark head nor Elisabeth's blond one swiveled at all. Antonio's jaw chugged up and down like a singing bullfrog's, as if he were drinking some needed substance from Elisabeth's mouth, and one of his hands spread across Elisa-

beth's head, fingers snarled in her gleaming hair. His other hand dug at the flat surface of Elisabeth's rear pocket as though he had lost something there. Though their heads barely moved, their mingled bodies, identically dressed (in white cabled sweaters and corduroy pants), rubbed and bubbled like boiling soup.

Ruthie watched for several minutes, holding her breath, sticky as if she were joined into this incredible activity herself. Then she tip-toed bravely past them, taking refuge in the kitchen, where she paced the dish-littered room without purpose. Soon Aunt Leonora came in, rattling a stack of cups and saucers. These she exchanged for a plateful of grapes, ignoring Ruthie.

Ruthie shadowed Leonora out of the kitchen. With alarm and even disgust, she saw the couple still cleaving and heaving in their well-lit, public corner.

"Now, now," clucked Leonora, pausing with the grapes. "That is enough, I should think."

The two heads stretched apart reluctantly, like taffy, leaving a sad, airless hole. Elisabeth turned toward her mother politely, but without recognition. Ruthie saw, as anyone behind Leonora would have seen, that her cousin's face had blurred, melted, the lovely eyes and lips and chin no longer defined but smeared and blended into flushed pink skin, while Antonio's face was pale and icelike, extruding manly black dots of beard, his chin deeply split, the wings of his nose rigidly hewn. Even his feathery eyelashes now jutted like spikes around eyes that earlier had resembled melting chocolate but now contracted into charcoal snowman eyes.

And Ruthie, sad hair furrowed by her plastic headband, stomach squeezed over the waistband of her plaid skirt (unevenly fastened with a decorative gold safety pin), fat legs weighted by collapsing kneesocks, Ruthie was choking on lumps of admiration and jealousy. That *was* jealousy finally, grabbing her by the throat and squeezing, as she would willingly have strangled her beautiful, dazed cousin had there been any chance she could have her place next to the boy, who was taking his time extricating his chest, his hand, his thigh from

Elisabeth's. Meanwhile, Aunt Leonora lectured, "This isn't the place for that! Come now! What behavior! That's quite enough," as if she imagined that any of them were interested in her opinions.

It was clear to Ruthie that Leonora, short and square, had been squashed by the details of her life: bent by the weight of bad memories, the multitude of Thanksgiving guests and the complex menu, and her husband, Uncle Sol, who at any moment might forget where he was and fling himself into a closet, since his demons refused to leave him, preferring to hover nearby, waiting to overpower him. She was overburdened by her counters full of dirty dishes, and by the old relatives, who, lacking sufficient English, needed help negotiating their visas, their reparations, their rental agreements, their excursions to stores and to doctors. (Aunt Leonora shouldered these crushing tasks rather than her brother, Daddy, because she was capable with money and bureaucrats, understanding how to manipulate and negotiate to advantage, while Daddy's concerns were loftier: his lectures and papers, his research, his views of the state of the world.) She was crushed by her own difficulties seeing over the steering wheel when she drove, and even by the heavy grapes on the platter in her hands. Such loads rendered Leonora indifferent to Love, epic Love, Love which requires only that you take a step back and admire it from afar. Ruthie recognized Great Love from mythology, Renaissance paintings, and movies, but Leonora was unimpressed by True Passion, and kept pecking and clucking about their naïveté, their foolish idealism, their family backgrounds.

She informed the unhearing lovers that while Elisabeth came from fine people and most certainly Antonio came from fine people, too, no amount of smooching could change the fact that the two of them didn't belong together. Didn't they care that what they stood for, the very sight of them together, was repulsive, made her sick, and would surely sicken Antonio's parents, too? They were a slap in the face to all their fine people on both sides, especially those who were no longer living.

Briefly Ruthie saw those fine people appear in Aunt Leonora's dining room, rising from mausoleums and crypts and cemeteries and mass graves, lining up behind their respective offspring. Roman soldiers and buxom Caravaggio peasants with feet purple from stomping grapes, mustachioed barbers, opera singers, and painters painting ceilings while lying on their backs, pinstriped gangsters with machine guns, heavy dark women with mustaches and black dresses, robed monks with bald circles on their heads, nuns, and even a pope crowded behind Antonio Vitarelli, while behind Elisabeth the entourage contained wild-bearded prophets in sackcloth and ashes, men wearing wide fur hats and curled earlocks, a king with a harp, doe-eyed girls with jugs balanced on their heads, women with kerchiefs and aprons swinging chickens by the feet, peddlers pushing clunky carts, bankers in spats and starched white collars, sharp-nosed women in furs, spectacled students carrying volumes of Spinoza, tanned pioneers in wire-rimmed glasses and kibbutz hats, and hollow-eyed wretches with shaved heads and yellow stars on their tattered striped uniforms.

The two mighty hordes pulled at their respective offspring, clawing them apart, so that even though Elisabeth and Antonio did return together to Brandeis University, it was evident to Ruthie that doom awaited them, as it did all Great Lovers.

⁓

ON HER WINTER break from Brandeis, Elisabeth spent the three weeks at home pining for handsome Antonio, who was with his own family in New Jersey. She wasn't herself at all, fighting with her parents over everything: she didn't wish to visit the relatives and wouldn't eat the foods Aunt Leonora prepared for her. She sat alone in her room, playing records, claiming she had no patience for her high school friends. She took long walks by herself, in the snow, without boots.

"Call her, Ruthie," Mommy ordered. "Ask her to spend an afternoon with you. Maybe it would make her feel good to spend time with a cousin near her own age."

Ruthie's hands shook as she dialed, aware of her presumptuousness—at eleven she was hardly Elisabeth's contemporary, even though Mommy always fantasized that they had a special relationship—and she stammered out the invitation, would Elisabeth take her to a movie or shopping.

"Really, Ruthie, you need to find some friends your own age!" Nastiness crackled into Ruthie's ear.

"I do! I have friends my age!"

"You can't sit around waiting for me to entertain you. If you have friends, you should call them."

"I have lots of friends!" Didn't she? As soon as she said it she had doubts. How dare she imagine Elisabeth would turn to a friendless creep like her? "I have plenty of friends to play with!" Probably her friends didn't really like her. Elisabeth's sigh wafted through the phone.

"I'm sorry, Ruthie. I don't feel very sociable. I wouldn't be good company."

"Oh." Ruthie tried to sound like she understood exactly.

"I miss Antonio so much. I didn't know being in love would be like this."

"Oh, sure."

"When we're apart I can't function, I'm not myself . . . I'm not anything!"

"It sounds awful!" said Ruthie, indignant that such love should be sundered, even temporarily.

"I've never been so happy in my life." Elisabeth's voice was weak, as if she were falling asleep. "Someday you'll understand."

But Ruthie was sure she understood already, thinking of Antonio, what it would feel like to be kissed the way he had kissed Elisabeth on Thanksgiving. Her lips would mash against her teeth, his cheeks would scratch her face. "Ruthie Ruthie Ruthie," he whispered, his eyes narrowing, seeing only her. She hugged herself, digging her fingers into her shoulders, shuddering with longing.

AT THE END of January, after failing to contact Elisabeth for five fretful days in a row, Aunt Leonora succumbed to a "strange feeling that something was wrong." She alerted Elisabeth's dorm house-mother, who grilled Elisabeth's roommate, a tough New York girl who claimed ignorance of her roommate's whereabouts, remaining loyal to Elisabeth even though she knew all. The girl broke only when subjected to higher officials and intensified questioning, which in Ruthie's understanding had taken place in a soundproof room lit by one dangling light bulb. The roommate, blindfolded and bound by bandannas that dug into her wrists and flattened her wiry New York hair, chewed her lips as burly professors in mortarboards sneered accusations at her: "Is it possible that there's been foul play? Isn't it a fact that you're an accomplice?" Finally, still refusing to speak, the terrified girl produced a wrinkled paper on which Elisabeth had scrawled, "We're off to Florida, ta-ta!"

It was that "ta-ta" which, to the family, signaled a rat—would a girl so serious, so sensitive, make light of such a grave situation? For her parents were certain that their only child, their miracle con-ceived and born in the ashes of a DP camp, had run off to marry *that Italian boy.* The family gathered, again at Sol and Leonora's house, but for what? A wedding? More like a tragedy!

"BE QUIET!" AUNT LEONORA greeted Ruthie's family at the door, her finger to her lips. "Sol is on the phone. With the FBI!"

"Can I see the puppy?" asked Marvin, who did not care that Elisa-beth had ruined her life.

Ruthie's family tiptoed through the house, Mommy heading toward the kitchen with a bakery box while Marvin went to the basement to play with a puppy Sol and Leonora had recently acquired. You wouldn't expect Uncle Sol and Aunt Leonora to have a puppy. One of Sol's patients had given it to him, and Leonora thought it would make a nice diversion, a small consolation for Elisabeth's being so far away at Brandeis. But it wasn't much comfort. The puppy's yipping and yapping made Uncle Sol even crazier than usual, so they kept it locked in the basement where it cried all the time.

Daddy headed for the living room, with Ruthie right behind him. She did not immediately notice Tante Hilde knitting in a dark corner among the overstuffed furniture, despite the immense bulk overflowing the armchair. "A fine mess that brings us here, *nicht wahr?*" she greeted Daddy. Ruthie started to back out of the room. "Tell the child to bring me a glass of water," Tante Hilde said.

"*Go,* Ruthie," Daddy ordered.

Ruthie fled down the hall. The kitchen contained several other aunts, laying rolls and cold cuts out on trays. She opened the refrigerator to search for a bottle of seltzer, but Leonora pushed her aside.

"Ach, Ruthie. Why are you holding the refrigerator door open so long, spoiling all the food? Zena, why did you bring the children?"

The basement door opened a crack. At once a small beagle head lunged out, but Marvin grabbed it back and followed it into the basement.

"A family should be together at difficult times," Mommy answered, rolling her pretty eyes a bit. "And when in all the years did you ever leave Elisabeth at home?"

Leonora's round peach face twisted. "Elisabeth!" she moaned. "*Gott, mein Gott!*"

"Is there any news?" Mommy whispered in German. From the dining room one heard the thunderclap of Uncle Sol's voice.

"WHAT DO I CARE IF IT'S 'AFTER HOURS'! DO YOU KNOW THIS NAME: VITARELLI! SHE WAS TAKEN BY A VITARELLI! MAYBE MAFIA! DON'T YOU KNOW WHAT IS THE LAW!" Since he had spent the war changing papers, identities, hiding places, he was never entirely certain what year it was, what country he was in, what form of government prevailed.

"It's not so bad that he's an Italian." Leonora collected herself. Her fingers gleamed from touching cold cuts. "I just don't understand why they had to run away."

From the dining room: "I TELL YOU SHE IS TAKEN!" After all, he explained, Elisabeth, so beautiful, so accomplished, so reliable, his daughter—surely she wouldn't choose to disappear?

"You should sue the university is what you should do," said Aunt Cidi. "Then they'd find her quick."

On the stove, a pan of sausages ignited, shooting smoky flames to the ceiling. Women gasped and leaped out of the way: "Call the firemen!" Ruthie shrank back against the refrigerator, ready to throw Tante Hilde's glass of sloshing seltzer into the advancing inferno, but Leonora was already holding the pan under running water. Smoke and oily black rings floated upward. Squealing, scratching, and yipping came from inside the basement door. "Come back down here," Marvin's voice pleaded.

"Oh, that would have been a real disaster," Leonora said.

"Why are you fussing so much at a time like this?" Mommy scolded her sister-in-law. "Who will eat all this food, so much *braunschweiger,* so much *blutwurst?*"

"Everything will be fine," Leonora said. Only a few black spatters greased the wall over the sink. "We shouldn't get so excited." She took the dripping, charred sausages from the sink and lay them on a dishtowel. "I'll dry them off and they'll be just fine, good as new."

Ruthie headed for the living room with Tante Hilde's water, not particularly caring how cold it was. Women trooped ahead carrying trays, the meats, the cheeses, the cakes needed to pacify them this evening.

"You will hear from my congressman! He has met me!" Sol shouted. You could hear him crash the phone and the receiver together, like cymbals.

Tante Hilde took the glass without looking up at Ruthie's face. "Why did you take so long?" she scolded. "Every time I see you you seem less capable. You are at that stupid age, I imagine." Ruthie had long ago learned not to respond to this great-aunt by breathing deeply and shutting her eyes. ("She means well," Daddy always said, as if Ruthie should acknowledge Hilde's goodwill.) The aunts were subdued, sampling chocolates, speaking of Elisabeth in the past tense as they comforted Leonara: she was always such a good girl, a boy would respect that; she still loved her parents, you could be sure, no matter where she was; many women survived youthful mistakes, sometimes they even turned out well . . .

A pale and wrinkled Uncle Sol settled on the sofa near Mommy. "I don't know . . . ," he sighed, pinching his nose. "They say in America things are different, but everywhere it's the same . . . a person disappears and no one lifts a finger . . . bureaucrats, criminals . . ." He began to shake—his entire family, taken: father, mother, brother, another brother, the two wives, all the children, babies, the youngest brother shot as they all looked on, no one left, no one left, no one . . . "Taken," he muttered.

"Stop this, Sol!" Leonora ordered. "Elisabeth wasn't taken away, she has run away! She will come back!"

"WHAT! RUN AWAY!" He stamped both his slippered feet under the coffee table so that the sausages trembled on their platters. "When they took my family, *I* run away! For years I run away! My daughter doesn't have to run away! She was TAKEN!" He began pacing the room, waving his arms and muttering.

This awkwardness didn't silence the room for long, because the family was accustomed to Sol's behavior. Daddy changed the subject.

"So how does a girl find an Italian at Brandeis University?"

"Italians are not good husbands," Tante Hilde declared, setting aside her needlework. "They drink and chase after other women as soon as they make the first child." She added that all winter long in Italy they shot migrating birds out of the sky. Bluebirds, larks, thrushes: no bird was too small for Italians to cook into their puddings and stews.

"Really!" Daddy said. "They shoot songbirds?"

She nodded her large gray head. "It is known." She had heard that so many were slaughtered during their winter migration over Italy that barely a bird remained to return to Germany in the spring.

Who could respond to that? There was no sound other than Sol's pacing and the clink of ice cubes.

"I wish I knew how to reach Elisabeth." Mommy refreshed her lipstick without a mirror. "I have a feeling she would confide in me. I haven't forgotten what it's like to be young."

"We followed all the advice about raising children: Dr. Spock, Ann Landers," Leonora fretted. "It's not like we kept her locked away." Her eyes puckered, real grief that made Ruthie want to cry, too.

"Still, she's afraid to talk to you." Mommy took a nail file out of her purse.

"A girl unmarried belongs with her parents!" Sol said, still moving, raking his sparse gray hair into alarming points.

"Such a beauty," Aunt Cidi added. "And she was smart about boys, wasn't she? She knew not to let them take advantages?"

"Great beauty can be a curse," Tante Hilde said. She was knitting again. "Perhaps in Elisabeth's case it has led to her downfall."

"Downfall!" Mommy snapped. "What a way to talk about your niece!"

"It's because she *is* my blood that I know. Some women can cleverly manipulate a man, but others are softer and easily fooled. Oh, I know very well what it is to be led astray by a man!"

Ruthie sat forward, wishing to hear just how Tante Hilde had come to be led astray. What man would have even dared toy with the woman buried fifty years into that hulk? She must have exacted terrible retribution. (But it had to be lies; if Ruthie never found a boyfriend, she thought she might tell such lies. She imagined herself old, headband scraping her sparse white hair away from jowls that wobbled as she told her bored descendants tales of ardent lovers and spurned suitors. If you told a lie often enough, it began to seem true . . . would she finally believe her own stories?)

From the kitchen a crash, splintering wood. A whiz of beagle flew into the living room, changing course every few seconds to avoid the densely packed furniture. Leonora rose from her chair, but though her square figure darted here and there, it never managed to occupy even the same quadrant of the room as the puppy. Marvin, running in pursuit, smashed against a curio cabinet, causing several teacups to spill onto the floor. Ruthie reached down and caught hold of surprisingly loose dog skin. She pulled the flailing puppy into her lap.

"Is nice doggy, no?" Sol observed as everyone caught their breath, straightening the results of chaos.

Ruthie lifted the puppy by its armpits and looked into the shaking spotted face. His eyes were deep and tragic, telling of early trauma: separation from his mother, random painful whacks on the nose, isolation in the basement.

"It's a good idea to have a watchdog," Leonora said.

"What does he watch locked in the basement?" asked Daddy.

"He must stay there until he becomes housebroken."

"My heart is broken!" Sol declared. Apparently the pacing potential of the living room was exhausted, for he opened the front door and strode outside, not bothering to take a coat or shut the door.

"Perhaps you should go to Boston," Mommy said, turning to Leonora and the business at hand. "You should talk to her friends. They will know more than anyone."

Leonora said she was considering it, and wondered if she could leave Sol alone in the house for a few days. At this, the puppy leaped from Ruthie's lap, pausing only to grab the string of blackened sausages, and catapulted against the storm door, which gave away.

"Marvin! Ruthie! Catch him!" Mommy ordered, but the two children were already after the animal, now a dark shadow running in ever-widening circles in the spotlit dirty snow. This startled Uncle Sol, who was also navigating the front lawn.

"Your coats! Your boots!" Mommy shouted. It was glorious, the sting of snow melting into their shoes as they ran. The aunts bunched together by the door to watch the flailing, shouting, even joyful chase. Moments later, Uncle Sol leaped after the puppy. It veered, disappearing under the advancing headlights of a large dark car. The car slowed for a moment, during which all was quiet, then gunned its motor and sped away. The puppy lay in the road on its side, flattened, the string of sausages still clamped in its mouth.

"Oh, dear." Aunt Leonora wiped her mouth with her hand. "*Mein Gott*. Poor, poor thing." Marvin burst into tears and ran to the house, to Mommy. Ruthie didn't want to go in, but she was getting cold.

Someone said at least it was quick. Outside, Sol was heading toward the body—approaching the animal, she was certain, not as a grieving owner or even a doctor but as a collector, looking to augment that extensive taxidermy collection in his study. Leonora ran after him, her squat body quick in the cold, and pulled him away, back into the house.

Mommy was preparing to leave: it was late, the children were tired, so much excitement, they should not have come.

"The boy should not have let the animal out of the cellar," Tante Hilde observed. She had not gotten up from her corner, because she did not move easily. "A wild boy has no more sense than a wild animal."

It was true, Ruthie thought, shocked to find herself even partially agreeing with the mean old woman; even so, anyone could see that Marvin was terribly sorry, more than anyone else.

"It's not his fault," Daddy said, putting his coat on. "How could you blame Marvin? What happened was perfectly clear. I hate to say it, but this is the first time I have ever seen such a thing—an animal committing suicide."

⌒

WITHIN TWO WEEKS of the dog's death, Elisabeth was returned home, transferred to Case Western Reserve, to lead a "quieter life and concentrate on her studies," according to Aunt Leonora.

As if Elisabeth had ever neglected her studies! Her life was a parade of awards and honors: besides being in the usual honor societies, she'd won a citywide competition for her essay "President Kennedy: Changing America's Youth Forever," and a chapter of the

VFW had chosen her as the first girl to receive the America's Best Hope award. For years already she had sipped coffee among the adults, crossing and recrossing her grown-up legs in their nylon stockings to explain precisely (pressing together the thumb and forefinger of her right hand) the flaws and dangers of the domino theory, the posturing of Madame Nhu. Naturally, she hadn't neglected her studies (hadn't Case Western accepted her at once, unconditionally, in the middle of the term?), and in the end it turned out she hadn't really "run off" with Antonio Vitarelli either. Rather, they had gone to a cottage his parents owned near Boca Raton, just for one week, because she greatly needed some sun. She explained this to Mommy with Ruthie right there in the room, but Aunt Leonora out of earshot.

Perhaps the escapade had been impulsive, Elisabeth allowed, lifting her beautiful, heavy-lidded blue eyes to punctuate her true telling of events. But she had been so tired just then, from all her classes, a pinching headache that never went away, and a scratchy throat more often than not. And Boston had been so cold that week, all fall really, cold and bleary except for Antonio, from her Principles of Psych class, who had loved her, whom she had loved. (And she made it seem reasonable that one couldn't survive under that kind of hardship, Bad Weather in Boston. Who else could get away with such melodrama: "From the beginning we were so close; so, so close," first willing and then holding back tears to puddle the blue, blue eyes that stared far away over Mommy's head. Her pink unpainted lips trembled as she spoke, so bravely it would break your heart to see it.) Antonio Vitarelli had suggested the vacation, just for the week; they could both easily make up their schoolwork, he was worried about her health and knew she needed rest, a week of hot sun . . . "And was it really so terrible that I went?" she asked them, her serene features a study in rationality. "I didn't mean to cause trouble. I really loved him. Could anyone have expected me to ask my parents?"

"No, not with their old-fashioned ideas." Mommy slandered her sister and brother-in-law while widening her eyes to show her comprehension of Elisabeth's grief. "Still, in the end you'll see your decision was good."

"Of course," Elisabeth agreed, one siren to another. "I have no regrets about anything, though."

"No, you shouldn't. There are always more men. You're entitled to adventures."

Ruthie sat quietly, hiding the excitement stirred by these womanly opinions, this affirmation of female wiles. She could feel Antonio's arms around her as if she had actually been in them . . . he was the most beautiful man she had ever met.

"I've realized how much I don't know," Elisabeth confided, and Mommy nodded: "You're wiser than you think."

She was studying psychology, seriously now, Aunt Leonora bragged; even though Elisabeth was only a freshman she was working closely with one of her professors who recognized her superior abilities, her seriousness . . .

"And she has read Freud?" asked an aunt. Leonora snorted. Freud! Of course Elisabeth had read Freud, long ago. To study psychology one read Freud, that was basic. Freud!

The aunt nodded, satisfied . . . if Elisabeth had read Freud she knew what she was doing, her commitment to the field was unquestionable . . .

In the library, the adult section, Ruthie looked for books by Freud. They were about sex, Ruthie thought; *Totem and Taboo* would be about forbidden things. Although, why "Totem"? What could Freud have cared about Indians? And she had heard that Freud wrote about how girls wanted to have penises (you were allowed to say that word for scientific purposes if you didn't giggle or act silly), although she did not want one and could not recall ever having wanted one. She sat down to read one of the books, but despite the occasional word that titillated her interest (eros, phallus), she found her mind wandering away from the thick, incomprehensible words. She was certain it was not for this that Elisabeth had given up Antonio Vitarelli.

Down These Mean Streets

BY RUTH KNAFO SETTON

But down these mean streets a man must go who is not himself mean—who is neither tarnished nor afraid. . . . —*Raymond Chandler*

Tata Zizou thought it was Bogie we needed. I knew deep in my heart it was me.

SHE HIJACKS ME after school, when I'm standing in the schoolyard. Of course she picks the exact moment when Carlos Rivera finally comes over to talk to me for the first time. He stops in front of me, lights a cigarette—even though smoking isn't allowed on school property—and gives me the long-lashed, slow hard look every girl in the eighth grade yearns for. I'm so stunned that I just stare. It's as if one of my night dreams has moved to daylight. Carlos—standing in front of me, close enough to touch. My friends, Missy and Karen, try to look cool, but their mouths hang open, and their excitement hums through me.

Carlos says, "So—what are we supposed to do for history class tomorrow?"

Before I can answer, he blinks, then narrows his eyes, and steps back.

"What?" I say. "What?"

I turn and look behind me. Advancing like a monster from a swamp: my aunt, her hennaed hair Medusa-snakes, biting and forked in the wind, brown eyes splintered and bloodshot—what Mom calls: *le regard de la folie,* and Dad, simply: Zizou's crazy eyes.

"Sophie," she screeches. "Sophie—" Breathing through her nose, voice desperate and raw. She's a mess, a long muddy feathered scarf looped around her throat, Dad's brown leather bomber jacket, and what look like his striped pajama pants. The fuzzy pink blanket from my bed wrapped around her shoulders. I don't have to push up the jacket sleeve to see the blue numbers screaming down her arm.

Why now? Why here? Oh Tata Zizou, please disappear, walk backwards, end this scene. Start again. Go back home, talk to Mom, light candles, do one of your exorcism chants—but leave me the hell alone!

Carlos half-smiles, but his eyes are already somewhere else, and Karen and Missy watch me pityingly. I'm so embarrassed that without a word, I turn around and walk away, shoving Tata Zizou ahead of me. We're the same height, and from the back, it must look as if I'm walking with a bag lady. As if it's not enough that we live in a cruddy apartment above the Couscous Caboose, the stupidest restaurant in town, probably in the world, and that most of the kids call me Jungle Jew because I'm from Morocco.

"This way," says Zizou urgently. We're at the corner of Second and Ridge, where I usually turn right to go home. She points left, toward the heart of downtown. "I have to show you something!"

"What? Let's just go home." I yank her arm, but she pinches my wrist with fingers that claw. For the first time, I look at her face closely. She's so pale it's scary, lips almost blue. Eyes dilated and starting to roll back the way they do when she shrieks at night.

"What is it, Tata? What's wrong?"

I watch her swallow, try to catch her breath. "He—" she says finally, a gasp more than a word. "*He's*—back! You have—to—save me. Sophie!"

~

I HATE TATA Zizou with a truly profound hate. I hate the way her dark brown eyes crack when *la folie* hits and she forgets who she is. I hate when she calls me a dirty Jew in front of my friends, complains to clients in the restaurant that we mistreat her, periodically draws blue numbers on her arm with my marker—then cradles that arm as if it were a lost, weeping baby. I hate coming home from school and seeing her on the sidewalk in front of the Couscous Caboose, handing out scribbled maps on napkins to her birthday party. She calls out to complete strangers, anyone who passes by, "Such a good time we'll have: saltines, pickles and ginger ale, and maybe I will sing, songs from Mogador, when I was a girl and the sea was young." Most of all I hate how she stands in the middle of the dining room at the dinner hour—our busiest time—draped in my old pink blanket, eyes wildly searching the restaurant until they lock on me. She almost runs to me, breathes garlic and lemon over my face, and sings a broken song in French and Arabic—about how sand blows in your eyes, shoes beat time, a woman screams, the bird dies in a cage, and the beast howls at the town walls.

Only Mom can soothe her then. She leaves the kitchen and hugs Zizou, and gently—murmuring in Arabic—leads her out of the dining room and upstairs to the bedroom—the one she shared with me until her nightly moans and screams made Dad move me into the tiny attic room above, so that I could sleep a whole night without interruption. But the strange thing is that even in the attic, where I sleep alone, I wake up hard and trembling in the middle of the night, the moan sweeping through me like the desert sands she sings about.

She moved in with us when I was eleven—three years ago—after her husband, Uncle Ray, died. It was around the time that Dad had the brainstorm of transforming the failing Sahara Stews into the

Couscous Caboose. "Who doesn't like couscous?" he asked. "Who can resist fourteen varieties of couscous?" He saw Mom and me exchange looks, and he said, "You'll see, this will be our key to Easy Avenue."

I was in sixth grade, and every Friday night Mom, Dad and I went to the Electra Theater, the little theater at the corner of Seventh and Allen, that showed old and foreign movies on a screen that spluttered and oranged as we watched. One night we went to see *The Diary of Anne Frank,* and when Mrs. Krapp, my teacher, talked about the movie in class, I raised my hand and announced that my aunt, who had just moved in with us, was a survivor. She had blue numbers on her arm. Mrs. Krapp told me to invite her to our class. When I got home, I told Dad—who was standing on a ladder, tacking silver and blue foil stars to the ceiling—"to make you feel you're in the Sahara." He grunted and took the tacks out of his mouth. "We didn't go through the camps in Morocco," he said. "But we could have."

I stared up at him, thick curly black hair falling over his eyes, lips tight, stars bunched in his hands. He sighed. "I'm not saying she didn't suffer. We all suffered. We were next in line, and there was no reason in the world to think that the French would save us from the Nazis." He pushed back his hair with his wrist. "We lived those days on the edge of terror, not knowing when they'd call us, not knowing if they'd kill us first, or send us to Europe to die—" He stopped, stars drifting like leaves down his shoulders and arms. "But Zizou is not a survivor. She draws the numbers on with a blue marker. She's crazy."

IN THE FIRST few months when Tata Zizou moved in with us—on her good days, her misty evenings—she insisted on giving me baths, even though I argued that I was far too old, but Mom pleaded with me: "Be patient, Sophie. She's never had a child of her own, and she loves you. Never doubt that. I think she loves you most of all."

Zizou scrubbed me "hard but fairly . . . to scrub the Jewish dirt from you," and told me how Hitler entered her life, or how she entered his.

It was 1945, and she and her family had moved from Mogador to Casablanca, where work was easier to get. They'd all suffered from the deprivations of the war, and the horrific anti-Semitism of the Vichy government, worse even than the Arabs. "The French loathed us," she said. "We were poor, no one had enough food, and we were locked in our houses." I sat in the tub while she scrubbed my back and shoulders, pausing now and then to stroke her faint mustache, or dig her thumb into the dimple in her chin.

Suddenly she sat up straight. "I'm going to tell you about what happened to me the night before the war ended. I've never told anyone else. They wouldn't understand."

I tried to disappear under the water, not wanting to see how her voice pierced the bubbles, her words dripped yellow down the tiled wall.

"A man came to me that night, in my room, in my parent's house. How could he enter? My father locked the door. I shared a room with your mother, but she slept so soundly—or he put a spell on her so she wouldn't hear—and she snored through it all. I awoke at dawn with the feel of this man crushing me, his mouth on mine, his tongue coiled like a snake on mine. The smell of musk and *h'rmel* rising from his dead-cold body, suffocating me. He bit my ear, and I leaped from the bed. He glistened pale, like an onion. Eyes glittering like the silver scales of a fish. I didn't know if he was real, or one of my visions.

"'Who are you?' I asked him.

"He sat up in my bed. 'I am a saint,' he said. 'We'll set up shop together. I'll wait in the back room while you heal in the front room. You can trust me: Rosina sent me.'

"'My sister never sent you!' I cried.

"'Don't fight me, Zizou. I am going to make you the most famous healer in Morocco. You already have the touch, but every healer needs her male spirit, her saint to give her the answers.'

"I dressed and went to the door, then turned back. 'You're no saint,' I said. 'You don't fool me. You're a djinn!'

"He laughed. 'I'll find you wherever you go.'

"In terror and rage, I slammed the door behind me, ran through the house, and out to the street. Made myself slow down, straighten my dress, bra straps, garters, adjust the seam in my stockings. I was human again, a young woman of twenty-one, innocent and normal like any other woman in Morocco, not one who had just spent the night thrashing under the sheets with a pale demon who called himself saint. I still felt his clammy, rubber-smooth hands, and his body covered with downy white-blond hair.

"It was an April morning, spring in Casablanca. But people on my street, the Boulevard de la Gare, were screaming. For a moment I thought they were screaming at me, that they knew about the blond, blue-eyed ice-cold djinn I'd spent the night with. Then I realized they were shouting that the war was over. 'La guerre est finie! La paix! Liberté!'

"Allied soldiers in uniform marched down the street like gods, laughing as they scattered chocolate bars and packs of gum and Life Savers. Benny Goodman blasted from the soldiers' club on the corner. Everyone was shrieking, dancing, singing, praying. I felt dizzy, strange. I walked, head down, the way I'd always learned to walk, to meet no one's eyes, neither Christian nor Muslim, because you never knew what could happen. Suddenly I saw a shadow spread over the ground before me: the evil shape we all dreaded, the swastika.

"I stopped and covered my mouth to keep from crying out. A hand reached out to me. I glanced up: a tall blond American GI—a blinding vision under the glare of sun. The djinn! Disguised as a soldier! 'Dance,' he said in English.

"I shook my head and took a step to the side. I didn't want to cross the black shadow—where the djinn-soldier now stood—but he grabbed my wrist with icy fingers and said again: 'Dance . . . belle . . . dance . . . please.'

"I let him pull me into his arms, and we danced. All around us, the soldiers danced with Moroccan girls, even with children. Everyone was so happy. I'd never felt so alone."

Zizou dried me with rough, brisk moves—and watched me put on my pajamas with a critical eye. "You are not as pretty as Rosina and I were. It's better. You stand a chance."

We went to the room we shared. Tata Zizou pulled the dangling chain that turned off the light, and curled up next to me on the bed, and pulled my fuzzy pink blanket over us. We listened to the sounds outside—car doors slamming, a shout, pounding footsteps. In the dark her wild red-gold hair crackled like lightning, her endlessly gesturing hands looked menacing.

"He got sick on my mother's food," said Tata Zizou. "I brought him back home—he insisted—and we had a family meal, everyone celebrating the end of the war. My mother and aunts had been cooking all day. It smelled pungent, sweet and spicy at the same time. My uncles and cousins were there, the kids playing and dashing around. He looked so shocked that I tried to see us with his pale blue eyes. All of us dark, olive-skinned, moving like the Mediterranean, slow and graceful. My mother, short and fat and smiling, with gold teeth, a checked scarf covering her head. My father, black-eyed and bearded. They sat Ray down in the place of honor, and plied him with food, course after course—sweet, sour, salty, hot, cold—in no order, and all of it oily and thick and dense—to someone who's not used to it. My brother Moshe kept filling Ray's glass with burning mahia. Moshe's thick black hair and mustache, his dark hand pouring the mahia, made Ray look even whiter, chalkier, like a man of snow or ice. I'd never realized how dark we all were, how swarthy and dark, next to this—this Aryan. The sounds of laughter, Arabic, French, my father swaying front to back as he prayed in Hebrew in a corner—the smells of the never-ending stream of food, the mahia, sizzling oil, perfumed heat—he stood abruptly and grabbed my arm. 'Quick! Outside!'

"I led him to the courtyard where he vomited on the tiles, near the hungry cats. I felt sick myself. His vomit pooled on the tiles, in the shadow of the swastika. And I knew that it was his mark. He was the djinn, Hitler, the enemy of the Jews, the one who had come to torment me."

"But why you?" I asked, shivering next to hjer. My teeth clacked, so cold. She tightened the blanket around me and hugged me. She smelled like burnt wax, the blanket horsy and fierce.

"Why not me? I had certain powers. I was already getting known as a healer. Women came to me to touch their inflammations and sores, and cure them. And I understood dreams. But I made a big mistake, one that spread the way the shadow did: I let my family convince me to marry him and follow him to America."

"Couldn't they see that he was bad?" I remembered Uncle Ray and his mother. They looked alike: both red-faced, with bellies lurching out over their pants, both thick-necked and fingered, foreheads low and ridged. Both stinking of cigarettes, beer, sweat. Uncle Ray smiled with his frosty eyes when he pinched my cheek, twisting his knuckles till he formed a knob that throbbed long after he let go.

"You have to picture how we lived, always bent over in fear. The end of the war only meant the war was over. It didn't mean that life for the Jews in Morocco would get any better. And there was every sign that it would get worse, as the Arabs rebelled against the French—and we Jews were stuck in the middle, everyone's scapegoat. And scary as Ray was, he was less scary than what could happen to us. My father and brother thought it was a way out for me, to rescue myself. That America would soften him and free me. And then, maybe I could send for them." She let out a deep, ragged breath that shook the bed. "After that day on the Boulevard de la Gare, everything I touched, everywhere I walked, left a stain."

"LISTEN," TATA ZIZOU says in the hoarse voice that grates my flesh. "I came for you at school today because there's something I must show you. I have to warn you."

She trudges next to me, hooded with the pink blanket. November wind bites my cheeks, makes my eyes water, as I try not to see Carlos's eyes when he saw her. Leaves rain as we walk, forming a carpet beneath our feet—gold, red, purple-black and cornstalk-beige. We crush and crack them with our shoes.

"I'm warning *you* because you're the only one who has any sense. I'm being punished because I lied in my letters to bring you and your parents here. I told you it was wonderful here because I was scared of being alone with him. They thought he died in Germany. He didn't, Sophie. He disguised himself as an American GI and came to Morocco, and found me. My bad luck—bad luck since the day I was born—means that I was destined to step into his path. It was sunny that day. Music played, people danced. You think nothing bad can happen on a day like that, but that's exactly when it does happen. He caught me, snared me in his trap."

I see how people stare at us, as we get closer to downtown. She looks like a witch from a fairy tale. Her blanket flying like a cape behind her, her dark sad face lowered.

She turns abruptly, eyes dilated. "We're almost there. Are you ready?"

⌐

AT FOURTEEN, I lived in dark corners, jumped at every sharp sound, looked behind me on my way home from school, certain I was being followed. I trembled in the dark, imagined the cardboard people of Tata Zizou's stories walking up and down the sloping walls of my room. I imagined someone poking a knife into the shower long before I saw *Psycho*. Alone in bed, I recalled things I'd never done, screamed in alleyways I'd never entered, ran and ran from the man with the mask. I never raised my hand in school. My wish was to remain unseen and unnoticed, to move so fast that no one would pin a name or identity to me. When Mom and Dad asked me to wait on tables, I never met the customers in the eye. Everyone thought I was painfully shy. No one understood. Only Tata Zizou, in her quiet moods.

By day I was a wimp, but by night, I was the bold, fearless avenger of all wrongs. Bogie and I worked together to solve cases. We knew that Edgewater was a facade. At any moment the redbrick buildings and phony signs and storefronts would crumble, and the true world would rise: harsh African sun, cold green sea, winding cobbled streets, stone archways that beckoned, painted doorways that teased. At night, I raged through locked doors, broke through barriers, demolished walls. No one dared keep me out. My rage was hot, violent, uncontrollable. I murdered my enemies without a second's hesitation. And then I laughed.

"Zizou was always scared of her own shadow," said Mom while we worked together in the kitchen, slicing and chopping vegetables for the spicy soup, *harira*. Mom's hands were sturdy, strong, and quick. I loved watching them move so fast, never a mistake, cutting cleanly through every vegetable, slices so fine they were paper-thin.

She glanced at me. "Not that there wasn't enough to be scared of there. We lived with warnings, rules, boundaries. The whole world was a locked room we couldn't enter because we were Jews. Arab kids stoned us on our way to and from school. We ran and covered our faces and heads with our hands. And the French started looking like Germans. We heard the stomping of boots at night down the street. Everyone was worried. The French came to our school and marched all the Jewish kids to the *fourière,* the hot showers. They made us take off our clothes and washed them in sulphur. The smell was so horrible. And then, naked, we had to walk by them so they could see if we looked clean enough. They shaved some kids' heads because they suspected lice. Thank God, not mine. But I felt so dirty."

She stopped chopping for an instant. Pale light shone through the window, illuminated her face. When she looked back at me, her eyes glinted wet.

"Did they shave Tata Zizou's head?"

"No, not hers either. But she had nightmares that night, and for a few weeks after that. She woke up screaming about the boots."

"Do you think she's crazy, Mom?"

"No—" She hesitated. "No. But she saw things, heard sounds— that no one else did. I think it started the day she was almost kid-napped by an Arab. We were about ten or twelve, on our way home from school. The whole way there and back, we had to duck and cover our heads because the Arab kids threw stones at us every day. We were used to that. We learned to run. But that day someone reached out from a doorway—in one of those streets so narrow you can touch both sides—and pulled Zizou by the hair, started tugging her in. I heard her scream and turned around. A man wearing a hooded djellabah, with a face bleached and colorless, like an albino. His fingers covered with rings, he was choking her, pulling her into his house. Now here was another of the dangers we'd been warned about—how Arabs kidnapped Jewish kids and raised them as Mus-lims. If Zizou was pulled into that house, I knew without a doubt I'd never see her again."

"What did you do?"

"I leaped at him, and scratched and kicked and shouted—and Zizou bit his hand—until finally she was free, and we ran like wind."

Mom scooped up the chopped vegetables with her cupped palms, and tossed them into the pot of simmering water. "But she was dif-ferent after that. She was afraid to go to sleep. She'd keep me up talking all night, trying to keep from closing her eyes. I tried to reas-sure her, promised I'd stay near her all night, but she said, 'It's what I see when I close my eyes.'"

Mom pinched and sifted fragrant spices into the pot with her fin-gers. "She'd wake up and cry out: 'I thought they set me on fire!'"

———

EVEN AFTER I moved to my attic room—about a year after Tata Zizou began living with us—she often came up to find me. I sat, hunched forward on my bed, doing my homework. I couldn't sit straight because the walls all sloped towards the center, under rafters that crisscrossed to form a pointed roof. The windows were smudged, impossible to clean: when I kneeled on my bed and peered out, it always looked like rain, or as if I were on the top deck of a ship sailing away from Edgewater, far far away.

She sat on my bed and examined her arms. If the blue numbers covered one or both arms, I knew she was in the grip of *la folie,* and I'd clear out. Dad was furious that she always focused on me in her fits, and he yelled at Mom: "It's not fair to Sophie to put her through this! If I hadn't pulled her out of that room, you'd have let your daughter keep sleeping there, with a woman screaming and grabbing her in the night! Zizou may be your sister, but you have to think of your daughter!"

But if her arms were bare—scrawny olive-tinged, with the same sturdy hands as my mother—she'd wait till I finished my homework, and together, we'd go to the Electra Theater, and watch whatever was showing. Mr. Grimm, the manager, was a Humphrey Bogart fan, the way Tata Zizou and I were. On weeknights, he indulged himself and kept replaying Bogart films—to a theater that was usually empty, except for Zizou and me.

I remember one Halloween, right before I turned fourteen, we went to the Electra. The *Casablanca* posters in the lobby were still up, next to new ones for *The Big Sleep.* That night, the feature was *The Maltese Falcon.* Zizou and I sat on the floor, jammed between two rows of seats, knees against the back of the seat before us—alone in the theater, as usual. When the lights went out and the movie started, she clung to me, sitting so close that her lemon-garlic breath clouded my vision. She watched the movie so intently that I felt her absorbing it into her pores, but all the way through, she muttered, poking me with her elbow at her favorite lines. Meanwhile I entered my own recurring daydream, in which I saved Carlos Rivera from his enemies. It was midnight, puddles glimmering after rain, when I arrived on the scene of the crime. As brave as Bogie, fedora tilted forward, trench coat belted, toothpick in the corner of my mouth, I pointed my gun and snarled. I was in my element. When it was all over and I'd ridded the world of a couple more evil characters, Carlos approached, eyes blacker than sin. "Sophie! I'm so glad you made it. I couldn't have held out much longer!"

I chewed the toothpick and spit out the wood tip—clear across the street, into the night—without using my hands, and maneuvered the toothpick back to the corner of my lips.

"Wow," said Carlos.

I smiled modestly. "It's all in a day's work."

After the closing credits, Tata Zizou grew melancholy. "Where is Sam Spade when we need him? A tough guy, with street smarts—but with a heart that's clean. You set him on the Boulevard de la Gare, or the Champs-Elysées, or Liberty Street, and within two hours, he will know who's who, who's done time, who'll spy for him, who needs to be protected. Like King David going out there with his slingshot and snapping off the giant's head. Doing what he has to do."

"Sam Spade wasn't a Jew," I reminded her. "He wouldn't even care about us."

"You're wrong," she said triumphantly. "Sam Spade would have been with us. He knows the way out of every prison, even Alcatraz. He knows how to fight and win."

"Don't we?"

"Jews? We only know how to lose." She shrugged. "I wish Sam Spade could hear me now! We need a hero!"

As usual I got impatient with her. "Maybe you should be our hero, Tata."

"Me?" She brooded for a moment, then sighed. "No, I'm from the old batch of Jews. The ones who creep in the mud from town to town, who never show their face, who don't cry out till they're dead."

"Why don't you cry out now?"

"Now? While we're at war? We should be hiding in a shelter."

"What do you mean we're at war?"

She whispered, "I thought you saw it too—don't you?"

"What?"

In the dark silence, shadows prowled the screen. Others lunged from the corners to slouch over the chairs.

Her voice was a thread of sound. "Do you want me to reveal our whereabouts? To the enemy?"

"Yes." I wasn't sure what I was saying, not sure I understood any of this.

"If *you* say so, Sophie." She grabbed my hand, took a harsh breath, and let loose a howl that blazed through me, made me feel I was bleeding everywhere at once.

Her howl echoed through the empty theater. Outside, on Allen Street, it must have sounded like a wild beast trapped inside. We watched the echo smash around the walls until it sank, disappeared, and we were back in the black silence, jammed against each other, gripping each other's hand so hard it hurt.

ZIZOU STOPS, PANTING, at the corner of Fifth and Liberty, near the old Courthouse, across the street from the large central Post Office. "Sophie, wait! Just a minute, before we go in. Did I tell you about my first year in America?" Her voice is frantic, rushed. "I didn't speak a word of English. I didn't know anyone but Ray and his mother. They called me a filthy Jew and always kept their eyes on me, never let me out alone. They starved me. She watched while he beat me. When I wouldn't kiss the cross she wore around her neck, they kicked me out and left me in the snow, barefoot, in my night-gown. Pregnant. I walked in the snow that night to the river, bare feet cracked and aching. I walked to my death, to throw myself in the water.

"A man saw me at the river. He had a thermos of coffee. He sat me in his warm car and served me coffee. I cried while the tears froze on my cheeks. He wanted to take me to the police or the hospital, but I knew it wouldn't help. 'Please let me die!' I begged him.

"He was listening, I know he was listening, but then we heard a knock on the car window. I turned and saw *him,* glaring through the window at me. I screamed and screamed—"

She shakes her head violently, and grabs my hand. We cross the street, heads still lowered against the wind that blows grit, torn newspaper, crumpled leaves in our faces.

"What happened?"

"I don't remember how it happened now. Somehow they got me back. But I lost the baby. I'm glad he didn't get the baby. I fought them both with my powers—but I had so little strength left. Just enough to keep myself alive. And then to my surprise, they died. One after the other. She choked on her own food—heavy cabbage dumplings she gobbled like a starving animal. And he fell a few weeks later, from a ladder where he was working on the roof."

We stop in front of the Post Office. "They waited until I forgot and felt safe again," she whispers in my ear—a hiss that burns. "And now he's back, watching for me to make one mistake, turn a corner without looking, and walk right into him."

We enter the large concrete building through heavy swinging brown doors. Tata Zizou freezes in the foyer. She pinches my upper arm. "Look!"

Ahead of us people stand in lines, waiting to get to the postal employees sitting behind a long counter. The Post Office is vast and long, with dully gleaming brown and black walls and floors.

"Down," she mutters. "Look down."

A pattern is repeated across the large brown scuffed marble tiles: four thick black lines in the form of a cross. Each of the four lines curves at the outer end, following the line before, in a dance that leads nowhere. I stare at it but don't really make sense of it until she pinches my arm even harder and says: "Swastika!"

The instant she says the word, the black lines rise from the floor with gleeful malevolence and tighten around my neck in a stranglehold.

Sky and street blur into a gray wash: nothing clear, every surface tarnished. How can I save us? We wait, hands tightly clasped, at the red light that blinks in warning. I make the mistake of looking down: cracks in the sidewalk gape and leer, hungry for one misstep, to swallow us.

We wait forever for the light to turn green.

"Ascent"
from *The Lost Land*

BY GÖRAN ROSENBERG

Translated from the Swedish by the author, Lena Karlstrom,
and Peter Stenberg

At the end of April 1962 we ascended to Israel. The ascent, *alija,*
is the figurative term for the emigration of Jews to the
Promised Land. In our case it did not only signify that Jerusalem was
a higher place, but also that we were departing from a low point. At
only thirty-seven, my father had left us two summers before, finally
caught up by the disaster that for fifteen years he had managed to
escape. On the outside he was handsome and lively, with fine features and a warm smile, but on the inside the wires were as fragile as
glass. A strike of bad luck, a few disappointments, and it all broke to
pieces. Father was sick, very sick. He tried very hard to conceal it
from us, but at night I heard him call out strange names. A few
months before he died, he was given a provisional leave from the
hospital in Strängnäs, during which we all stayed with good friends
in a summerhouse on a beautiful sea bay south of Södertälje. The
doctors had perhaps imagined that a large dose of bright Swedish

Spring would drive out the darkness in his soul. In the early mornings, when the sun was up but no one yet awake, he would silently get up and row out on the bay. I asked him to take me along, but he never woke me up. The third or the fourth time he returned with a large pike perch, which was left to swim in a bucket all morning—as the rapidly fading memory of a dawn's forgetfulness. After lunch the pike perch turned belly up. A few days later Father was brought back to the hospital and we never saw each other again.

I was thirteen years old when we left Södertälje, where fragments had begun to heal, and roots slowly were reaching soil. With desperate determination two survivors had decided to hold on to anything that seemed to give support, and to hold off anything that seemed to open the abyss again. I was given a name, which my parents could never learn to pronounce, and spoken to in a language which they could not yet master. At the age of two, I was put in one of the first day care centers of the welfare state. I quickly learned to become a supporter of Södertälje Hockey Team and to steal apples from the neighboring villa gardens. I began to long for the Lucia festivals in the assembly plant of the large truck factory, for the midsummer holidays in the small boarding house at Näset, and for the walks to the still-fashionable seashore establishment beyond the forest. I saw my father do his military service in a quartermaster's uniform and watched Mother tiredly hurry off to her job as a seamstress at Tornvalls. Slowly but surely a place was being bent and wrought together which could have been anywhere and in any realistic calculation should not have been at all, into something that at times seemed confusingly reminiscent of a home.

One summer I found a dead swift on a neighboring villa lawn and learned that swifts cannot lift themselves into the air while standing on the ground. One winter some of the neighborhood kids threw snowballs at our window yelling "Jews," wherever they had gotten that word from. Jews were about as common in Södertälje as blacks, and I was as ignorant as the kids outside, but Mother's face had turned white. Another few years my parents could sometimes still laugh as if the world was new again and Södertälje their home on earth. How could I have known that what seemed like a home was an unreleased state of shock?

Father's death was the end of the fiction. The path through the forest, leading to Torpa and the seashore, where I knew every blue-berry shrub and every patch of cowslip, turned into an alien trail of unfulfilled memories. The baths, smelling of salt and tar, with their ten-meter trampoline, their creaking boardwalks and their separate pools for men and women, one day burned to the ground. Or actu-ally were set on fire by Lång-Erik, who apparently had a screw loose, and who lived at the far end of the rowan-tree alley, until they locked him up at an institution for young delinquents at Hall. By that time the water in the bay had been contaminated by city sewage and swimming was at your own risk. The wooden dance pavilion fell into disrepair. The mini-golf course was closed. The beach rested silent. For the fragile remains, fate and city hall had an oil harbor in store, while the forest gave way to warehouses and mini-malls.

Most of my dreams and plans had been linked to Father. He had brought home the great travel books, the exciting adventure stories, the boyish surprises. One evening he took me to the Roxy and we saw Charles Lindbergh fly over the Atlantic in *The Spirit of St. Louis*. Another we went to the Castor and saw Danny Kaye in *Up in Arms*. I really liked Danny Kaye, who somehow belonged to us and whose actual name was Daniel Kaminsky. Father looked like Danny Kaye. In particular when he laughed.

Father was our tie to the outside world, to friends and fellow workers, to grand dreams and wild plans. But it was a tie that was fastened to the most fragile of foundations. And when the founda-tion broke, our ties broke with it. A few months later the remainder of the family, a widow and her two children, left Södertälje for Stockholm, and after yet another year, with our suitcases barely unpacked, we ascended.

How deep down were we? We were probably a bit more rootless than most people around, but we weren't really in a bad situation.

Our grief was great, but grief can be overcome. The ties broken could have been restored and restored again. Many that we already had would prove to be for life. In our case, emigration was not a final desperate choice, but one of many possibilities. Materially and socially, Sweden actually seemed to promise more.

But who has never fancied beginning a new life, in a higher place? Seemingly firmly rooted Swedes emigrated too—to Australia or the USA. Restlessness was not a Jewish monopoly, and at this particular junction of my life I was restless for other than historical reasons. Mother was getting reports from her Jewish neighbors that I had taken up with a bad crowd down at the kiosk near the Hägersten subway station. Which in one sense was true, but not really. We were thirteen and in the seventh grade and smoking on the sly and discovering our bodies and fondling our curiosity, awaiting something different and better, which almost certainly we knew was on its way. On the other hand, we weren't all that certain what that something might be. And even more uncertain about what that was which we actually had. Sweden was already pregnant with that great existential boom which was to be discharged a few years later and bring forth a whole new generation of rootless beings. Nobody of course saw it coming yet, but it must surely have had some impact on a young boy's dreams and yearnings. In any case, there were very few of those which I could not easily extend to a new country and a new life.

⌒

WITH ALL SAID and done, perhaps it wasn't the low starting point that seemed to make our ascent so steep. Perhaps it was the height, after all. We were about to climb nothing less than the summit of all Western dreams, to where the air was so thin that you could see whatever you wished to see. To the mountains of Zion, the gates of Jerusalem, the fields of Saron, the house of David, the walls of Jericho, the garden of Gethsemane, the deserts of Judea. To a meadow flowing not only with milk and honey, but with millennial dreams of divine justice and human redemption. To the mother of Utopia, the cradle of Messianism, the soul of Salvation, the fulfilment of prophecy. This was the Promised Land, and no other land had ever promised so much, to so many, for so long.

To what had been promised to the Jews, I will return. What had been promised to generations of Christian nonconformists is described with incomparable brilliancy and sensitivity in Selma Lagerlöf's epic about the pilgrimage to Jerusalem by a group of Swedes from the parish of Nås in Dalecarlia:

> The call reached them one after the other, and at the same time all fear and want left them. There was a great, great joy, which came over them. They no longer thought about their lands and their kin. They thought only about their community which would bloom anew, they thought about the splendor of having been called to the City of God.

I was of course still as ignorant about most of these promises as I was of the disappointments that inevitably had followed in their wake. But I was nevertheless mythically prepared. Not in vain had I spent five consecutive summers in the Jewish children's colony at Glämsta, where the glittering swimming bays and lush football fields were eventually to be surpassed by even more striking vistas. Almost every week we assembled at nightly gatherings to look at pictures and listen to stories about the latest and greatest of miracles upon the height—the Jewish state of Israel, *Eretz Israel*. I probably didn't quite understand what was so fantastic about it, and it didn't really seem very material and urgent to me. But the people in the pictures were all muscular and lean, and their eyes were always directed at a point slightly above the horizon. And it didn't matter whether they were carrying a gun or a shovel, since it was made perfectly clear that they above all were carrying a Mission. Ascending to Israel, we were led to understand, was to assume one's responsibility for the fate of the Jewish people, to ensure its survival in the face of further persecutions, to prevent its final physical and spiritual destruction, and to bring to fruition two thousand years of national and spiritual yearnings. And if you didn't make the ascent personally, which hardly anybody in Sweden seemed willing to do, you had the incontestable duty to support those who did with all the means at your disposal. In between pillow fights and athletic tournaments we learned to dance the *hora* and to sing the melancholic and stirring songs of the new Zion.

I think most of us reacted with skepticism, if not pure disinterest. Ten years after the Shoah, a new faith in progress and the emerging institutions of a benevolent welfare state seemed ready to embrace even little Jewish kids. Through the still-smoking ruins of Auschwitz, we could see the limitless horizons of the modern, secularized society open up to our eyes. Whatever a twelve-year-old Jewish boy could possibly dream of, could suddenly be dreamed of freely and uninhibited, here and now. Especially when the dreams were small and were about blond-haired Brittmarie up front in class, or about a spot on the hockey team. Or about getting on that express train, which made a daily stop outside our window on its way to somewhere else.

Later, when the dreams became more demanding, and history came back to darken our sight and senses, and it no longer seemed all that obvious who we were, a few of us returned to the Israeli dream. Some eventually emigrated, others started to supplement their fragile Jewish identity with that of the Jewish state. If there was not yet an unambiguous answer to the question, "Who am I?" there were at least some ambiguous ones.

The concept of Israel was of course charged with considerably greater anticipations than I at that age was able to assimilate. As I now go back to the memoirs and writings of the first postwar decade I realize that many non-Jews probably had greater anticipations than Jews. Not that Jews lacked in anticipation; on the contrary. During these years Israel became the crucial instrument for receiving and sheltering the scattered and homeless remnants of the war, the belated rehabilitation of Jewish dignity, the guarantee of sorts against the return of history, the natural center for Jewish cultural and religious renaissance. In most Jewish homes, a little blue-white savings box with the map of Israel was prominently displayed. Into most Jewish homes flowed letters and greetings from surviving relatives and friends in the new country. News of and from Israel became of greatest importance. During the Sinai war in October 1956 Father sat glued to the radio, deeply worried about what would happen, and not only about what would happen in Tel Aviv.

~

To many non-Jews, the State of Israel soon assumed a different and more complex meaning. The early Swedish writings on the subject are charged with mythical overtones, lacking all criticism and distance, and permeated by an unctuous sentimentality obviously nurtured by the still unspeakable and taboo-laden significance of the Jewish catastrophe. The survivors are quickly induced to silence, the newsreels are stowed away, as a new world soonest wants to forget and go on as if nothing has happened.

In this context, Israel is actually perceived as a happy ending of sorts, or at least the promise of a new beginning. Through Israel, the past will be atoned for and the future legitimized. Through Israel, the new world will prove itself different from the old. Through Israel, the European civilization will be absolved from confronting its own moral numbness. The historical shame and the utopian yearnings of a non-Jewish Europe thus largely form the early images of Israel.

In 1957, Herbert Tingsten (the influential editor in chief of *Dagens Nyheter,* who ten years earlier had been critical of both Zionism and Israel) wrote the following: "Through my studies and recent travels I have become convinced that the founding of Israel is one of the greatest events of our time. I am so absolutely convinced of this that I find it hard to believe that anyone approximately sharing my general values and having at least some minimal knowledge of the matter, must not come to the same conclusion."

With almost religious passion, Tingsten depicts Israel as nothing less than an earthly Utopia, a state whose "learned people" not only are making plans for their own country, but for "humanity" as a whole, and where "a restless activity is exalted and made holy by a pathos of mystical and religious conviction. . . . Never before has our culture reached a higher level of synthesis and power."

This is not very far from the openly biblical interpretations of the Israeli foundation that at the same time are emerging in Christian circles. An envoy from the Pentecostal church traveling to Israel, Johan Hagner, eagerly looks everywhere for the anticipated signs of the world's forthcoming salvation and the founding of a "future theocratic age." According to certain interpretations of the prophecies of Ezekiel and Isaiah, the Kingdom of God will be preceded by the return of the Jews to the Promised Land and their massive conversion to Christ. And Hagner of course finds what he is looking for: "The tool for achieving God's great victory on earth is now being created by God himself. And what a tool! If Saul of Tarsus was able to shake almost the entire known world at that time by encountering Jesus and becoming Paul, to what end will not God be able to use a whole people!"

Equally noticeable these years is the emerging role of Israel as a socialist Utopia, not least in the eyes of Swedish Social Democrats and co-op activists, whose various delegations enthusiastically reported on the triumph of union-owned enterprises, the implementation of far-reaching cooperative ideals and the establishment of miraculously functioning agricultural collectives characterized by "a simple, healthy and strengthening life without the class differences that have created so deep-seated conflicts in the Western societies, and without the central coercion which is so inherent in authoritarian states."

The new Israel is now expected to deliver both religious redemption and social salvation. It is perceived as a fresh path, away from egoism, materialism, urbanism, capitalism; a cure for all those human ills that the Western reformers so long have failed to vanquish. From Israel, a new morality, a new man, and a new society will come forth. Rapidly the cause of Israel is becoming the cause of the whole Western world, and the Jews, in their Israeli guise, being transformed from its pariahs to its social and moral alibi. "It is the undeniable duty of the western civilization to extend to this people all the assistance it needs for a peaceful and prosperous future in its historic homeland," concludes an envoy from the Swedish cooperative movement in his confident account from 1957.

Analyzing the various non-Jewish visions and utopias that were attached to the Jewish state, one would soon find that they were all based on the emergence of a wholly new Jewish man: blond, blue-eyed, stub-nosed, harsh, practical, strong, and unintellectual. The books of the time are filled with Riefenstahl-inspired portraits of young, muscular men and women in sharply contrasting light, standing next to a tractor or a gun. In his book, *Murslev och svärd* (*Trowel and Sword,* 1955), the Swedish journalist Agne Hamrin tries hard to find some biological and environmental explanations to the phenomenon of the un-Jewish Jews, or as he provocatively puts it, "the anti-Jewish Israeli." The desirability of such a mutation is however beyond dispute. He finds the "small, pale, bearded East European Jews" appalling, but is slightly shocked when he soon thereafter realizes that Jews and non-Jews alike are all idealizing a Jewish type looking distinctly like a German: "When you time and again run into this paradoxical ideal, you begin to ask yourself whether this is not the reflexion of an unconscious 'anti-Semitism' among the Israeli Jews."

The grand expectation in the air these years is that the Jews are about to solve "the Jewish problem" on their own, not by changing other people's stereotypes of Jews and Judaism, but by radically changing the stereotypical Jew. The European "Ghetto Jews," the ones persecuted and exterminated, had apparently been of a different breed, and if not actually deserving extermination nevertheless an understandable object of hate and disdain. Anti-Semitism had had its dubious sources, but sources they were nevertheless. The new

Israeli Man, the resurrected Hebrew, had now freed himself from the shackles of his ghetto-Jewish past—and his former persecutors from guilt. Israel had opened the way out of the past, to the delight of all those who wanted to get out of it as quickly as possible. Israel was the mortgage payment, or perhaps even the final installment, of the West's debt to the Jews. Israel was the culmination of a historical sacrificial drama where the Jews were "the lamb slaughtered, six million sacrificial lambs: an awful sacrifice that freed [the Jews] of all imaginable guilt and created a new balance in their favor. Through this sacrifice Israel has been safeguarded as the land of the Jews. The world owes this to the Jews as a compensation for the great ritual murder. Before all mankind they have won the moral right to Israel, to their own state."

It was not only a few occasional emigrants from Sweden who in these years aimed too high.

I think that our step was perceived as bigger than it really was. Emigration from Sweden to Israel was still an exception, especially at a time when most survivors had more or less settled down, or at least didn't want to open up the wounds again. In the early fifties, the restlessness was still more apparent. In the summer of 1953, my father had traveled to Israel to explore our prospects, but had encountered food coupons, overfilled immigrant barracks, and people shaking their heads. Do you want to come now? Are you out of your mind?

So we stayed in our mind as long as we could. Which is to say until the earth shook and the move to Israel seemed safer and more secure than many other things. In Israel lived the only surviving remnants of my once numerous family: one uncle on my father's side, one aunt on my mother's side, my grandmother's sister and brother on my mother's side, and four cousins. In Israel we were all awaited and longed for. So what were we waiting for?

On September 23, 1961, on the thirteenth day of the month of Tishri, in the five thousand seven hundred and twenty-second year of creation, I stepped forth in the great synagogue of Stockholm, to let my trembling voice follow the silver-plated hand's journey across the Torah, and thus becoming a *bar mitzvah,* a man ready to fulfill his Jewish duties and his covenant with God. As a saying to take along the journey, my rabbi, Emil Kronheim, had chosen a passage from Deuteronomy (32:4):

> *The Rock, His work is perfect;*
> *For all His ways are justice;*
> *A God of faithfulness and without iniquity,*
> *Just and right is He.*

On Easter Sunday, April 22, 1962, we boarded the train for Venice in order, as we saw it, never to return.

As ON ANY trip to a high and preconceived goal, there are many things that can go wrong at the ascent. The goal can prove to be a mirage, or the first view can give rise to something else than love. For a long time you reached the Promised Land through the port of Jaffa, where centuries of Ottoman lethargy had left their mark and where consequently many feverish fantasies had ended in insanity and resignation. Not that Jaffa was a particularly ugly or unfortunate city, but it was certainly not a paradise. Neither was it Jerusalem. Which even not Jerusalem always was. Selma Lagerlöf tells about the Jerusalem traveler Birger Larsson, who dies a few days after his arrival to the city, out of sorrow and disappointment for not having reached his goal. Where were the walls of gold and the gates of glass? Where was the city of glory and splendor? Could Via Dolorosa be a stinking alley? Could the Gate of Zion be lined by rubbish heaps? Could the City of God be inhabited by beggars and lepers?

> Birger Larsson beckoned Halvor over to him and took him solemnly by the hand.
> "Now you must tell me something, since you are related to me," he said. "Do you really believe that this is the real Jerusalem?"

"Oh yes, this is certainly the real Jerusalem," said Halvor.

"I am sick and by tomorrow morning I may be dead," said Birger. "You do understand that you may not lie to me."

"Nobody is going to lie to you," said Halvor.

In our *alija* nobody had to be suspected of lying, other than we to ourselves. Both the journey and the arrival eventually fulfilled even our most unrealistic expectations. I have since then made several trips to Israel, also several by train and boat, but none of them can compare with our trip in the spring of 1962 aboard the beautiful white *Enotria* of Venice; its gentle flight across the Adriatic Sea, its magical millimeter-exact passage through the vertically hewn walls of the Corinthian Canal, its inexhaustible supply of spaghetti and grated cheese, its descents on glittering Dubrovnik, palm-lined Brindisi, noisy Piraeus, and slumbering Limassol. It was a journey which in perfect pace and good comfort swayed us through time and place, away from something that increasingly felt like a cold dead end and toward something which in our dreams took the shape of an ever warmer and ever more open embrace. There was something definite and irrevocable about that journey, a satiated sense of fate, which no later journey in my life could ever recreate.

As mentioned, the first view of the goal can destroy it all. If the myth is not ever so slightly confirmed, it will die. The travelers to another paradise, America, eventually had a Statue of Liberty to which they could pin their hopes, which kept many hopes afloat for a long time. In our case, the arrival gate to Israel was Haifa, which seen from the sea on a clear day offered a much more inspiring vision than even Jaffa. And this very morning not even Jerusalem could have competed. Against the still verdant slopes of Mount Carmel, the city glimmered chaste, white, and clean. Elegant villas and exclusive neighborhoods hovered weightlessly under the still sparsely populated summit range. In the midst of the city, slightly above the most cluttered quarters, bordered by cypress trees, the marble white Bahai temple with its golden cupola shimmered in the low morning sun. At the entrance to the port a swarm of prosperity-promising passenger and freight ships lay at anchor, while at the docks, energetic Israeli police and customs boats with the Star of David proudly flapping from the sterns kicked up white wakes every which way in the clear blue water. Along the low coastline to the north rose the smoking refineries and brimming cisterns of progress, gradually giving way to the sun-drenched walls of Akkos, the green beaches of Nahariya and the white cliffs of Rosh Hanikra. Wherever I looked, I saw what I wanted to see: vitality, challenge, purpose. The air was filled with it, the clamor in the harbor signaled it, the uniformed policeman and customs officers who clambered on board and made us wait patiently for several hours commanded it with their assured gestures, buttoned-down khaki shirts and nonchalantly confident behavior.

Not even after having gone ashore, and the houses had taken on a more normal ash gray shade, and the somewhat irritating pulse of traffic had become noticeable, and the people proved to be of all kinds, and the sandy dust whirled in through the open windows of our small Volkswagen as we headed south toward Tel Aviv, our arrival did not lose any of its original magic. There was absolutely nothing that did not seem to confirm my view of how everything should be.

For a long time I was thus convinced that the reason Israelis drove like maniacs, which they did already back then, was because they had divine protection. In Israel there could simply be no traffic accidents. Whatever other miraculous occurrences there were, I would soon enough find out, but the dogma of traffic with no accidents was long kept alive. Partly because I never saw a traffic accident occur, despite all the ones I saw that should have occurred, and partly because I could neither read nor hear about the many that in fact did occur. Perhaps I also did not want to. Another, more short-lived, misconception of mine was that there were no criminals in Israel. There was simply no cheating, no stealing and no murder. Consequently, there were of course no prisons. I still remember my shamefacedly repressed amazement when I first noticed the huge rolls of barbed wire surrounding the prison of Atlit, along the road to Haifa. Such big prisons in such a small country?

In retrospect, I cannot reconstruct how these childish idealizations came about, except that they must have been the fruit of long-nourished child fantasies. And perhaps of a child's need to rationalize a life transformation, which could not easily be rationalized. During the months leading up to our departure I uncritically swallowed every argument in favor of breaking up, especially the romantic ones, and cautiously pushed away those holding me back—comrades, emotions, memories. With a pounding heart I read Leon Uris's newly published blockbuster *Exodus,* not as a fiction novel but as a real and ongoing drama. Israel was a live heroic epic waiting for my appearance, and I certainly did not intend to wander in on stage with my hands in my pockets. Here was to be offered hard work and camaraderie, courage and sacrifice. And girls of course, but of a completely different type than those at home, tough, boyish and modest, serious and dedicated, which of course, as in every heroic epic, made them harder to conquer in the short run, but with the promise of greater rewards later. My first Israel was a boyhood fantasy, a Scout dream, an endless summer camp.

My first self-studies in Hebrew were conducted with the help of a bilingual Bible. This may sound weirder than it actually was. The Bible, as we all know, is organized in a such way that each and every line in it can be located according to book, chapter and verse. Each verse in the Swedish version of the Old Testament, which I had received for my *bar mitzvah,* thus exactly matched a corresponding verse in the beautiful Hebrew *tanach* with a metal relief cover, which I found in the bookcase at home. In this way I could for instance easily make out the meaning of the Hebrew word *bereshit* since it stood in exactly the same place as "in the beginning" in the Swedish Bible. Even if the phrases and the vocabulary often seemed archaic and had no exact corollary in modern Hebrew, the step was much shorter than one would expect. The rough-hewn archaic phrases from the Bible desk at home were quickly polished up to date on the street and in the schoolyard. By no coincidence I asserted myself in the mandatory Bible classes in the Hebrew school, long before I asserted myself in anything else. Although my Bible reading obviously had utterly prosaic motives, I would not discount the possibility that this early drilling of archaic phrases and myths further reinforced my romantic view of Israel. The country's still governing patriarch, David Ben-Gurion, regularly used to quote the Bible as if it were a contemporary historic and geographic document.

Departure and arrival, ascent and initiation, absence and longing, promise and fulfillment, were the heavy building blocks of a new Israeli identity, which rapidly replaced whatever identity had been there before. After only a year, Sweden had become a foreign country, my Swedish had taken on a Hebrew accent and Hebrew had become my home tongue. An identity swap of such radical nature can probably only occur under very special circumstances and at a very particular age. I wanted to become someone else, breaking with a past that seemed to have lost its meaning, and I was still malleable enough, at least on the surface, to go through with it. It certainly was an identity with coarse contours and large voids, since about the real Israel I of course knew very little. And for a long time would very little know.

The Right Nose

BY DORON RABINOVICI

Translated from the German by Dagmar C. G. Lorenz

Inadvertently Amos had run into a crowd that had coagulated in the pedestrian zone; a mob of people, women and men, mostly older ones, who had gathered here to get rid of their loneliness and to mingle, in order to emit their respective little gas explosions of displeasure. The latter soon began to cloud the atmosphere. Amos Getreider intruded quietly upon the vapors of complacency. Initially he thought that it might be entertaining to stroll by, detached, unconcerned, and unperturbed. He carried a vain smile on his lips.

Only an instant earlier a political event had taken place on this very square. The masses were already disintegrating into individual human clusters, when sounds of dissatisfaction disrupted the universal harmony and opposition made itself heard. A few individuals had tried to distribute flyers with discomforting questions among the people. However, the leaflets were torn from their hands by the angry crowd, and somewhere a sign had been torn from the hand of a counterdemonstrator and smashed on his head. Now he stood there, numb, holding his head, his glasses lying on the ground, and the police had already arrived to take down his personal data. Bewildered, the young man felt his skull and realized that he was bleeding. He did not respond to the inspector who was about to reprimand him. Desensitized, he kept looking at the blood in the palm of his right hand and felt his pain with the left. Two policemen in uniform suddenly twisted his arm behind his back while their superior continued to question him, but the man did not understand, be it that he was a foreigner who could follow the language only when spoken slowly and was altogether unfamiliar with the regional dialect, be it that the pudgy gentleman who had thrashed him yelled at the police officers in a loud voice, demanding the arrest of the counterdemonstrators. The stranger looked around in confusion. Startled, he cried out when his arm was yanked up. He resisted his arrest and had to be forced into the police bus.

In those days the customary unified silence, that perfidious tranquility among people, was disrupted. Those elements that had constituted the basic consensus, the decorum and the "good tone" of society, had degenerated over the years into a cacophony. In order to drown out the scandal the people had gathered here today. However, what spoke out of them revealed the very thing they wanted to cover up.

Amos, who had merely wanted to stroll through the commotion, had soon become involved in the flow of the debates. The majority considered the crimes of the past the decisive issue, a small minority, however, focused on the timelessness of the crimes. A short man yelled at Amos: "If you don't like it here, go to Israel or to New York."

"New York is more fun," Professor Rubinstein of Columbia University was to assert with regard to Vienna a few weeks later when he asked Amos one day if he wanted to stay here—in this city, in this country. "After graduating from high school I want to live in Israel," Amos had replied suddenly and to his own surprise. "New York is more fun," Aron Rubinstein responded with the same sentence and in addition chewed forth the German translation in his American accent.

For several weeks already Susi, Professor Rubinstein's black-haired daughter, had sat next to Amos in class. His mother had been taken with the girl from Brooklyn and had invited the American family to her home for Pesach dinner. The Rubinsteins were neither traditional nor sentimental, but they savored the *chale,* the kreplach soup, the gefilte fish, and the rest of the traditional dinner menu. Although they did not understand a single one of old Mr. Getreider's prayers, they found the Hebrew songs and other folklore utterly delightful.

Susi spent the few months during which her father lectured in Vienna with Amos and grew increasingly fond of him. As her return to America was drawing near, he became increasingly special to her. Even though his mother had already given her verdict the morning after the feast, "Such a beautiful young girl," Amos, too, had fallen for Susi.

Susi was so little concerned about her grades in a school that she was to attend for only four months that her desk pal Amos too fell hopelessly behind in his achievements—he had never been a diligent student. She tried to see Amos as much as possible, in order to learn German, she emphasized. Maybe the lonely American with the kinky hair hoped to mirror herself in this pale and scatterbrained young man.

Professor Aron Rubinstein said, "New York is more fun," and when Amos wanted to contradict him and come to the defense of the state that had been founded to prevent Jewish suffering, the professor contended, "I love Israel. It represents a process of self-purification for us. All the racist, narrow-minded Brooklyn Jews who hate blacks travel to Israel in order to hate the Arabs over there for even better reasons. I love Israel. It represents a process of self-purification for us. New York is more fun."

"W E D O N ' T H A T E the Jews," said an older gentleman in the
midst of the crowd. He had a full white beard and smiled pensively.
He had spoken in a loud voice in order to make himself heard in the
general excitement. He wanted to drown out the noise to return to
the main theme of the gathering. He ignored the crowd's shrill
attacks against a young woman, a critic. With a glare he reproved
insults and, with a gesture of his hand, dismissed any polemic in a
conciliatory manner. He spoke very deliberately: "We do not hate
the Jews. But the Jews—*ja?*—the Jews hate us, perhaps not even
unjustifiedly, perhaps I would hate us too, but the time has come for
this hatred to end."

The counterdemonstrator interrupted him. With an expansive
motion of his arms and in a well-modulated voice, the older gentleman replied, "But, my dear young lady, I beg your pardon." He
jovially folded his hands over his round potbelly and continued, "We
do not hate the Jews. All that is a propaganda campaign: Fear aligns
itself with hatred in a disastrous alliance." "You may wonder, which
fear?" he preempted her question and went on to inform her, pointing his index finger, "The fear of the loss of power. Which hatred?
Well, which one could it possibly be?"

For the time being, he kept the answer to himself, but when the
young woman still did not understand, he declared, "The hatred of
the Old Testament. An eye for an eye, a tooth for a tooth." Now his
eyes were wide with meaning, and all of a sudden he had become
very quiet.

Now she understood what he had meant, what he had talked
about—and against what. He rebuked her succinct objections with
an air of kindness: "Listen, my dear young lady, we actually like all
races," and while others nodded in agreement, the man with the full
beard and a full head of white curls continued, "Isn't it beautiful that
our world is so colorful? However, with all of its array of colors, it
needs to understand itself as a whole, just as all colors together pro-

duce white light. Would it not be stupid if blue and yellow hated one another, or red and green? It is equally stupid when the Jews hate us and we hate the Jews."

After his last words the critic had fallen silent, but the old man, an expert in the theory of harmony, found himself exposed all of a sudden to overenthusiastic agreement. His appeal was complemented by demonstrative statements against a particular person, a politician, a Jew.

Immediately he placated the impassioned gentleman, "Yes, we have to love him too. *Ja.* Because he is not our enemy, only the hatred is." "Which hatred?" the young woman asked, outraged, but he continued, "*Ja,* and we must overcome their hatred. There is only one way. We must love the Jews until they stop hating us, regardless of how long it will take."

AMOS'S MOTHER WAS hoarse when talking about these things. She said, "I want you to beat him up. Do you hear me?"

Early in the morning she woke him up with her loud singsong, and Father implored her, "Not so loud. The neighbors," but his mother continued trilling. When she yelled at him immediately thereafter for not having gotten out of bed yet, Father pleaded, "Not so loud. The neighbors," and he reassured Amos, "Don't annoy Mommy. Get up."

She wore her tightly woven and twisted abundance of hair meticulously amassed on her head; this is how she sternly looked down at Amos, how she laughed at him, how she beheld her son, her little one, who was precocious and tried to tell jokes at an early age, who asked, "Papa, am I funny?" and whose father decided, "Yes, you are very funny," while she kissed and reprimanded him, "You are a little clown." Already as a nine-year-old he tried to teach her lessons in politics and later asked her: "Mommy, am I smart?" and she would sigh: "You are a little clown."

At the age of four Amos was already in the habit of metrically scanning his opposition: "No, we appest! No, we appest!" a phrase the boy had invented. When his father had told him that he mispronounced the word, he had called out to his mother the next morning when she was about to take him to kindergarten: "No, we protest." Thereupon the dark-haired woman had assured him, "The correct word is appest." "Protest! Protest!" It surged up from within him in despair. "No, appest. Appest," she laughed at him, as she tied his shoes. "Protest! Protest!" he chuckled in resistance, but she insisted, chortling, "Apest! Apest! Apest," and, giggling, they tiptoed down the steps of the stairwell.

She screamed until she was hoarse, "I want you to hit him the next time. You hear?" A fellow student named Helmut had told him during the break that he had been forgotten in Mauthausen. Amos had taken the boy to task and discussed the matter with him, which had been usual practice since he was nine, and he had tried to explain.

"I want you to—are you listening?—beat up such a person the next time around. Discuss, schmiscuss! No. If someone tells you something like that I want you to beat him bloody. Do you hear me? Bloody! I couldn't care less if you come home bleeding as well. I'll take care of your wounds. But you are supposed to kick him and scratch until blood flows, until his clothes are torn, so that his parents ask him who did that, so that they go to the principal to complain about you. Do you hear me? I want them to go to the principal, and then I shall go to your school and explain that I told you to do that. Don't worry, I'll take the blame. Do you understand me?" she screamed, and Papa, unsuspecting, walked into the kitchen, saw Amos sitting there, his head lowered, and said, "Go ahead, obey your mommy. You know what she has been through."

But Amos did not want to get into fistfights. He trusted the power of his words, the eloquence of his speech. He had never tried to settle for any kind of dialect, any other jargon but the standard language because he was afraid that he would fail to master the local accent. At least he wanted to be in line with the written language.

In Hebrew he was a different person. There his voice and his expression seemed to have a particular sparkle, as if his own timbre resounded in this language of the south, of the summer, and of the shining ocean. Idiomatically this language rang forth from him in deeper registers, and he felt so secure in it as if he were behind tinted windowpanes, as if he were armed with sunglasses, as if he were leaning against an olive tree, a blade of grass between his teeth.

Something within him believed that he would be able to gain access to a more exclusive circle by way of Hebrew, a circle that had nothing to do with W., nothing with his school, nothing with his non-Jewish or Jewish friends, and also nothing with the pious Jews whom he saw occasionally passing through the streets in dark clothes. Regardless of how uniquely packaged they seemed, in Hebrew Amos felt as if he belonged to the prouder edition, the nobly bound luxury edition of the Jewish assortment.

All of a sudden Peter Bach had emerged from the crowd. The muscular, slender youth bent down to the older gentleman with the white full beard and said, "What is that supposed to mean: the Jews? The Jews, you proclaim, hate us. We are supposed to love the Jews. The Jews? All of them?"

Peter, the lanky, giant boy had stood behind the slightly built Amos. A smile twinkled between the two fellow students, while a short gentleman with a brown hat and a black suit began to chatter excitedly.

⌒

THAT DAY BOTH Peter and Amos had not walked home immediately after school, and they had not, as was their habit, walked toward the subway together with Georg Rinser. In the afternoon, the 150 meters between the neo-Gothic building and the subway that Georg—a habitual latecomer—crossed every morning in a few seconds took the three friends at least half an hour. Actually, Peter Bach was only an accompaniment for the duo, whose antics amused him and whose pranks he let go on with delight. Amos and Georg, on the other hand, had to admit with envy Peter's head start regarding amorous adventures. Amos even asked his advice when thinking about Susi Rubinstein and the apartment that would be available for a late-night rendezvous with Susi during the few days when his parents were going away.

Peter Bach said to the stout little man with the hat, "Listen, what you are saying is clearly anti-Semitic." But the short man merely sniveled, "I am no anti-Semite, I just don't like the Jews." "But that precisely is anti-Semitic," Peter explained, but he was put in his place by a fat adult: "So what? A little more tolerance, young man. Let the gentleman have his opinion."

Amos: The name was a billboard. As soon as it was mentioned, there was enough material for a two-hour conversation. Because of it there was no denying his descent; on the contrary: He learned to enjoy the alienation he caused others by being exotic. He had a potentially imposing attitude concerning these matters, but it came across as a pose, a production, because his righteousness had little to do with character, and he could always be certain of his parents' support.

"He talks a good line, our little Amos," Peter asserted, but Georg added, placing his arm around Amos's shoulders, "He sure does. Incessantly. Without listening. What he likes to do best is to listen to himself talk." Amos smiled, and at home he told his mother, "Peter says that I have a good way of talking, and Georg thinks that he is right in a way." However, she just looked at him sternly and sighed, "You are and always will be a little clown."

A few people were still standing on the square in small, scattered groups. The conversation rustled on and soon congealed once again. It crackled and then flared up high again, as if the square in the Inner City, close to the cathedral, had been seized by a turbulence. All of a sudden a swarm of pigeons fluttered up into the air. The birds circled close above the crowd and ascended in an arrowlike formation.

An older lady in a dark dress and white lace gloves reaching up to the middle joints of her fingers and leaving her fingertips exposed, an umbrella tucked underneath her arm, had forced her way into the front row of the dispute. A little hat was attached with a pin to her bluish-gray hair. She was excited, her hands fluttered swiftly through the air, and Amos was reminded of the rapid and diligent movements of Flemish lace makers. Gesticulating, she seemed to be spinning, while airing her indignation in the nasal sounds of a highbrow accent tinged with status consciousness.

Amos talked himself into a passion during the debate, and now articulated his countercharges in a penetrating staccato.

"How can you possibly say that I am anti-Semitic," the lady erupted. Amos: "Because what you say is anti-Semitic." "But," the woman smiled piquedly, "one can smell anti-Semites." She had placed a particular emphasis on the word "smell" and turned up her nose. Amos followed up by asking her in a friendly and encouraging tone, "And Jews probably too?" For an instant the old woman stopped the movement of her hands and her words. Musing, she said, "Yes, Jews probably too."

The crowd panted, be it that it dawned on some of the people that the old lady had given herself away, be it that some of the others were tickled by a statement that resembled a dirty, forbidden joke. Then a man in his mid-fifties bent forward and proclaimed, "Please, that is not true. One cannot smell Jews, except for the Polish ones."

Peter jerked forward, but Amos Getreider simply said in a very low voice, "My mother is a Jewish woman from Poland."

For a moment there was silence. Then the man hastily seized the hand of the seventeen-year-old and said, "Oh, I'm so sorry."

Amos, shaking his head, could not but laugh out loud.

THE CONVERSATION HAD petered out. Amos looked at the Plague Column towering over the pedestrian zone. The monument had been erected as a warning and a reminder of the black plague. It was a prayer of gratitude made of stone on behalf of all those who had been spared by the epidemic.

In the final decades of the seventeenth century the pestilence was again making its rounds through many parts of Europe; it mingled with the people and infected thousands. The disease divided the population into those who were still counted among the living and those who had already fallen ill and, there being hardly any hope for recovery, were counted among the dead. Whoever was seized by the plague was quarantined. The clothes of the infected were burnt. Their bodies were interred in mass graves. Only the money—the coins—was saved from destruction. It had to continue circulating despite the epidemic.

The borders of the country were closed off, and it was decreed that henceforth they were to be crossed only with a health certificate. It was the task of the army and the government to drive the disease away. The Jewish people, who had been suspected of poisoning the wells since the Middle Ages, had been expelled from the city many years before.

Amos looked at the Plague Column as dark figures dressed in old-fashioned attire walked past it. The group of people dressed in black crossed the square where a little while earlier the event had taken place and crowds of people had hollered and screamed.

Peter Bach followed his friend's glance and gasped all of a sudden: "You know, anti-Semitism is of course inexcusable, but when I see the Orthodox Jews: Why do they always have to isolate themselves like that? There is actually no reason for them to run about like that. And besides: Why do they only accept circumcised people? Considering all that, one can understand in a way why resentments arise. I mean, they are not particularly adept, not even when it comes to politics, for example those gentlemen . . . "

That was precisely the moment when both a friendship of long standing and Peter's nose were broken.

PETER'S FACE WAS to take a conspicuous turn after this right hook: The classical straight line that had characterized his olfactory organ up until that time was gone and bent. As for the problems that arose as a result of this incident in school, Amos did not have to worry about those; his mother, of course, took care of them. Amos had become the family hero with a single blow.

"The Purple Jew"
from *Jew Boy*

BY ALAN KAUFMAN

I n school he was average, inconspicuous, his somewhat silly face obscured behind thick-lensed black horn-rimmed glasses through which his walleyed stare rushed at you like some bizarre, near-blind cave fish from the ocean depths. But when the eighth period bell shrilled, Bruce Weiss rushed from our world into the pages of an animated Marvel comic book surreality with the zeal of a Kali-worshipping thug. Ordered to slay in the name of his panel-strip paradigm, he would surely have done so. A fan of Spiderman before most had ever heard of the troubled superhero, he emulated the wall-climber in every detail, down to a perfect imitation of the webhead's neurotically obsessed alter ego, Peter Parker. But after a time Bruce Weiss came to know that there could be only one true Spiderman in the world, and so he invented a hero for himself to inhabit: Voodoo Kid. And in a brilliantly tailored superhero costume he skulked about the neighborhood, performing deeds of mayhem and mischief that my brother, Howard, in his role as Bruce's personal cameraman, captured on an 8-millimeter handheld Bell & Howell. The footage was to be used in a forthcoming Voodoo Kid flick.

In fact, Bruce displayed a keen knack for cross-promotion. There was also a hand-drawn and -inked Voodoo Kid comic, self-published on mimeograph, as well as a Voodoo Kid plastic toy model made by Bruce's father, Bob Weiss, a professional illustrator who not only aided and abetted his son's fantasy world but encouraged Howie and I to become comic book collectors.

Father and son inhabited a dingy one-bedroom that had been converted into a workshop for their capricious pursuits and where they talked aloud of the Fantastic Four, the Incredible Hulk, and Doctor Strange as if they were blood relations. Supposedly there was a Mrs. Weiss somewhere, but one never saw her: Howie and I presumed her dead, murdered for her failure to indulge Bruce and Bob's obsession.

Atop every available inch of dusty furniture surface posed hand-crafted plastic models of superheroes, ranging from Spiderman to Superman to Daredevil. At a kitchen table spread with inkpots, drawing pens, and large panel boards, Bob drew the strips he published in "underground zines" out of San Francisco, all containing a grotesque superabundance of dripping snot, drooling lips, and penises of exaggerated sizes with human faces. Along the walls his rare comic archive filled enough shoeboxes to pack a store; these jostled for space with unmailed stacks of his personal newsletter, *Bob's Comix World,* which posted tips on rare comic book editions alongside fees of up to two and three hundred bucks per "collector's item."

Bob, his massive girth settled in a creaking chair, wiped his clammy face with a soiled handkerchief and said: "As you see, there's a lot of bread to be made in this comic collecting business."

To get rich, he explained, one simply hunted in secondhand stores or in the closets of one's own friends and relations for first, second, and third edition issues, stole or bought them, and preserved the booty in individual plastic sleeves bought for a nickel apiece from the Bronx Hobby Shop on Jerome Avenue. The treasures were then stored at room temperature in shoeboxes or manila folders marked with the series title and the numbered sequence. For example: AVENGERS #1–9, or X-MEN #6–15. The most prized issues were either the first edition or else that issue containing the origin of the superhero's transformation from an ordinary mortal into costumed avenger.

I loved the grandiosity of the word "origin"; longed for a day when I would be so famous that young boys in obscure places would speak of my "origins" as something exotically remote, fabulous.

Sometimes, though, the origins of a particular superhero appeared only incidentally in a publication series of a different name. For instance, the first appearance of Spiderman, containing the tale of his origins, debuted in *Amazing Fantasy* #15 in a trial run for only one issue before fan demand led to his very own series. Needless to say, possession of such an item was tantamount to ownership of the Lost Ark.

My personal hero was Captain America (origin in *Avengers* #4), whose red, white, and blue leotards symbolized an American essentialness I desperately craved as the son of a French-Jewish Holocaust survivor. Divorced from the realm of common American experience, not only by her accent but by her survival of an historical event of such extreme savagery and magnitude that it made the violence-prone Bronx seem rather innocent, I felt estranged from the country of my birth, ambivalent about my *own* origins. But Captain America, who had risen from a twenty-year frozen sleep after an earlier career in WW II as a fighter against the Nazis, understood quite well, it seemed to me, about gas chambers and mass graves. This brought him closer to my experience than other characters.

His boy sidekick, Bucky, had been blown up midair over London during the Blitz while trying to defuse a Nazi buzz bomber. In despair, Captain America dropped into the North Atlantic, where a glacier encased him. Two decades later a team of researchers thawed him out, still garbed in his red, white, and blue togs. As he came to, his old despair raged as fresh as a minute ago. Dazed, he found himself trapped between the present and the past, unsure, historically speaking, of what era it was or his place in it—my predicament exactly.

Bob held out as a reward for all this collecting that once our stock had grown fat, we could haul it off to a comic book convention to sell or swap. Not only could we make thousands of dollars, but through smart trading we could consolidate our holdings and multiply their value.

"Where are the conventions held?" I asked, amazed.

"All around the country," said Bob. "Boston, Miami . . . it depends on the collectors associations. But don't worry. I'll be glad to rep you. I'm sure I can cut you some great deals."

That settled it. Bob next showed us how he constructed plastic model superheroes, this a full decade before their like would roll en masse from a factory conveyor belt. For Captain America's basic form he used an existing model of a Roman gladiator and with a soldering iron and the melted wire of a clothing hanger such as my mother used to hit me, slowly, patiently sculpted muscles and mask. I shivered to see my hero emerge from the same painful instrument used to punish me. Bob's power struck me as Godlike. With slow, patient applications, he painted Cap's costume. He then fashioned little mask wings and Cap's shield from loose bits of plastic, wire, and opaque enamel paints. He had brushes of such delicacy that you could paint an eyelash on the head of a tiny figurine. He showed us a brush with a single hair. "Look at that," he said, turning it before the light, a tightrope across which dreams and heroes walked against a backdrop of dirty Bronx kitchen walls perspiring with gleams from a naked ceiling fixture. . . .

THE FIRST THING I would need as a budding comic book collector was investment capital. So I got a job for two afternoons a week in the local stationery store. My mother fully approved of this, and even my father nodded and yawned at the supper table and said: "Oh, yeah? That's good. It's good to work."

But at work I found it difficult to understand instructions or to concentrate on tasks. The shop was narrow, crowded to the ceiling with cheap toys, greeting cards, notebooks, etc., and there was nowhere to sit. The owner was Mr. Shwab, a pudgy bald man with a very pink face who wore the same short-sleeve shirt and bow tie, day in and day out—the shop stank of his perspiration. He explained to me at great length how to find things on the shelves and in the stockroom, and my head even nodded with a kind of dim comprehension, but the instant he stepped away I forgot everything. Consequently I stood frozen to my spot, ears burning with shame and heart thumping as he called out with weary impatience: "Alan? Are you going to bring me the Number Two pencils I asked for? Our customer is right here waiting." This drove me to make a desperate rush at the shelves, where I pulled out rolls of crepe paper as boxes of rubber bands tumbled to the floor and the customer's precious time was wasted to the loud drumroll of my heart, and finally the stationer was at my elbow, whispering in a huff: "Here! The pencils are here! Just follow the code the way I showed you." I groaned: "Ohhhhhhhhh! That's where it is," flooded with the relief of sudden insight; but moments later darkness again descended and I waited, hands in pockets, dreading the next customer.

Once my mother came in, expecting, no doubt, to find her boy genius perched on a high stool behind the cash register, ringing up sales with a smile and exchanging pleasantries with the customers while directing a battalion of clerks rushing about with No. 2 pencils behind their ears and the owner seated in a chair behind the counter, beaming with contentment. Instead she found me hiding timidly behind a revolving display stand of Magic Markers in a side aisle.

"What are you doing back here?" she asked, disappointed. "Why aren't you up front, helping Mr. Shwab?"

"This is where he wants me," I lied.

"Go," she said crossly, "introduce me to your boss."

He had no time for small talk, was busy with a customer, but my mother's voice droned on as Shwab nodded stiffly. I heard her say the words "He's brilliant" and "a little Einstein." Shwab's face looked unconvinced, but he offered a tight-lipped smile. She cooed effusive thanks. He apologized for being so busy. A week later I was fired. . . .

Also at this time I began to draw a comic strip of my own: *The Purple Jew.*

One morning I took out some paper and colored pencils and drew the origins of my own hero, with balloon boxes for him to speak in. He was a poor Bronx boy, went the narrative, walking up the Grand Concourse, minding his own damned business when suddenly for no reason a gang of teenagers beat him to a pulp. They left him dying on the sidewalk. No one came to his aid, though traffic flowed by and pedestrians stepped around him. By nightfall, he still lay there, about to die when, suddenly, the voice of God broke the silence. "Jim! Jim! Stand up!" said the voice of God. Jim stood up, miraculously all right. "I have saved you for a special mission," said God. "You will fight evil! You will be my champion, a modern Jewish knight, with the strength of a lion and the prowess of a cat, and you will wear purple fighting togs bearing the Jewish star on the front. You will be: The Purple Jew!"

I drew all through the morning while my mother slaved over pots steaming with boiled potatoes, corn, broccoli, and a meatloaf baked in the oven. Despite the intense heat, I drew on, oblivious.

"What is this, Abie? A cartoon? You should only do your math homework with the same kind of patience. Four hours you've been sitting there. Enough already. Go outside. Play! There's not so many days left in the summer. Then school starts and, believe me, you won't have time for your cartoons!"

"I'm OK, Mom," I said abstractedly, "thanks." My disposition grew kindly. I felt well disposed toward everyone. A pleasant sense that I had been blissfully emptied spread through my body. My smile was genuine.

"What's this?" asked my father when he shuffled in for lunch, dressed in white T-shirt and boxer shorts, his house slippers slapping on the floor. His thick fingers isolated a page of panels and his brow wrinkled. A slow, condescending smile spread over his face as he read. "The Purple Jew?" he chuckled in disbelief. "Do I read correctly? The Pur-ple Jew?" enunciating each separate syllable slowly to better savor the preposterous whole.

"Whatzamattah wit it?" I asked sullenly, my vision deflated. "It's a comic book. I'm gonna try to publish it."

"Publish? Tee hee hee! The Pur-ple Jew! Hee hee hee hee! Sure, you'll publish! Sure. Tee hee hee! Sure. Tee hee! The Pur-ple Jew!" but I received this stiffly, said: "That's right. The Purple Jew."

That he read comic books, was something of an early aficionado himself, familiar with Superman, Captain Marvel, and Batman, lent his devastating weight to his sarcastic critique: here was yet another world, like that of sports or of the streets, the nature of which I just didn't "get" according to him, but which, of course, he did.

Still, I had gone about my collecting in deadly earnest, inspired by Bob Weiss's confidence in its lucrative benefits, worked hard to save, and felt myself to stand on more solid ground than I had ever before, so I said to this man who had never, according to my mother, succeeded at anything: "You can laugh, but I'm gonna make a lot of money from the comics. You'll see!" And this sent my father into paroxysms of laughter, as though it was all too much for him and he couldn't bear a single minute more. "You'll see!" I repeated, voice rising angrily. I stood up, gathered my papers together, tears springing from my eyes. "I'm gonna collect comics, become a millionaire, and draw my own comic books! That's right! The Purple Jew will make me rich!"

When I left him, he was close to choking.

And that's how summer went. Absorbed in collecting, drawing the Purple Jew, shooting films, and tolerating my father's constant gibes. Ridicule lurked in other quarters, too. When filming we avoided the schoolyard, the potentially painful contact with other kids our age who wouldn't understand. They were beginning to trickle back from summer vacations in greater numbers as fall drew near.

My life became an adventure imagined by the writers and artists of Marvel Comics. Each week's newly purchased issue explained me to myself. Lying in bed on my side, with flies buzzing in the blast-furnace heat of the room, I stared at . . . no, *fell into* each panel on the page, where I experienced life in the character's ink-sketched skin and lived more intensely than I could ever hope to as myself. Reading Captain America, I felt like him: knew myself as stiff around others, unable to relax, haunted by a painful, private sense of special destiny. Like him, I fought against the phantoms of the Nazi past, and like him, the battle took place entirely in my own mind. We each mistook the present for the past and the past for the present. Like him, I had lost a dear loved one when I was just a child—his loss was his young sidekick, Bucky, mine, my own mother, who even before I was born watched her own childhood and faith in humanity mur-dered when *she* was still only a child. . . .

ON THE FIRST day of class I showed up squeaking in stiff black clunkers, rustling in polyester, my pale blue long-sleeved shirt already malodorous with perspiration and an excremental musk ris-ing from the seat of my old-fashioned black trousers. I, who had worked in two stationers over the summer, now bore garish Looney Toons–illustrated vinyl school supplies. Dragging my feet, all hopes shattered, I waddled to secure a seat in the back, where I could hide from view all year.

Mrs. Shwartz lifted her face only to squint as we filed in through the door, point her pencil at a student, and attempt to guess the name.

"You're . . . Kaufman."

"Yes," I said sadly, "I'm Kaufman," which seemed to irritate her.

Clearly she had formed an opinion of me based on previous discussions with Mrs. Adler. But she held her peace, checked a box on the document laid before her on the desk, and said: "Just find yourself a seat. Keep in mind that you're tall and that the person behind you might have trouble seeing the blackboard."

Her eyes followed me with such approval to the last seat of the last row in the classroom that in a sudden blush of pride I doubled back, waded in among the desks in the middle row, chose the most centrally located one I could find, and plopped myself down in it. Her face grew hard at this, and I could tell by the sudden opacity of her eyes that she was making a mental note for herself.

Minutes later, three girls in a row entered, the prettiest in the class—Michelle Hyman, Vickie Cantor, Laura Winkler—and took up in a cluster of nearby seats. My body odors now seemed to roll off me in spreading waves. I couldn't be sure, but I thought that Laura Winkler stared hard at Vickie Cantor, shot a look my way, then back at Vickie, and wrinkling her nose made a face. She then put a hand quickly to her mouth to smother a laugh, and Vickie Cantor did the same.

Naturally, Mark Steinberg took up his throne in the front row, right under Mrs. Shwartz's nose. He had the added advantage of being not only weak-sighted but short. Mrs. Shwartz, of course, welcomed his arrival with a smile that still contained the warmth of her recent dinner in his parents' home. She did not want to seem biased, though, so she quickly composed herself, but by that very effort magnified her preference. As for him, he wore a secret little smile too: there was so little wrong that he could do and he knew it.

When the full class was present, accounted for, and all the rules spelled out, she launched into the first lesson. Covered the blackboard with chalk strokes that seemed to spring from a demonic core of cold rage. She put up an incomprehensible equation with such fury that I felt my heart rate increase. I looked around at the bowed heads of my fellow students. Their pencils moved furiously to keep up. A raging symphony was in progress: she the conductor, they the orchestra. I sat there like a janitor stumbled somehow into the pit during a performance and waved into a chair. I should pretend to play, I decided. Slowly I opened my loose-leaf binder, began to take notes. But as I wrote I could not shake the feeling that others around me were gagging secretly from the smells of my body and clothes, and I felt a painful urge to leave the room. My hand shot up.

Mrs. Shwartz glared. "What is it?"

"I need to go to the bathroom, please," I said.

"Not now!" she snapped.

"I gotta go bad," I whined. Giggles down the rows. Only Mark Steinberg's pen scratched ahead uninterrupted, his cheek resting on fist, brow furrowed with concentration, a model picture of intellectual effort and in his H.I.S. shirt with button-down collar points, corduroy Levi slacks, thick tartan plaid wool socks and buff-polished loafers with a bright new penny wedged into the bowstrap of each shoe, as at ease as in his own living room. Of course it was his gold wire-framed spectacles that—more than scholastic achievement, his structured and enlightened home environment, or inculcation with the finest middle-class virtues—guaranteed his future attendance at Harvard University, a college about which I knew nothing more than that my acceptance there would heal my mother of cancer if she should ever contract it, and also would probably end world hunger for once and all.

"All right! Go!" said Mrs. Shwartz. "But be warned! This is difficult material. I am not going to repeat myself! If you miss out, then it's your responsibility to find another student to explain it to you, but only after school! And there will be a graded quiz today . . ."

"Awwwwwwww!" the class groaned in unison.

"That's what I said. It will be a graded quiz. Every week we will have one. The grade will be part of your cumulative card grade. And if you fail you must bring the quiz back to me signed by a parent."

The room now had grown perfectly still. We were like the soldiers of a new unit formed from high-spirited recruits who have just learned that some of us would probably not return home alive from the war. Everyone looked at each other as though trying to guess who wouldn't make it. The decisive pity evident in the eyes of those peering my way was virtually unanimous. Like an innocent man condemned in the field by a kangaroo court of officers responsible for a failed offensive, I stood to my feet, a half-smile of unconvincing gallantry on my face, shuffled self-consciously past desks, odors emanating from my tush, brushed Laura Winkler's knees, smiled a doltish grin of apology and, clutching the lavatory key ring in my unwashed hand, my body apologized its way out of the room. When the door slammed, faintly rattling the glass window in its insecure frame, the chalk resumed its flogging of the board.

I returned home after school on that first day, tears welling up in my eyes alternating with gasps of disbelief and exclamations of "Darn it! Oh, darn it!" At Walton Avenue I hurriedly departed from my usual route, trying to avoid as far as possible the spreading pool of students spilling from the school, my brother Howard somewhere back there among them.

I moved up toward Mount Eden Avenue at a huffing trot, stopped, pulled the quiz from my pocket, again gaped at it walleyed, and shook my head. I walked up to a building, the quiz dangling from one hand and my fingertips gently grazing the dirty ochre-colored walls, leaned my forehead against cold stone and uttered a moan so deep that it seemed to rise from within the belly of another, second person hidden within me whom I failed to fully recognize yet knew, with a kind of peaceful acceptance, was me.

Perhaps victims of criminal abduction, realizing their imminent execution by torture in undiscoverable waste places, groan this way, with the same surprised discovery of their innermost being poised on the verge of annihilation. It was not only an emotion; the dread I felt of what I faced at my mother's hands found no consolation in anything around me, and questioned everything with a kind of mournful reproach. From where would help come? From the owner of that green-and-white Bel Air convertible parked on the curb? Was the owner a family person? How would he or she feel to know of the torments that lay ahead for me? Would such intervene for a complete stranger? Would anyone take my mother aside and say: "Mrs. Kaufman, your Alan is a wonderful, gifted boy. He is not a Nazi. He is not the enemy. He is only a child who likes comics and is having problems with math." But there was no one in the world who would help me.

"George! Sheshi! Come in to eat! The imbecile is home!" she shouted as I plodded through the door, head bowed, hands hanging at my sides, incontinent with the utter futility of it all, shoulders sloped so badly that they practically begged to be saddled by a humiliating posture-corrective brace from some mail-order house in Georgia. I was hoping to communicate, by an ashen, worried expression, that my scholastic condition resulted not from a defect of character but from a genetic deficiency of some sort, one that warped my back and slowed my mind, made me cretinous.

She wiped her hands angrily in her apron, flushed face drenched in perspiration, shiny blue eyes dimmed to an inhuman opalescence like eggs from some nearly extinct species of predatory bird that were at any moment about to hatch their full-blown menacing brood.

"Where were you? Do you know we were worried about you? Did they keep you at school? What happened?"

"No" is all I said.

She stared at me, her eyes dancing with the movements of mine, which waltzed to avoid her direct gaze. "So, what is the matter? Did you get into trouble already with that big mouth of yours? George, look at your son. He's standing there. Something is wrong but he won't say what it is. Did they beat you up, those stupid kids? Gosh, they raise them like animals in this country. People have no brains. So? Say something!"

"I failed a quiz."

I was careful not to say "test," to assert the distinction in the way I drew out the word "quiz" in an incredulous tone of voice, as though to say, Can you believe it? I went to the post office to buy a stamp. I handed them my money; they handed me back a tomato.

"So, he failed a quiz. So what?" said my father as he shuffled past us through the almost kinetic field of her sudden anxiety and swiftly mounting anger. Already sensing her changed mood, he tried to defuse it, not for concern for me but because he had to work tonight and wanted to catch a few hours more of undisturbed sleep after supper.

"Go, wash up," he said to me with a meaningful look. "Your face is all dirty."

I touched my fingers to my forehead where I had leaned against the building. "Go, fer cryin' out loud," he said, sitting. "What, you been cryin' over a stupid quiz?"

"What are you telling?!" my mother exploded. "What do you know, with your fourth-grade education! You want him to end up like you in the putz office working all night on a cold deck, like your father did?!"

Under the dinette table his white, oak-solid legs underweared in boxer shorts and his callused feet shod in house slippers shifted uneasily.

"I told you," he said, his voice sounding younger, pleading almost, "don't talk to me like that in front of the kids or I'll rap you in the mouth!"

"Oh, yes? You will hit your sick wife? Like that crazy brother of yours, Arnold, the *meshugener,* hits his wife, Ray?"

"Hey!" he barked reflexively. "Leave my brother out of it!"

She turned suddenly to me like an actor in a sitcom confiding low-voiced to the studio audience: "Look at the trouble you're making between your father and me. You won't be happy till you see us divorced!"

The thought that my math performance could be responsible for the destruction of my parents' marriage filled me with despair. "Nooooooo!" I urged. "Please don't say that! It's not true!"

Just then, Howie brushed past. "What happened? You failed a test?"

And she: "You told me it is a quiz, not a test! Did you fail a test?!"

"No, look!" I unfolded the sheet of mimeographed paper. It bore only a few questions and answers, but the words "Very Poor" and the grade 45% were written boldly in bright red ink, as well as Mrs. Shwartz's angry red-ink cross-outs, made it seem important.

"Oh, Gosh!" my mother moaned softly, all her college dreams for me shattered by the proof of failure in her trembling hands. Then her face grew hard and she looked at me without pity. "So. What do you want me to do with this?" She held it out for me to take. "Here. You don't have as much of my family in you as I thought. You're more like your father's side. You should have seen how brilliant my brothers were in school. Sure. Because they studied. They didn't spend their time with stupid comic books! You know what the comic books will get you? Like your father and his father you'll end up, broke, illiterate! You watch! In ten years you'll tell me: 'Momma, you were right!' But by then it will be too late! Wait. You'll see. Here, take back this. Your life will be wasted. Go. Your father is right. Wash your stupid face. It's all dirty. Take it! Go. What were you doing, hugging the wall? Get away from there! Did you get the new clothes we bought you dirty too? Go. Take this away. Your father is hungry. He has to go to work tonight. Ten hours on his feet in the freezing cold. That's what you get with a fourth-grade education! Go read comic books like he did instead of studying. Hitler I survived, five years I was hungry, afraid, running, hiding, so that you could read comic books. Go, stupid! What do you know? All day I cooked."

I didn't accept the quiz back, swallowed hard. "I need you to sign the quiz. Mrs. Shwartz wants proof that I showed it to you."

"Forget it!" She laughed bitterly. "George look at this stupid son of yours. You watch. He's gonna get me in trouble with the Department of Immigration! He wants me to sign the test. Watch. It'll end up in the wrong hands! They'll send me back to France. Won't that be nice?"

"Your mother's here illegally, she don't sign no nothin'," growled my father. "Mash-a-la. Bring me some of that soup. I'm starvin' here, fer krissakes!"

He glared while Howie observed me, shaking his head from side to side with a sad smile. "What's wrong wit you?" my father said. "Why do you always gotta make trouble? You got a test, so pass the test! You failed the test, so study more. But don't bring here no tests from no teacher to sign. You tell that teacher that she should sign! She's the teacher, not your mutha! Is your mutha teachin' you or is the teacher teachin' you? Well, which is it?"

"The teacher is teaching me," I said, trying hard not to smile with relief that no physical punishment seemed in the offing.

"OK. So it is me and Momma's fault that you failed the test . . ."

"Quiz," interrupted my mother. "Quiz. It's not a test." Again she turned to me as to an audience to confide: "He doesn't know the difference. He's only got a fourth-grade education. He never made it to the sixth grade . . ."

My father had already heard this once too often and said, "What do you know about what I know or don't know? You know, you got a bigger mouth than that stupid kid of yours, you know that? Bring me the food already! I'm sick and tired of the both of ya!"

And that should have been that. She turned to the stove. He picked up the *Daily News.* Howie's face dropped to read the comic book hidden on his lap under the table. Suppertime's well-oiled machine was set into motion. The atmosphere resettled into a mist of steamed and charred food smells floating on a pond of stove heat. But it all came to an abrupt halt when I said again: "I need to get the paper signed."

My father's face grew crimson. "You know, now you're beginning to get on my nerves! I told you, no one's signin'! Your mother's here illegally. Now get out of here! Beat it! Discussion's over! You wanna go witout supper, you can go witout supper! But stop makin' trouble, ya hear, or I'll make you trouble like you'll never forget!"

"But it's gotta be signed!" I cried out. "Mrs. Shwartz said so! She's the teacher! I'll get left back! She'll think I didn't show it to you! Please! It's not my fault! I didn't know there was a quiz. I'm not good in math anyway! But this really screws me up! Please, oh, please, you gotta, you gotta." I removed a pen from my pocket, held it out, struck such a pathetic picture standing there, I thought.

And then my mother snapped. My father shoved his chair away from the table, the torn-out center of a slice of Wonder Bread swelling his cheek. I heard her mutter very low: "No more talk. Now I'll take care of this the way I know how," as she brushed past him with a glassy look in her eyes, as though I were a perfect stranger in no way connected to her plan. But I understood very well my place in it.

"Pop," I begged, talking very fast—there was so little time. "Pop. She's going to get the hanger. Please! Pop! Don't let her!"

"Too late, mister," he said, moving his chair back to the table. "You asked for it. And you know what? I hope she gives it to you but good!"

"Pop!" I pleaded. He was my last hope. "Pop, please. I beg you, Pop!"

"You beg me? Don't go begging me, I ain't got nothing to do with it."

I imagine that while she laid into me with the wire hanger, he and Howard helped themselves to warm food from the stove; supped with heads bowed low, not from shame but concentration, with my screams and pleas for help seasoning their ears.

What finally caught their attention was my appearance with a welt across my forehead to announce, in a drained voice of numb disbelief, that they had better go look, because she's throwing out our comic book collection.

They rushed past me even before all the words had left my mouth.

"Put that down, put that down!" shouted my father, as Howie stood beside him chanting: "She's lost it, Dad, look. She's nuts." Howie had convinced my father that some day, say five years from now, we'd all cash in on our *Captain Americas* and *Spidermans,* convinced him that the future lay in comic book investments, and he had looked forward to their eventual auction to the tune of tens of thousands of dollars. Having them was like owning stock in a commodities exchange, a gentlemanly form of speculation perfectly suited to a poor sort raised on Captain Marvel comics and Buck Rogers matinees and who had never gotten past fourth grade. Besides, he enjoyed reading them as much as we did. So, he said again in a voice of wavering conviction: "You're not throwing out nothin' until I say so. Put 'em down!"

Eyes crazed, hair wild, she had an armful of first editions hugged tightly to her breast, among which I recognized the cover of *Avengers* #4 announcing Captain America's star-spangled resurrection from the black sleep of war. She hunched her shoulders and neck when she spoke, like some deranged kidnapper backed into the corner on a rooftop and threatening to jump with the abducted babe in his arms.

"Out they go!" she shrieked. "I'm not going to have our kids' education ruined by putz office comic books! And if you make me trouble, I divorce you! I leave! You make your own food! And raise these sons of yours! Don't you try to stop me! . . ."

"She's crazy, Dad," Howard muttered. "Get them out of her hands. They're worth money. Do something. In five years we'll be rich!"

He looked at her, then back at us, torn between future prosperity and the current state of peace, and said to my brother: "Five years? Who knows if we'll even be alive in five years? Let this be a lesson to the two of you. Your momma works hard. All day she's been slavin' in that kitchen to make you food. We don't need no trouble. Your teachers got papers to sign, let them sign them. Your mother wants to throw out the *fa-cac-tah* comics, so throw 'em out. It's time you two grew up already. When I was your age I worked for a living."

And that was it. Howie followed her out the door wailing indignantly as she marched to the incinerator chute in the corridor. I stumbled after, while my father returned to the kitchen mumbling to himself: "I'm telling ya, they're a bunch of goddamned nuts, the whole lot of 'em, and they're driving me crazy."

The incinerator for garbage disposal was located in the corridor by a dim window, just before the dark stairwell. It was only large enough to squeeze an arm into and stuff trash down the cast-iron chute. It opened like an oven mouth by a wooden handle to reveal a brick throat glowing below with fire, and sparks shot past like tracer bullets. It reminded me of the pictures of the crematoria that I had seen in the book about death camps, in the Grand Concourse public library. Whenever I threw out the trash I'd stand for a moment staring into the fiery darkness, trying to feel what it meant to be shoved dead—or worse even, alive, as some of the prisoners had—into such a space. But I could never quite grasp it. Here she now stood, Howard behind her, pleading, while I watched coldly from a distance as she stuffed down comic after comic, all first editions still in their plastic sleeves, and at one point I glimpsed the tricolor costume of Captain America before he too was consigned to the flames, killed a second time by the war, first by its villains, now by its victims, and it seemed to me that none of us could escape from what had happened in WW II to Jews like my mother, everything was burning in the ovens of Time, my childhood too, and there was no escaping, no rescue possible, from the ultimate destruction awaiting us all.

The Adventures of the Purple Jew
Gun in hand, I kicked down a door behind which sat a table full of bald Nazis in suspenders and riding boots, playing poker and smoking ill-smelling cigarettes. "Take that, you Nazis," I shouted as I pumped them full of lead. Then, cloaking myself in an overcoat I found hanging on the wall, I slipped out of the building with my collar turned up. I strolled over to a guard stationed at the gate of the camp, put a cigarette to my lips, and asked in perfect German: "Gotta light?"

The guard responded, "Yes, mein Commandant," and with the automatic gesture of an obedient robot brought out a cigarette lighter and complied.

"Thank you," I said and blew a smoke ring in his face that hung on his big nose like a ghostly horseshoe and dissolved. "At ease," I said, and drawing my revolver I shot him too.

Now the sounds of sirens, barking dogs, shots, and the boots of alerted troops charging down steps clamored in the night and spotlights lit up the sky. I shrugged off the coat to reveal my purple fighting togs, adorned with the emblem of a Jewish star, and melted into the shadows of the woods.

I next showed up in Stockholm, Sweden, at the home of its most famous math professor, Dr. Olaf, an old man who lived in scholarly solitude with Brigitte, his voluptuous daughter.

When he saw me at the door, gaunt with fatigue, dirt-smudged and smelling of gunpowder, he gave a start and gasped: "Why, you're Abie Kaufman, alias The Purple Jew! Good heavens, what on earth has happened to you!" His beautiful daughter appeared at that moment at the head of the stairs, saw me, and came hurrying down, holding up the hem of her gown to keep from tripping.

"Good evening, Dr. Olaf," I said grimly, brushing past him. "Would you mind terribly if I sat down? I need a rest."

"Mind?!" exclaimed the doctor. "Why, I am honored! Brigitte! Brigitte! The Purple Jew in the flesh! Bring him something cool to drink. Sir, what is your pleasure?"

"A tall glass of milk mixed with some Bosco chocolate syrup will do just fine, thanks. And here, you can put this away somewhere. Don't worry: it's not loaded. I won't be needing it for the rest of the night."

The touch of cold gun metal sent a thrill through his pudgy soft white hands as he bore my gun to a cabinet and stored it in a drawer.

"I see you've been up to your usual business of killing Nazis," he said with admiration, returning.

I nodded grimly. "They're out there all over the place. I kill one and two more pop up." Then I chuckled and added, "Heh! Doesn't leave me as much time as I'd like for math. But, it's gotta be done."

"Oh, I wouldn't worry about that, Abie. Why, tomorrow you're to get the Nobel Prize!"

"Funny," I said, "I'm only twenty. They've never given the prize to a mathematician so young."

"How does it feel?" asked the good professor, "to be so brilliant and so early recognized?"

I shrugged.

Just then Brigitte returned with the milk. Also, she had slipped into something more comfortable, a Frederick's of Hollywood black silk baby-doll pajama outfit.

Her father smiled his approval. "Ah, I see you've made yourself nice for our guest."

She leaned over me to hand me the glass, cried "Oooooh!" and the glass crashed to the floor, shattering and turning the costly beautiful rug dark-stained with chocolate milk.

"Your shoulder," she said tearfully, "it's bleeding," and with manicured dainty fingers turned back the torn fabric of my costume to expose a hole in my flesh. "You've been shot!"

"It's nothing," I said. "I caught a slug as I made my escape. Just a flesh wound." But in no time she had my togs off and was bandaging the hole as I sipped a fresh glass of chocolate milk prepared by the professor. "Look," I said to both of them when the dressing was done. "Whatever you do, don't let on about my injury to my mother. She's gonna be there tomorrow. I don't want her to worry."

Both nodded deferentially that they understood.

The next day the professor and his daughter helped me into my tuxedo and rode to the King's palace for the awards ceremony. In an auditorium very like the one in my old grade school, P.S. 64 in the Bronx, the world's greatest mathematicians sat assembled. In addition, my parents, my uncle Arnold and his family, my grandparents (all four risen from the dead and sitting as happy as Topper up in the balcony), plus just about everyone I had ever known and who had doubted the special nature of my destiny, including all my classmates, were there. Mrs. Adler was there and Mrs. Shwartz. When I entered they all rose to their feet and sang "God Bless America" as I sauntered nonchalantly to the stage. Then they burst into a din of thunderous applause and shouted, "Bravo! Bravo!"

The King, after a brief, dull speech, handed me the Prize: an enormous trophy and a check for a million dollars. "I trust," he said, "that this will make you comfortable for a long time to come. You were very brave not to follow your mother's silly suggestion to become a teacher and marry rich. Instead you became an avenger, went hungry, and, learning math on your own in dingy basement rooms, wrote your name in the stars. . . ."

"Don't talk bad against my mother or I'll knock your head in," I snarled, and the King bowed his head in shame.

"Of course," he said, "I never intended . . ."

"Right," I said, and he skulked off stage.

I now stood at the podium, the trophy in one hand, check in the other. A hush fell over the hall.

"Mom," I said, looking down into her eyes, which glowed with pride, "now you can rest. This one is for you. The Nazis put your childhood in a concentration camp, filled your heart with dead people and fear, and in turn you did the same to me, but that's over now. I'm gonna build you the house you shoulda had. And I'm gonna send you to the Sorbonne for that diploma you always wanted. And I'm gonna get you the best doctors money can buy to take care of your high blood pressure, kidney stones, and rectal polyps. Because what happened to you is not fair! And there's God and he gave me the talents to make it right! So don't you ever cry again, my little momma, and don't you worry no more about no Nazis either. I'm taking care of that!" I allowed my tux jacket to slip aside, revealing underneath the costume of the Purple Jew and the blue steel handle of my gun. I grinned handsomely.

"Oh, Abie! Be careful!" she shrilled. "Is it loaded? Oy! Don't hurt yourself!"

"Goodbye, Mom," I chuckled. "Goodbye Professor, goodbye Brigitte." I slipped behind the curtains, melting back into the shadows, underground, to calculate groundbreaking equations on the run as I made my vengeance raids on the enemies of innocence.

from *Summer-Long-a-Coming*

BY BARBARA FINKELSTEIN

Towards the end of June, Lalke and Mendl Decher came to the farm and occupied the spare bedroom on the second floor. Lalke was a third or fourth cousin to my father, his closest living relative, but sufficiently distant so as not to pollute our lineage with her misguided taste in men. Lalke and Mendl had sold their blue jeans stall at the Long-a-coming Farmer's Market and Auction a few months earlier, and having lived out the lease on their apartment in Pleasantville, near the south Jersey shore, were now preparing to ship themselves and their Country Squire station wagon to Israel, which, as Lalke said, was the only place for a Jew to live.

Lalke and Mendl were the two largest Jews I ever saw, looming tall and wide over the dollhouse Szusters. I imagined them as a pair of walking salt and pepper shakers, fit for Goliath's table, or as larger-than-life-scale figures in a natural history museum. They weren't simply tall; their bones, muscles, coloring, angles, and curves were lost inside dunes of fat. Their elbows and knees were dimpled, their chins terraced into three pouches. Our house was inadequate to withstand Lalke and Mendl's long strides and heavy-footed plodding to the bathroom in the middle of the night to gargle, and contained them as a glass bottle contains a model ship. A child resulting from the union of these two behemoths could only be something as remarkable as the Jersey Devil, but the only child Lalke ever had was with a first husband before the war. A Polish teenager with celebration in his yelp had hurled the child into the air and shot it dead along with its father in a kind of target practice.

From my earliest childhood days, Lalke and Mendl visited us every Sunday evening when the Auction work week ended. They bought Perel, Sheiye, and me Wrigley's chewing gum and hexagons of dark chocolate. With my parents they dined on onions, sardines, and rye bread. Lalke's eyes invariably moistened when she beamed down at Perel and me sitting together, thigh to thigh, in the same armchair, watching *The Ed Sullivan Show*. "Do you know how much your mama and papa love you kids? Do you know what your parents went through?" she asked us in accented English. Our answer was always the same uncomfortable grin and an unspoken prayer to leave us alone. Mendl would position himself between the TV and my sister and me, his simian arms akimbo like those of the Jolly Green Giant. In his half-English, half-Yiddish baritone, he thundered, "Ah, you little monkelach!" He uncrossed his arms only to perform along with Ed Sullivan's comedy routines, particularly ones involving Topo Gigio, the talking Italian mouse, until Lalke summoned him back to the kitchen to discuss business and the war with the adults. Crestfallen, that's how Mendl faced his wife.

Like Sheiye, Mendl had a number of unusual talents. He improvised polkas and ballads on his ever-present accordion; he spoke fluent Yiddish, English, Polish, Russian, Ukrainian, and German, and knew enough Hungarian, Spanish, and Hebrew, as he put it, "*tsi flirteven*"—to flirt with the ladies. I assumed this facility with languages constituted a kind of streetwise genius, a genius that had enabled him to survive the war. But aside from these musical and linguistic gifts, Mendl was a bungler. Nothing demonstrated this more convincingly than his talent to wring misfortune out of a placid five seconds. He would walk past a perfectly sturdy table and suddenly its wooden leg would crack. He would lay his mitts on you for a kiss and accidentally slam you in the ribs. A car ride with Mendl at the wheel was best spent in reestablished dialogue with a personal God; in his most attentive moments, Mendl drove with one hand on the steering wheel while the other skoaled wild toasting gestures across the expanse of the front seat. His recklessness stemmed, perhaps, from the half gratitude, half resentment he felt towards Lalke, for her business acumen and his parasitic reliance on it.

Mendl, I observed, shrugged off all concern for personal safety and, as a result, endangered us. I remember one case in point three summers before Lalke and Mendl stayed with us. Lalke was sitting in the kitchen, a blue denim apron shielding her voluminous skirt and blouse, complaining about a Puerto Rican couple who had teamed up to steal a shipment of denim caps. Mendl stood in the doorway between the kitchen and living room and gurgled at an Italian trapeze act on *The Ed Sullivan Show.* "O solo mio! Tra-la-la-la-la!" Mendl boomed. He roared at his prankishness and at the embarrassment on my face and Perel's. I looked into the kitchen and caught my father's eye. He snorted his throaty laugh as if to explain that sometimes adults are children. Lalke yelled, "Hey you, *komiker!* Hey you, lover boy! Get your sexy body in here! *A shlak zol dekh trefn! Kim aher!*"

"Sure! Sure! Sure! Sure!" Mendl answered. "Sure" was the latest expression he had picked up at the Auction. Mendl delighted in rolling the English *r* behind his lower teeth, and with each new "Sure," the muscles of his face arched into a new clownish contortion. "In a minute!" he called to Lalke. Imitating one of the Italians tiptoeing daintily across a high wire, he bent down to avoid the low-hanging chandelier that my parents had bought at the Long-a-coming Lighting Supply Store. Mendl pretended to lose his balance and totter. "Ah, you little monkelach!" he bellowed, and before she knew what had happened, Mendl scooped Perel out of the chair and into his bearish arms.

Against the backdrop of the TV trapeze act and a Strauss waltz, Mendl floated the nine-year-old Perel through the air. "She flies troo de air with duh gradets of ease! Ha! Ha! Ha!" he syncopated with a howl. Perel's eyes turned from brown to black with terror. Her chubby body involuntarily turned rigid, and she strained her head as far from Mendl's lips as possible. When our eyes met, she wordlessly begged me to wrench her free of this madman. In the midst of Mendl's footwork, he bounced Perel's head into the fake brass cone of the chandelier.

The bump Perel received scared her less than the realization that Mendl was truly a danger, and she started to wail. Mendl stopped singing, my mother jumped out of her chair in the kitchen, and a forlorn look of apology filled Mendl's eyes. Perel tore free of Mendl and threw herself around Mama's waist like a five-year-old. Mama stroked her daughter's head, and couldn't contain her anger at Mendl. "*Farvus firste zekh uhp vi a kind!*" Why do you act like a child! she jabbed under her breath.

By now Lalke had heaved herself out of the kitchen seat to investigate the turmoil in the living room. "Whas going on in here?" she asked with a little laugh, assuming that Perel and I had attacked each other over seating rights, or that Sheiye was starting up with us again. When she looked at her husband she understood immediately the source of the problem and cursed, "*Ay, Gey kebenye matre!*"—a half-Yiddish, half-Russian oath that meant something like, "Go lie where your mother lies," which in Mendl's case suggested Auschwitz. "*Antshildik zekh!*" Apologize!

Papa, meanwhile, continued to add dollops of sour cream to the fresh strawberries he and Mama had picked after slaughtering chickens that day. He glanced through the kitchen door, saw that no blood had been spilled, and decided to let us fools thrash out a conclusion, content to learn later from Mama secondhand what had transpired.

In one of his well-considered commentaries, he addressed us all: "*Kinder,* Ed Sullivan *volt zekh gesheymt!* Children, Ed Sullivan would be ashamed! Do you know his wife is a Jew?"

⌐⌐

W‌HAT PUZZLED ME about Mendl was his expression whenever his wife chided him, or whenever my father insisted Mendl had read someone's character all wrong. It was the same glaze of chastisement you see in the round brown eyes of a dog who has trampled through a well-tended flower garden. I remember at least one occasion when that confused look covered Mendl's own brown eyes with something like the rubbery translucent veil separating the white of an egg from its shell.

The incident, which happened a few weeks before his residency with us, grew out of an argument about *The Ed Sullivan Show.*

Sheiye hated *Ed Sullivan.* He preferred *The F.B.I.,* with its dragnet episodes of interstate embezzlement schemes and foreign spies intent on toppling the American government. On that particular summer Sunday evening, Sheiye strode down the stairs from his room, headed directly for the TV, and switched the station Perel and I had been watching.

"What do you think you're doing?" I yelled. "Jesus Christ! You don't even ask permission!"

"According to the Bible, the man is superior to the girl," Sheiye said coolly. "I don't need a little girl's permission."

"Put Ed Sullivan back on, scholar," I said dryly.

"Brantzche," Perel whispered. "Don't say Jesus Christ!"

But Perel was absolutely on my side and ready for fisticuffs. She stopped inspecting her strands of brown hair and jumped up from the floor, where she had been sitting to cool off. Sheiye's hand held fast to the TV dial, and he blocked the screen with his thick waist. "Move!" Perel grunted.

"You better go play with your dolls if you know what's good for you, little girl," Sheiye said.

"You have no right to barge in here while we're watching TV," Perel huffed. "Go back upstairs and squeeze your pimples."

That was the instigation for Sheiye's first blow—and Sheiye's first blow beckoned Perel's return kick. "Who do you think you're kicking?" Sheiye barked, now giving vent to the acid brew forever simmering inside him.

"The last I looked, John Lennon didn't have pimples, so it can't be him!" Perel flung back, preparing to launch another kick at his shins.

Sheiye grabbed Perel's foot and raised it as high as it would go. "Let go of my foot, strawberry patch!" Perel screamed.

"We'll see who's a strawberry patch!" Sheiye blustered. He shoved his face, covered with a sheath of acne scars, into Perel's, holding her leg all the while. To her discredit, Perel started screaming in earnest, for we both knew that screaming only incensed Sheiye. In fact, Sheiye's sole victory as a high school wrestler had come after his opponent shouted in an attempt to distract him. "First the bastard screamed at me, and then he ripped a hole in my T-shirt," Sheiye had gloated. "That was the final straw. I had him pinned in three moves." Now Perel's cries unnerved Sheiye; when Perel's mouth was open, Sheiye spat into it. Perel looked as if she had bitten into a piece of putrid meat. She didn't dare swallow or say another word lest Sheiye's saliva roll down her gullet.

"Taste good, little girl?" Sheiye laughed.

Perel spat Sheiye's saliva back at him, and it landed on his mouth.

"Right in the kisser!" I cheered.

"Who said anything about kissing?" Sheiye said. "If kissing's what you want, little girl, kissing's what you'll get!" And he dove towards Perel's lips.

This time when Perel started screaming, she turned her head to the side. Not content with spitting at Perel's neck, Sheiye pushed her against the TV. Weary of the domestic quarrel, the TV whined, and a tiny white dot sucked its image towards the center of the screen, making it disappear like the powder cleanser that concentrated a household's dirt into a pinpoint and whisked it away inside a white tornado.

When the audio spiraled down into a steady low buzz, the four adults in the kitchen, who had been reconstructing the war's chronology, bustled into the living room. First came Mama, her cheeks bulging with challah; behind her followed Lalke and Mendl; last came Papa, whose appearance at all warned that his patience had finally been challenged, and that as a result he could rationalize any unpleasant consequences. This moment was always the pivotal point in any of our intersibling battles. Whose side would Mama and Papa take? Their son disappointed them; he preferred go-carts to *Gemara*. A scene like this could provide an opportunity to take a potshot at Sheiye's failures. Or Mama and Papa might feel responsible for their son's academic limitations, in which case they would rage at Perel and me for highlighting them. Oftentimes the causes of our conflicts were irrelevant. What mattered most was our parents' momentary disposition towards each of their children, and the point at which they had been interrupted in their war chronology.

This time they took their cue from Mendl. He was genuinely shocked by the sister-brother hostilities; this evening was the first time ever he had viewed them outright. His eyes widened, and he swallowed with effort. You could see the fantasy that Mendl had cultivated about our family disintegrate into horror at Sheiye's bullying. "*Farvus nemste eym nisht tsen* a psychiatrist?" Why don't you take him to a psychiatrist? Mendl asked. His jaw dropped. "A boy his age shouldn't act like this."

Towering above, Lalke reminded us, as she always did, "Do you kids know what your parents have been through?"

My mother was ashamed that outsiders had witnessed our bellicose intimacy. She sighed, "We should have enrolled him in a yeshiva. We have friends in Brooklyn . . ."

"*Makh zekh nisht narish,*" Papa said, opting for the sympathy stance. In Papa's eyes, ganging up against a petty mischief-maker was an act of cowardice. "He'll outgrow it," he reasoned.

"He's already eighteen years old," I protested.

"An eighteen-year-old is barely out of diapers," Papa said. "The only thing an eighteen-year-old boy can do is beat you up, and that's what Sheiye did."

Sheiye smirked, but Papa turned towards him and said, *"Ti mir a toyve 'n trug zekh up."* Do me a favor and beat it. That was Papa's way of democratically expressing his displeasure with all of us. Perel, meanwhile, had already pressed herself against the wall, just in case Papa held her responsible for disrupting the evening's peace.

Sheiye had been counting on a victory, and disappointment lodged in a tic under his eye. "You all make me sick, sick, sick!" he said angrily. He headed out into the night.

My mother blanched. "Where are you going? It's dark outside!"

"I'm obeying my father," Sheiye said, enunciating each word. With his chin thrust forward, he added, *"Yekh trug zekh up."*

At such moments, I could never predict my father's reaction. He would raise his eyes not quite heavenward but lower, more likely to the bathroom upstairs. You might debate whether he was about to smile or begin raging. His thin lips, shiny with sweat and supplication, seemed uncertain how to respond to the present situation. If anything, they looked about to question God's sanity in parceling out such a bad lot of children to him, especially in light of everything he had already suffered. With a look that said God's wisdom is not often apparent, Papa returned to the kitchen, the neutral zone.

Perel was satisfied with Papa's judgment. She said through the screen window, "Yeah, Queero, take a walk."

"Kinder, please!" Mama pleaded. "A brother and sister should love each other. *Alevay!* If only I could have my brother near me now!"

"Mama, you and your brother love each other so much that you're here and he's in Israel," I said.

More exhausted from fighting with us than from working in the slaughterhouse, Mama concluded, *"Luz mekh tsi-ri."* Let me be. She returned to Lalke, back in the kitchen, to my father, and the sardines. I had the feeling she wanted to whip something more caustic at me but decided that silence was wiser. Immediately I regretted my nastiness, but knew my behavior wouldn't alter much in the future. This, I realized, was the attitude my father described when he said, "Children: That's their nature," just as he would say when a chicken scratched him, "Chickens: That's their nature."

Mendl, his eyes bright with undeserved guilt, was so distraught by the recent episode that he walked outside with his accordion, settled himself and the wheezing instrument on the bench behind the house, and played "Moscow Nights" to the fireflies and mosquitoes. I looked through the kitchen window to see him, and possibly Sheiye too. Against the silhouettes of the three chicken coops, Mendl swayed slowly from side to side. When the accordion expanded, Mendl leaned back to encourage the flow of air; when he closed it up, he nearly collapsed over it, proprietary, hugging the sound to his massive chest. The squat, wide box instrument was made in Mendl's image like a son, a friend who understood him when no one else did. He went on playing lullabies and folk melodies, dotting his meaty fingers gracefully on the Chinese-checker pattern of the accordion, consoling himself for Sheiye's behavior as if he himself had spat on Perel and broken the TV. When the stars cordoned off the streak of clouds in the black sky, Lalke stole up behind her husband and cushioned her pillowy arms around him.

$$\rightharpoondown$$

As the move to Israel drew closer, Mendl became giddy. He danced across the kitchen floor, singing to Perel and me in the living room, "I'm going to be a *halutz!* I'm going to be a pioneer! Watch out, you Arabs! Oh, sure! I'm gonna get you!" He pantomimed loading a machine gun and took aim at Lalke's head. "Very funny, buster," she said in English, and returned to a Bashevis Singer story in the *Jewish Daily Forward.*

Lalke's silent concentration just then was atypical. For the most part, the seriousness of her current plan did not sow a pensive attitude in her, and she still talked up a storm. I discovered how easy it was to muffle the Yiddish language into gibberish. I did not want to listen to Lalke or my parents; all their thoughts were stuck, glued like feathers to the revolving cylinder of a slaughtering machine. If I wasn't careful, this language would transmit their ugly obsession to me and derange me as it had deranged them. Yiddish, with its strictures and death tallies, was a poison. Nobody healthy, nobody carefree, spoke it. I panicked that so much Yiddish had already seeped into my consciousness and wondered if I could possibly achieve total illiteracy in it. After all, my father claimed that the Polish language visited such unbearable memories on him that he had obliterated it from his mind.

My program for amnesia was not successful. In spite of my intentions, I, and Perel, could not help but understand one of the adults' more pragmatic discussions: To whom would Lalke and Mendl sell their white '62 Cadillac?

Mendl wanted it to go to someone at the Auction, a Puerto Rican woman with hoop earrings and red lipstick. My father tried to persuade Mendl rather to sell it to a man named Lonik, a war survivor, who delivered eggs to grocery stores and farmers' markets throughout south Jersey. Lonik had recently had a run of bad luck: His wife had changed the lock on their front door and demanded that he never cross the threshold again or she would have him arrested for trespassing. The title deed was in the wife's name, and Lonik had no recourse but to obey. At least Lonik's children stuck by him. He said that the children had always wanted a Cadillac, and to reward their loyalty he would buy one for them. In the course of the story, Lalke dabbed her eyes with the corner of her skirt and agreed that Lonik should get the car.

"Mendl," my father said, as if to a child. "If you can help a fellow Jew, why not do it?" Shaking his head to clear away pictures of past adversity, he added, "You remember how much the *goyim* helped us. . . ."

"But I promised," Mendl persisted stubbornly. "She's my friend."

Mama and Papa stared at each other in amazement. The concept of friendship bewildered them. Adults didn't have friends; they had a husband or a wife. Lalke stood up to reach for a toothpick in the dish cabinet, sat down again, and began picking at her teeth. "You'll be better rid of such 'friends,'" she winced. "I've put up with your 'friends' long enough."

"She cares more about me than you do," Mendl said, defending himself in a battle he knew was already lost.

Sensing her advantage, Lalke continued, "That's right; I have to put up with your 'friends' long enough and now it's my turn to throw some weight around." Turning towards my father, Lalke said, "Get in touch with this righteous Lonik and tell him the car is his for four hundred dollars." She underscored her resolution with a spontaneous burst of sympathy: *Got zol eym up-hitn!* God protect him, poor soul!

"Okay, sister," Mendl said in English. "You win this one, but you're not gonna make me sell the guns."

"The guns?" my mother echoed. She focused alternately on each face at the table. "What guns?"

Lalke may have been a big-mouth, but she also possessed a candor that could momentarily humble her. Embarrassed, she stated simply, "He has guns. A pistol and a rifle. He target-practices in Pleasantville with the *shvartse* and Puerto Ricans he meets at the Auction."

"And now you're gonna ruin my life by taking me to Israel," Mendl shouted. "The least you can do is let me protect you from the Arabs."

My mother: "A Jew should own guns? For pleasure?" Stunned, she sat forward, and her elbow jostled a glass of iced tea. A line of light-brown liquid streamed down its side and onto the tablecloth.

"Now you know what I've put up with all these years," Lalke lamented. "Other women . . . *shvartse* . . . Puerto Ricans . . . guns. Mendl doesn't care about his own kind. He never did." Facing her husband, Lalke said bitterly, "A Judenrat bum! That's what you were and that's what you still are!"

"My friends are all better than you!" Mendl fumed. The impending isolation, which life in Israel threatened, threw Mendl into a panic, and he cried, "The Jews—the Jews are scum! I'm not going to Israel and that's that!"

"Yeah, yeah, sure, that's that, lover boy," Lalke said. "That's that and you'll do as I say or end up a fat bum on the street. Then we'll see where your friends are!"

Simultaneously, my mother and father demanded, "Mendl, you have to sell the guns."

"They're my guns," he said.

Whereupon Mama, Papa, and Lalke began discussing the issue among themselves. In a hushed voice, Mama said, "Lalke, if you don't sell them now, you'll have trouble in Israel. Who knows what he's capable of doing?"

"Who are any of you to tell me what to do?" Mendl cried. That bright, guilty look returned to his eyes and suddenly Mendl understood: He had nothing in common with Lalke or the Szusters! Mendl belonged in south Jersey, at the Auction, on the Boardwalk, at the gun club, with people who accepted him. What good were the Jews? They were choking him. In a rage, he burst out, "I'm taking both guns with me and I'm gonna kill as many Jews as I can!" And with a rebelliousness as much impotent as fierce, Mendl picked up Mama's glass of tea and hurled it to the floor.

From my vantage point in the living room, I saw Mama's lips part, about to order him to clean up the mess. But she was too afraid and wouldn't look Mendl in the eye. Perel began splitting strands of her hair, and torn between eavesdropping and hiding, she compromised by taking off her glasses to handicap at least one of her senses. Papa looked in at me and burst out laughing, maybe to assure me that Mendl was only temporarily acting flooey and there wasn't anything to worry about.

Mendl flew out of the kitchen door, this time without his accordion. I wondered how long he could entertain himself solely with his anger. The accordion would have kept him occupied indefinitely.

With Mendl out of earshot, Mama looked earnestly at Lalke, now on her knees collecting the broken glass, and said, "He's a maniac!

Why didn't you ever tell me? Lalke, you have to get a divorce. You're still young enough to find another man in Israel. Divorce Mendl in Israel. The government will take care of him. You've done your share."

"I can't divorce him," Lalke said. "He needs me. Who'll take care of him the way I do?"

"Lalke, do you know Mendl propositioned me once at the Auction? He set up a mattress behind a curtain and expected me to—to do you know what!"

I tried to catch Perel's eye, but her face was now completely curtained by her long, brown, splitting hair.

"Promise me you'll get a divorce," Mama begged. *"Er iz meshige!"*

Unable to surrender this picture of Mendl as a lunatic, Mama looked at no one in particular and suddenly announced her revelation: "He doesn't have a brain. He's just an inflated piece of meat that you have to feed every day." Mama puffed out her cheeks to underline the point.

Lalke looked tired. Her admission of shame after so many years of secrecy carved out a lull in this interfamily battle, and with her only soldier gone AWOL, the major general admitted defeat. Her shoulders sagged and her blue-winged glasses slid down her hefty nose. She shook her head sadly. "I can't put him out in the street like a dog. He wasn't this bad in the beginning. I swear he wasn't. The war made him go a little off his rocker, being a policeman for the Nazis and everything, but I thought that in time, with someone to take care of him, he would recover his senses. I just didn't know."

Lalke wrapped the pieces of broken glass in an *Inquirer* and threw the bundle in the garbage. Mama started to continue her imprecations, but Lalke cut her off. She looked squarely at my parents and said, *"Vi volt gekent zahn andersh, az Hitler, yimakh shemoy, iz dokh geveyn der shadkhn?"* What do you expect, with Hitler—God damn him!—as our matchmaker?

The three sat in a kind of silent memorial to the war dead, until Mendl finally walked through the screen door, determination in his eyes. "If I have to go to Israel, I'll kill the Jews," he said. As Mendl passed Mama, he kicked at her chair. "You're so smart you tell yourself when to bleed! You hear me!" he yelled, on a rampage against all manifestations of female intelligence. He thudded past Perel and me, up the stairs to the guest room. Perel's glasses forded the river of hair covering her face. She still refused to look at me and studied the grating on the window fan, as if it mattered more than anything else.

"I'll kill you! I'll break your neck!" Mama screamed. "I'll kill you if you talk to me again!"

Papa laughed at Mama's hysteria and told her not to talk *narishkeyt*.

⌇

As far as I know, Mendl never killed anyone, either Arab or Jew, though rumor has it that he was arrested once for wielding a sawed-off pipe through Ramat Gan. And Lalke never divorced him, though she had ended up promising my mother she would.

I guess it takes a person like Lalke Decher to understand endurance. Only someone who has married out of penance or pity, or out of physical love, long past, can believe that loyalty must override expedience. And so Lalke has always tried to reunite me with my parents, convinced by the example of her own life that no man should put asunder what God hath wrought. If not for Lalke, I might have either glorified or excoriated Mama and Papa. But she alone has kept my parents life-sized for me; she has shown me that their flaws were often honeycombed with goodness. It is thanks to Lalke that I received a brown mailer last summer containing cassette tapes and a note in misspelled English: "I always taut you kits shud no wat your parents wet troo. It is not to lat for this taps to do som god."

Lalke, for the first time I did not shrug off that silly, worn phrase of yours. For the first time I saw you as a canny mediator, not just as a fool who married the wrong man. I suppose a woman who has lived nearly forty years with "an inflated piece of meat" works around obstacles.

Every few weeks I listen to those tapes the way observant Jews listen to their rabbi's sermon on Shabbos. I pore over the stories and their possible interpretations, flicking on fast forward and reverse, just as yeshiva boys burn their eyes out over *Pirke Avot*. In case my parents think my soul abandoned my body and that the Szusters and the farm are only remote oddities to me, I designate you, Lalke, as intermediary to tell them it isn't true. Tell them this kid wants to understand what we went through.

Part II

Excision

BY SAVYON LIEBRECHT

Translated from the Hebrew by Marganit Weinberger-Rotman

When Henya extracted the sharp scissors from the green plastic sheath with the picture of the dissected chicken sketched on it, her eyes started glazing, and when she put her hand to her granddaughter's head and parted the shining, golden hair, which tumbled like curled laces under the clicking scissors, her face had already turned into a mask.

"Come closer to the window, baby, so that Grandma can see better and won't hurt you. Grandma loves you and never wants you to feel pain. Bend your head a little so that Grandma can do it properly."

There was a note of urgency in Henya's voice and the child, sensing the importance of what was being done to her, stood for a long time motionless and obedient, her head bowed, her hands tucked behind the belt buckle of her short dress, and her eyes staring at the long blond clumps of hair piling up around her sandals.

"We'll do this properly," Henya whispered promisingly to the pale, slender nape exposed to the light. "Nothing will be left on your sweet head and all the dirty stuff will drop off." Her left hand burrowed in the small child's extraordinary long hair, and her right hand quickly manipulated the scissors; her body was arched like a bow over her grandchild's head. Thus she worked with a frozen glaze, like a woman possessed.

The parting between the two golden curtains was getting more and more jagged until at last the entire head was shorn; short stubble, like mown stalks of wheat, stood on the pale scalp, exposing the tender white skin that had not seen the light since the hair first grew on it.

Henya emitted a feverish breath and her whole body was seized by a tremor. She returned the scissors to their sheath, dropped exhausted into a chair as if after great exertion, drew the grandchild to her, hugged her with all her might, and covered her nape with kisses, as if they were about to part. Her voice regained its soothing tone, despite the turmoil that had overwhelmed her. "Everything will be all right now, baby. You don't have to worry anymore."

The child raised tender hands to feel her head and recoiled from the new sensation. Then she looked at the heap of hair on the floor and turned her head away, her face contorted with crying. "You cut off all of my hair. Now I look like a boy."

Henya pulled the child to her bosom and stroked the anguished face. "We had to do it, baby."

"Why?"

"Because of the note from your teacher. You remember she pinned a note to your shirt collar? That's what it said. But now everything will be fine. Your hair will grow quickly and be very, very clean."

The girl ran to the big mirror in her parents' bedroom and returned to her grandmother sobbing. "I look ugly without my hair. I don't want to go to school like this. They'll make fun of me, 'cause it's ugly. It's even shorter than Hedva's hair. I'll tell my mommy on you. She won't talk to you, and then she'll stick my hair back on."

Behind the glazed look, Henya's irises started flitting. "Baby, come here to Grandma. Closer, closer to Grandma. I want to tell you something. I know tomorrow is your birthday and you're a big girl now and you understand a lot of things. So now I'll tell you something that only big children can understand, and then you'll see that we had to do what we did."

THE FIRST TO see it was Zvi. For a moment he stood there flabbergasted, his head tilted back as if he had been slapped. Then he looked as if he were about to burst into tears: his lips were sucked in and his eyes clouded over. He lowered the cardboard box he was carrying and put it on a bench in the hallway without taking his eyes off the girl caught in Henya's arms, as if trying to figure out what a strange child was doing in his house being embraced by his own mother. Then his gaze wandered to the puddle of golden hair and his hands shot to his head, clutching his temples.

The girl tore herself from her grandmother's arms and started to cry, her little hand groping on her scalp. "Daddy, look what Grandma did to me; she cut off all my hair, and it's not nice at all. The children will say I look like a monkey."

Henya rose briskly from her chair and spoke to her son as she used to when he was a child, "Zvika, come with me. I want to show you something."

Zvi put his hand on his daughter's head, and his palm, feeling its way like the palm of a blind man, stroked the coarse, straight spikes on the child's head. "Mother, I don't know what came over you. This time you're really out of your mind."

"Look what it says here." She held the note before his eyes. "Read for yourself and then tell me if it isn't a shame and a disgrace that a thing like this should happen in our family."

Zvi read the note, and his hand wandered in the air and stopped on his brow, as if he were struck by an excruciating headache.

"This is a note from the teacher," he said. "She sends such notes to all the kids every Friday."

"You didn't read it, Zvika! Read it first. Read carefully what it says."

"I already know it by heart. Every Friday I fetch Miri from nursery school and she has a note like this pinned to her collar. It always says the same thing."

"Zvika, it says she has head lice."

"I know."

"What do you mean, you know? As if it was a normal thing in our family. And the teacher knows and anyone who sees the note on the child's collar knows. People will talk. There are people here who know me from abroad."

"Mother, this time you really went out of your mind," he said. The girl wailed suddenly, frightened by the shouting between her father and her grandmother. She pressed her cheek to his thigh and hugged his waist.

"Look what you've done to her. She had the most beautiful hair in the school. We've never cut her hair since she was born. And you knew it, you were so proud of her hair. How could you do this, explain to me, how?"

"But Zvika, she has head lice!" Henya's eyes turned into two black rings in her face. "What does it matter if the hair is pretty or not if you have lice?"

"And now you argue with me. You refuse to realize what you did, and you're sure you're right. Don't you know that all the kids have lice? It's an epidemic. You yourself told me last month that you saw on television how they declared a nationwide campaign to wash all the children's hair that day, so that they wouldn't reinfect each other. Ziva washes her hair every week and treats it with a special chemical, and still she picks it up from the kids in her nursery school."

"Zvika, listen to me. I know what's good for my children. I've been through a lot and I know. When you've got lice, no chemical and no washing will do. The best thing is to crop the hair right away, down to the roots. Every hour there are more and more eggs and every minute counts."

"Cut it like this?" he asked, his voice on the brink of crying, and he pointed to the head clinging to his thigh. "If you decide to cut it, why like this, in a fit, why not at the hairdressers, in a straight line, so that it will look pretty?"

Henya looked at her grandchild as if seeing her for the first time, the shorn stumps of hair, the shrunken head, and the tender neck that looked like a plucked chicken's. Her head was still bent toward him as if trying to explain. Henya suddenly started to cry and to emit a strange sobbing sound, like a person who was born without the ability to cry but has learned to fake it, to reduce the distance between themselves and other human beings.

"It really didn't come out so nice," she sobbed. "It should have been more straight. But I was so agitated, I didn't pay attention. Will you forgive Grandma for doing such a poor job, baby? Will you forgive Grandma? You know, Grandma only wants the best for you, don't you? You know I have only Zvika and one Miri in the whole world."

The child lowered her eyes, unwilling to look at her, and a moment later turned her back to her, tightened her grip around her father's waist and buried her face in his trousers. When Henya put out her hand to pat the shorn head, the small body trembled, as if scorched by fire.

"It will grow again soon, baby," Henya promised her, her heart sinking at the sight of the recoiling girl. "You'll again have the most beautiful hair, and, more important, you won't have lice."

Zvi was staring at the felled hair scattered on the floor, beneath the window, like wisps of light. He said in a lifeless voice, "I really don't know what to do about this. Come with me to the other room, Mother. Ziva will be here soon; she only went out to order the birthday cake. What she will do when she sees this I really don't know. She'll blow her top. You'd better not be here at all. Go in there, and when Ziva gets here I'll take you home as quickly as possible."

⌐⌐

IN HER SON'S STUDY, with eyes staring at the darkness, Henya heard her daughter-in-law screaming, her granddaughter wailing, and her son trying to intervene, to explain, but his voice was drowned by theirs.

"Why should I care about that now?" she heard her daughter-in-law. "So what if that's what they used to do in the camps forty-five years ago. The world has advanced a little since then, and we are not in the camps now. Look at your daughter! Look at her! Tomorrow is her birthday. On this side she is completely shaven. And look here, she has a scratch. She cut her skin! Her hands should be broken so she'll never touch a pair of scissors again! Get that woman out of here or I'll kill her with my own hands. And tell her never to set foot in here again. I never want to see her face. Never again in my life!"

Zvi's voice struggled and rose, and for a moment sounded loud and clear and dominant in the adjacent room, but Ziva's voice immediately overpowered it: "Stop it, it won't do now. I'm telling you, it only makes me madder. I don't want to hear about it any-more! Those stories are prehistory by now. I told you not to ask her to baby-sit for us. She's crazy. You must realize that your mother is crazy. I told you a long time ago. She lost some screws in her head in the Holocaust. Look at the catastrophe she brought on us. A catas-trophe! I'll never let her near my child. And I don't want her to come here again. If you want to see her, you'll have to go to her house. She's crazy and you should put her in a nuthouse. Any doctor will agree to commit her right away. Look what she's done to our daughter. You remember what a pretty girl you had? Look at her now. She'll suffer for this all her life. Look here—and there. Turn around, Miri, so that Daddy can see. Can you take a child into the street like this? What shall we do with her? Put a wig on her? Shave her head? It will be at least a year before it looks okay. I want your mother out of my house now. I don't want her to stay for the birthday party. Anyway, we must call off the party."

Suddenly the screaming stopped and Miri's shrill voice was heard turning into a sob. "Do you hear what your child is saying? She knows what the lice did when people died in the camps. A four-year-old needs to hear such things? Is this a story fit for her age, I ask you? I want my child to hear stories about Cinderella, not about Auschwitz!"

THE TANGLE OF the voices stopped at the door of the study and Henya was enveloped by deep silence. The death rattle of the boy who was hanged by his feet in the passage between the men's and the women's camp had stopped a while ago, and since then only distant barking and rustling of leaves broke the silence now and then. In the corner of the barrack, near the only window overlooking the woods beyond the electric fence, a woman was tossing on her berth and groaning in her dream. The woman sleeping next to her moaned and turned too, so as not to find herself without the sack that served as a blanket, trying to warm herself against the nearby body. Henya raised her hand and with nailless fingers scratched her head; it made a dry, crackling sound, like a wooden floor scoured with a coarse brush. Her skull was itchy, the flesh of her nape inflamed, and she felt tiny bites in her armpits. In the morning, she will find that her neighbor on the other side, the one who had ceased to dream many weeks ago, died in her sleep. For weeks her face had borne the look of the dead, yet on the morning of her death she looked more alive than ever, serene, her eyes staring at the ceiling with a sort of curiosity. When the women hurry in the morning to line up in front of the barracks, the lice will start to leave the dead body; they will look like a black dotted line cutting across the forehead, feeling their way toward another body, looking for a new life for themselves.

Dancing at the Club Holocaust

BY J. J. STEINFELD

It was a clean, symmetrical, richly furnished office near the top floor of a large building driven into the heart of downtown Montreal. A double-sized desk, its surface protected by a sheet of polished glass, was in the center of the office. Only a long window that opened an unconscious eye over the city seemed to tilt the office away from symmetrical perfection.

"Where are your degrees and certification?" Reuben Sklar had asked after he had inspected the office during his first visit six months ago, certain no one would ever guess that this was a real doctor's office.

The doctor smiled widely without showing his teeth and said, "I don't like to be pretentious or construct unnecessary barriers."

Unsatisfied with the doctor's response, Reuben scratched his bearded face and said slowly, "Even dentists exhibit their credentials." When the doctor kept smiling, absently brushing the surface of his dustless desk, Reuben added in his usually rapid speech, "Latin mumbo jumbo on a scrap of paper makes you feel safe letting some stranger into your mouth."

The doctor motioned for Reuben to sit down in the chair to the left of the desk; it was a bold-patterned chair that a sideshow fat man would find comfortable. Tall and thin Reuben was swallowed into the cushions and began to think that this doctor did not fight fairly. The doctor smiled again, as if smiling were a neurological disorder, and removed two gold-framed university diplomas from the bottom drawer of his desk. "With honors," he announced, holding up the official documents to his new patient. "Now may I come into your mind?"

Reuben appreciated the attempt at humor, even found the doctor's ironic smile intriguing, but knew he would dislike this man anyway. Reuben could not forget that this neat, trim, restrained man earned a living excavating in a terrain only a fool would believe could disgorge truths.

"Of course, what I do isn't nearly as exact as what a dentist does," the doctor said and started to jot down a few preliminary notes in his new patient's thin file; later it would become a thick file, stuffed with notes about his thirty-six-year-old patient's dug-up terrain. After another session the doctor, less than four years older than his patient, would dislike Reuben as much as Reuben disliked him. They would not even develop the begrudging admiration of enemies who fight long and hard to a stalemate.

"If I had a son and he came home from school saying he wanted to be a psychiatrist," Reuben declared aggressively, "I'd castrate the kid on the spot." The doctor gave his ironic smile once more. He knew that his patient was a writer and the doctor was extremely tolerant of the creative mind. During the first moments of their meeting the doctor mistakenly thought that he had many worse and much more trying patients than Reuben Sklar.

After bluntly asking the doctor how much money he made a year, and the doctor good-naturedly boasting that it was a hell of a lot more than the Prime Minister made, the patient began talking about his mother without prompting: "My mother killed herself because she couldn't dance." When Reuben saw the doctor's indulgent expression, he raised his voice: "Goddamn it, she used to dance before the War. Her sister told me that at the funeral. My mother could barely walk as I was growing up. Until she killed herself she received *Wiedergutmachung* from the West German government for her crippled legs. You know what *Wiedergutmachung* means, doctor? *Making good*. Reparations straight from the Devil's ass. It's taken me all my life to comprehend that my mother had been a dancer before the War." Then Reuben Sklar the patient stood up and started dancing around the doctor's office like a madman . . . a very sad madman.

THE MONTREAL EXPOS were playing the New York Mets at Shea Stadium during the 1985 baseball season while Reuben was sitting in a smoky basement club and watching *Jud Süss,* just as hundreds of thousands of Germans had in the 1940s. It was the same movie that Heinrich Himmler ordered all German soldiers and SS men to see, or so the Club's host had said. Reuben wondered what the score of the Expos-Mets game was as a long-bearded Rabbi Loew huddled conspiratorially close to Josef Süss Oppenheimer on the movie screen. Comments jumped from the patrons at the tables, the words piercing the smoke and triggering more remarks and jeers. "Jew, Jew . . . " thundered like booing at a ballpark. "Jew, Jew . . ." turned into English and German curses. "*Jud, Jud* . . ." The rape scene began, Süss thrusting his vile Jew body onto the poor heroine Dorothea Strum, and the audience's hate for the defiler soared. The beautiful actress who played Dorothea in 1940 must be dead by now, Reuben thought, imagining her expiring peacefully in the comfort of a brass bed in Munich or Berlin.

How the frenzied audience cheered when Süss was placed into an iron cage, in preparation for his execution. "Hanging is too good for the Jew," someone would invariably call out in either English or German, and the chorus of "Jew, Jew / *Jud, Jud*" would start afresh, more venomously than before.

The Club was packed as usual, almost a hundred patrons. The tables in a semicircle by the small elevated stage afforded the best view, but Reuben always sat as far from the stage as possible, in a corner where the smoke drifted and hung like automobile exhaust. The Club, viewed casually, appeared almost ordinary: courteous and efficient waiters, Formica-topped tables of various sizes, a smooth wooden stage that was not so different from a theatre or ballet stage. Empty, the Club was nothing special, but at night it was never empty. Reuben usually arrived at nine o'clock on a Saturday and by then the evening's first film was well underway, the patrons absorbed in their drinking and time-defying world. At midnight the stage show would begin. Between, during and after the films the talkative host walked among the tables, greeting customers and friends, sharing a mug of beer, offering commentary about the films.

"Have you a good one tonight?" a blissfully drunk customer inquired. "A rabbi's eldest son," the host answered with a straight face. Laughter began and spread quickly.

The film ended to applause and the pounding of fists and mugs on tables. The host raised his arms and shouted, "*Deutschland erwache!*" his most commonly uttered slogan. He knew his audience and played with their emotions. "*Deutschland erwache! . . .*" One echo, ten, the entire Club eventually reverberating with "*Deutschland erwache!*"

"*Deutschland schlafe . . . Deutschland schlafe . . .* Go to sleep, Germany," Reuben whispered, but there was little chance anyone could hear his blasphemy amid the tumult. Then he mouthed "*Deutschland erwache*" in case he was noticed. He wanted to remain as inconspicuous as possible in his corner.

Following a long intermission and an introduction by the host, his accent markedly Brooklyn, the night's second film, *Der ewige Jude,* began. Jews observing their demonic Passover and studying their cryptic Talmud, the identifying of Jews with rats and the graphic ritualistic slaughtering of animals by Jews raised the audience to the same frenzy as *Jud Süss* had. This film was half the length of the previous feature and purported to be a documentary, but had no less of an impact.

Two years coming here now, Reuben thought, with both satisfaction and loathing. The first year there had been a large variety of German films, from the earliest to modern; but the last year only films from the 1938–43 period were shown, usually two an evening, on occasion three, some repeated often during a month. Reuben still remembered—and sometimes dreamed about—the first film he had ever seen at the Club: *Paracelsus*. Yet regardless of the film, to Reuben it appeared more tangible than the audience or the smoke or the never-silent host.

When *der Führer* appeared on the screen, speaking with arm-waving fervor about the need for a world conflict to hasten the demise of Jewry, the past completely vanquished the present for the audience. Soon the audience entered the slaughterhouse and witnessed what vicious and heartless creatures the Jews were, the slaughterer played as a butchering Satan. As the movie unrolled its grim montage, the host told the audience that when his father first saw this slaughterhouse scene in Berlin in 1940 many viewers fainted. Enjoying his role as cinema scholar, the host dispensed more and more details about the making of *Jud Süss* and *Der ewige Jude*. It was quarter to midnight and the audience grew increasingly restive.

Reuben sensed that it would not be much longer, one or two more visits to the Club, and he would act. He had long ago ceased to analyze his motives, no longer caring if what he intended to do was for revenge or justice or the memory of his parents; let the psychiatrist figure out motives. But then his psychiatrist did not believe that the Club existed; his own wife had never believed either. If only he could convince the psychiatrist to come with him to New York one weekend, to sit at a table in the basement club, then *he* would run to a psychiatrist, to a thousand disbelieving analysts. Instead Reuben was the patient with the thick file and the psychiatrist a wealthy man who believed that the Club was a delusion or morbid fantasy.

"Strange how things turn out," Reuben thought as he watched the host parade about the Club. "I was born in 1949, after it all happened, and now I'm caught in the madness of it all . . ." Reuben surely would have been better off going to the Expos-Mets game— baseball was once one of his passions—but this Club, at least for the weekend, made any other activity—sleeping, eating, writing—seem inconsequential and wasteful.

"*Deutschland erwache!*" the host exclaimed, his back to the black curtain hanging behind the movie screen. "One minute to twelve," he interjected with a clap of his hands, then turned and pointed to the curtain: "A rabbi's obedient, circumcised son awaits us. He studies Hebrew literature at Yeshiva University . . ."

Reuben knew what would start soon. He covered his eyes with his hands and saw the hideousness before it began. The screen was taken away and the curtain raised to reveal a man wearing an SS uniform and a naked teenage boy kneeling in front of him. "He can't be a Jew," Reuben thought, as he always thought when he saw another boy on stage. The audience oohed and ahed as if Marlene Dietrich was there as Lola-Lola, her silk-stockinged legs displayed for all to see and desire. Reuben wanted to gouge out his eyes but dropped his hands and watched again; watched with grieving eyes . . .

～

"I KNOW WHEN you've been to New York," the psychiatrist said before Reuben sat down. The doctor did not doubt that his patient traveled to New York—he speculated perhaps excursions into the city's pornography shops—but refused to acknowledge that Reuben had spent his time at his imaginary club.

"Do you now," Reuben said, exhausted and feeling belligerent. He had not slept in over two days.

"Look at your face . . . your eyes," the doctor ordered.

Reuben began to wander around the office in ludicrous pantomime, pretending to search for a mirror. Finally he ended his silence: "If I was at my barber's I could see whatever your magic eyes see, doctor."

The psychiatrist removed a plastic-handled vanity mirror from the same drawer in which he kept his university diplomas and held the mirror towards his patient.

"I'm working on a story. Creativity confounds the biological clock," Reuben said, attempting to rub his eyes into alertness.

"What are you writing about now, Reuben?" the doctor asked, more of an accusation than a question.

"A story about my mother."

"Another?"

"This one is different. My mother's one of your patients and you two are very fond of each other, doctor."

"I don't want that to be in your story."

"What are you scared of?" Reuben asked, smiling smugly, pleased to have placed the doctor on the defensive.

"I'm not comfortable with your literary vision . . . the way you *describe* people. Everything of yours you've given me to read might as well be set in hell."

"I've been to the Club Holocaust, doctor."

"Why do you keep calling it that, Reuben?"

"That's the truest name for it . . ."

Irritated by what he considered his patient's glibness, the doctor lifted the mirror higher this time and again ordered, "Just look at your face." Reuben slapped the mirror out of the doctor's extended hand, the glass shattering as it bounced off the desk and onto the carpet.

"Sorry," Reuben said immediately, glancing at his renegade hand; he thought he saw his mother's concentration camp number but did not mention this to the doctor.

"You have no chance of overcoming your problems if you keep going to New York," the doctor said matter-of-factly, little bothered by his patient's irrational act.

"I could go instead to a synagogue in town and masturbate as everybody is praying," the patient said, wanting to shake his doctor's composure. When he received no reaction, Reuben, stepping intentionally hard on some glass shards, walked over to the office's long window.

"What a great view you have, doctor. I can see Buchenwald, Dachau, Treblinka, Belsen, Auschwitz, Ravensbrück . . ." Reuben chanted in an accelerating rhythm, like a frightened shaman who knows his time is short and clings to any former incantation. With each name Reuben became more agitated. "I can see the concentration camps clearly. You have a look, doctor . . . Better yet, come to the Club Holocaust with me."

"Calm down, Reuben . . . calm yourself," the doctor said, turning only slightly in his chair.

Still looking out the window, Reuben said, "Would you have kissed Hitler's lips to keep yourself alive?"

"Back off that kind of talk," the doctor yelled at his patient. He scolded himself for becoming too emotional and easily regained his control.

"In the *Führerbunker,* who would see you?"

"There's a psychiatrist in Toronto who specializes in treating children of Holocaust Survivors. I've written him about you. Skip one of your New York sojourns and see him. To be honest, Reuben, I'm not helping you."

Reuben turned from the window and said, "I need you to base my story's lusty character on. I have to know you better." The patient started towards the doctor but stopped and picked up the largest piece of glass from the carpet.

"Why don't you get yourself a good German analyst, then your taunts and cruelty would make sense," the doctor said, unable to conceal his anger at his patient.

"You're the only one who can keep me sound in mind . . . functioning," Reuben said as he squeezed the piece of glass. His palms and fingers began to bleed freely but Reuben showed no pain or discomfort.

Recalling some of the messier and more grotesque suicides he had seen several years ago as an intern, the doctor said, "Let's clean up your cut." The doctor, however, did not leave his chair.

Reuben tossed the piece of glass onto the doctor's desk and said without a trace of agitation, "But you haven't answered me. Would you have kissed the Führer's moist lips to keep your practice alive? . . ."

TWO-THIRDS OF the way through *Jud Süss,* an elegant, elderly woman and an athletic young man from the audience stood up and began to dance. They glided carefully up and down the stage, their shadows joining the actors on the screen. No one in the Club complained, the couple was that enchanting. Another handsome couple walked to the stage and bowed to each other before commencing a sensual dance. The host started to sing "Falling in Love Again" and within a minute was accompanied by most of the audience. Several more couples joined those already on stage. There were only half a dozen women in the Club and soon each one was dancing with a partner. Two men stood and began to dance together by their table. More male couples followed their example, the movie of slight concern to anyone. A grey-haired man asked Reuben to dance, but he begged off, claiming in a careful German that he had injured his leg playing baseball.

Before the film ended fewer than ten Club patrons remained seated. Reuben did not know if the spectacle he was observing was insane or humorous. He thought of the incredible *Totentanz* performed in *Paracelsus* and his mood turned solemn. Recently he had dreamed still another time of the movie's juggler full of the baneful contagion and dancing, Death regaling in the marvelous, masterful dance. The host had stated on several occasions that Harald Kreutzberg was the greatest dancer of his time, the genius who brought the *Totentanz* to life in the 1943 movie. Reuben wanted to arise and do his Dance of Death, but could make no movement. His mother's legs were his; he was almost all the way back.

"Publish that story and I'll sue you," the doctor threatened as he tossed the thirty-page typed manuscript across the desk at his patient.

"You would sue a patient?" Reuben said mockingly, picking up his story and pressing it against his chest. His face was drawn and eyes darkly shadowed, but his voice was exuberant and clear.

"Damn straight. That story is nothing but filthiness, Sklar."

Shaking his head theatrically, Reuben said, "How can you say that to a man whose mother was in Auschwitz and committed suicide not two miles from your plush office and whose father died in a nut house run by nuns because he never accepted the fact that he had been liberated in 1945."

"You . . . you," the doctor stuttered angrily, "you still go to that Nazi bar."

Reuben smiled; it was the first time the doctor had spoken of the Club as though it were real. "If you sat with me at the Club Holocaust, you'd understand why I go there."

"You must find another psychiatrist," the doctor said. He could not take his mind off the scurrilous way his patient had portrayed him in the story.

"*Herr Doktor* in Toronto, right? . . . Another Jewish shrink."

"He went through what your parents did during the Second World War."

"But you're like an older brother to me, doctor."

"Reuben, you despise me."

"Only because you are a comfortable Jew . . . a forgetter," the patient said, placing his chin on the doctor's desktop.

"So why do you continue to come to me?"

"My wife, the comfortable Jewish wife, wants me to. As a condition to enduring me."

"Reuben, your wife left you two years ago," the doctor said, waving two fingers close to his patient's face.

Without showing any sign of surprise or being upset, Reuben proclaimed, "Well, it's a condition of my probation."

"*Psychiatric treatment,* not me necessarily." After a brief silence, the doctor leaned back laughing in his chair.

Confused by the doctor's outburst, Reuben stood up and began to pace around the desk.

"I didn't mean to laugh, Reuben, but I wish I'd been there . . ."

The doctor opened Reuben's file and flipped through his notes until he found the section describing his patient's arrest and subsequent firing from his teaching position.

"It's not easy to lose tenure," the doctor said, showing the wide, close-mouthed smile he rarely allowed around Reuben anymore. The doctor read and relived an early conversation with his patient.

That afternoon Reuben had begun by explaining softly, giving no indication that his story was anything but innocent: "The graduate students sponsored a Halloween bash. Students and professors had to dress as someone important from history. I went as Albert Camus. Unfortunately, no one recognized me . . . But are you ready for the zinger: there were two Hitlers at the party . . . *two.*"

"He was a legitimate historical figure," the doctor had argued, annoying his patient.

"Sure, but it seemed a bit disjointed—two overweight Hitlers in Montreal!"

"I thought that would appeal to your sense of the absurd."

"It did . . . for thirty seconds. Hitler number two was simply too keen on realism, if you can picture what I mean, doctor."

"Let me guess, Reuben . . . you punched a costumed Hitler."

"I could have gotten away with a little sucker punch . . . When the two Hitlers were sitting side-by-side cozy at a table, I hopped up on the table and pissed away. I got only one of them real good, but it was worth it. What a historical event: a Jewish professor from Montreal pissing on Hitler."

"You urinated on a student dressed as Hitler," the doctor had said

in an effort to redirect his patient's thinking, to fix reality in harmless place.

Joyously Reuben corrected his doctor: "I pissed on one of the big-
shot deans dressed as Hitler . . ."

REUBEN, SEATED NEXT to a stack of German newspapers on the
floor of his hotel room, finished the last drops of wine out of a bottle. Holding the empty bottle, he stared at the blank television
screen in the room, seeing the reflection of his unmade bed and
thinking of the oval-faced, obliging woman who had stayed with him
through the sleepless night but rushed out in the morning, after he
told her that his jealous wife would be arriving any minute.

Maybe he would not go to the Club tonight; maybe he was
stretching his luck too far. He lifted the German newspapers off the
floor and placed them on the bed. At the bottom of the stack was a
single, very old *Jewish Daily Forward.* Whenever he used to visit his
father at the mental institution, Reuben brought him a *Forward,*
including on the day the man died, screaming at his twenty-year-old
son, "You are the Gestapo, you are the Gestapo . . ." But Reuben
would go to the Club, certainly he would go; more certainly than
Gentiles go to church on Easter Sunday. I'm going to church, he
chuckled, then realized he was alone and laughing in a New York
City hotel room. Maybe, he thought, he should turn on the television set and fill the cheap room with noise and images, with the
strongest documentation that it was the 1980s.

Reuben opened another bottle of wine and went over to the
dresser mirror to practice his German. He had mastered the language and believed he could walk around Germany without anyone
knowing he was not a native. He addressed a crowd of emaciated
concentration camp Jews, assuring them help was on the way; he
addressed a crowd of Brown Shirts, lecturing them on the qualities
that make a person human; he addressed a room of dead, confessing

his envy for their tranquility . . . On the dresser was the cardboard sign he had printed: OUT OF ORDER, DO NOT ENTER/ZERBROCHEN, BETRETEN VERBOTEN. The newspapers, sign, adhesive tape, everything he needed . . .

Reuben pinched his cheeks and determined he was drunk; that was the foolproof test he used to measure his drunkenness. By nine o'clock he would be fine. He went into the bathroom and emptied the wine into the sink. Tonight he could not be too numbed, not tonight.

⚍

REUBEN SAT WITH the German newspapers piled neatly on his usual corner table. He had been driving back and forth from Montreal nearly every weekend for months with these newspapers in a suitcase. He read the headline of the top paper and was not disturbed that the news was stale. Each time he brought the newspapers to the Club, he intended to carry out his plan, but was unable to do it.

Der ewige Jude was not yet over but the host was speaking about the upcoming stage show: ". . . the boy's paternal grandfather died ignobly in the Warsaw ghetto and a maternal grandmother like a pig at Auschwitz . . . The maternal grandfather starved to death in a cellar . . . One of the boy's uncles perished at . . ."

Reuben took the newspapers and a pack of matches from the table—*German-American Cultural Society* was embossed on the matchbook cover—and unhurriedly walked to the bathrooms not far from his table. The displaced partisan taped his sign to the door of the men's bathroom. Inside, he crumpled up sheets of newspaper and scattered them over the floor. Next he struck a match and lighted the rolled-up *Jewish Daily Forward*. With his torch, Reuben ignited several newspaper pages and left the bathroom.

The curtain was nearly up when Reuben returned to his table. "*Deutschland erwache!*" sounded everywhere around him. He was certain that the teenage boy on stage was not Jewish, as counterfeit as the contrived scenes in the films shown at the Club. The boy began his sexual act, the SS-uniformed man's face rigid with delight.

"*Ich bin ein Jude,*" Reuben Sklar screamed as he walked between tables and towards the stage. "*Ich bin ein Jude* . . ." All heads turned to Reuben. The two performers on stage stopped their vulgar act and watched the approaching Jew. "*Ich bin ein Jude,*" Reuben screamed repeatedly, avoiding the hands that grabbed for him. Some of the patrons now smelled smoke. Reuben reached the stage and burst into his *Totentanz* as flames entered the room. He danced furiously, kicking at anyone who came near him. In the midst of the commotion and spreading black smoke and retributive flames, Reuben Sklar moved through a marvelous, masterful *Totentanz,* movement and heat and damaged decades coalescing, and for the first time in his adult life, he felt happy.

Cattle Car Complex

BY THANE ROSENBAUM

He pushed the button marked "Down." He pushed again. The machine ignored the command. Slowly he pivoted his head back, staring up at the stainless-steel eyebrow just over the door. No movement of descending light. The numbers remained frozen, like a row of stalled traffic.

For bodily emphasis, he leaned against the panel—pressing "Down," "Up," "Lobby," "Open," "Close"—trying vainly to breathe some life into the motionless elevator. But there was no pulse. The car remained inert, suspended in the hollow lung of the skyscraper.

"Help!" he yelled. "Get me out of here!" The echo of his own voice returned to him.

Still no transit. The elevator was stuck on 17. A malfunctioning car with a mind for blackjack.

"Remain calm," he reminded himself. "I'll push the emergency alarm."

Then he saw a conspicuous red knob that jutted out more prominently than all the other buttons. Adam reached and pulled. A pul-
sating ring shook the car and traveled down the shaft, triggering a
flood of memories he had buried inside him. He covered his ears; a
briefcase dropped to the floor.

"That should reach them," he said, running his hand through his
hair, trying to relax.

⌒

It was late, well past midnight. Adam Posner had been working
on a motion for court the next day. Out his window the lights of the
Manhattan skyline glittered with a radiance that belied the stillness
of the hour.

A lawyer's life, connected to a punchless carousel of a clock. He
hated being among them—being *one* of them—with their upscale
suits and shallow predicaments; those conveniently gymnastic
ethical values, bending and mutating with the slightest change of
financial weather. Gliding by colleagues in the corridors, walking
zombies with glazed eyes and mumbling mouths. No time to exchange pleasantries. That deathly anxiety over deadlines—the
exhaust of a tireless treadmill, legs moving fleetingly, furiously.

He played the game reluctantly, knowing what it was doing to his
spirit, but also painfully aware of his own legacy, and its contribution
to the choices he was destined to make. Above all else he wanted to
feel safe, and whatever club offered him the privilege of membership, he was duty-bound to join.

And so another night on the late shift. He was working on behalf
of a lucrative client, his ticket to a partnership at the firm. He was
the last attorney or staff member to leave that night, something he
always sought to avoid. Adam didn't like being alone in dark places,
and he didn't care for elevators either—especially when riding
alone.

Some of the lights in the interior hallway had been turned off, leaving a trail of soft shadows along the beige, spotless carpet. His Hermés

tie, with the new fleur-de-lis pattern, was hanging from his neck in the shape of a noose, and the two top buttons of his shirt stayed clear of their respective eyelets. A warrior of late-night occupations.

There was a car waiting for him downstairs, one of those plush Lincolns that cater to New York's high-salaried slaves. When he entered the elevator, he could think of nothing but returning to his apartment building, commandeering yet another elevator, and rising to his honeycombed domain overlooking the Empire State Building. He lived alone in a voiceless, sanitized shrine—his very own space in the sky. Not even a pet greeted him, just the hum of a hollow refrigerator filled with nothing but a half-empty carton of ice cream, a solitary microwave dinner, and a box of baking soda.

Sleep. How desperately he wanted to sleep. But now the night would take longer to end, and sleep was not yet possible.

"Behave rationally," he said, a lawyerly response to a strained situation. "They'll come and get me. At the very least, they'll need to get the elevator back," he reasoned.

Then with a nervous thumb, he stabbed away at the panel in all manner of chaotic selection. At that moment, any floor, any longitude, would do. Defeated by the inertia of the cab, he ran his hands against the board as though he were playing a harp, palms floating over waves of oval buttons and coded braille, searching for some hidden escape hatch.

The dimensions of the car began to close in on him. The already tight space seemed to be growing smaller, a shrinking enclosure, miniaturizing with each breath.

～

ADAM'S PARENTS HAD been in the camps, transported there by rail, cattle cars, in fact. That was a long time ago, another country, another time, another people. An old, trite subject—unfit for dinnertime discussion, not in front of the children, not the way to win friends among Gentiles. The Holocaust fades like a painting exposed to too much sun. A gradual diminishing of interest—once the rallying cry of the modern Diaspora; now like a freak accident of history, locked away in the attic, a hideous Anne Frank, trotted out only occasionally, as metaphorical mirror, reminding those of what was once done under the black eye of indifference.

Adam himself knew a little something about tight, confining spaces. It was unavoidable. The legacy that flowed through his veins. Parental reminiscences had become the genetic material that was to be passed on by survivors to their children. Some family histories are forever silent, transmitting no echoes of discord into the future. Others are like seashells, those curved volutes of the mind—the steady drone of memory always present. All one needs to do is press an ear to the right place. Adam had often heard the screams of his parents at night. Their own terrible visions from a haunted past became his. He had inherited their perceptions of space, and the knowledge of how much one needs to live, to hide, how to breathe where there is no air.

He carried on their ancient sufferings without protest—feeding on the milk of terror; forever acknowledging—with himself as living proof—the umbilical connection between the unmurdered and the long buried.

All his life he had suffered from bouts of claustrophobia, and also a profound fear of the dark. He refused to find his way into a movie theater when a film was already in progress; not even a sympathetic usher could rid him of this paralyzing impasse. At crowded parties he always kept to the door, stationed at the exit, where there was air, where he knew he could get out.

⌒

CONDEMNED TO LIVING a sleepless nightmare, he began to pace like an animal. His breath grew stronger and more jagged. He tore his glasses from his face and threw them down on the elevator floor. An unbalanced goose step shattered the frames, scattering the pieces around him. Dangling in the air and trapped in a box, a braided copper cable held him hostage to all his arresting fears.

"Where are they? Isn't there someone at the security desk?" He undid yet another shirt button, slamming a fist against the wall. The car rattled with the sound of a screaming saw. He yanked against the strip of a guardrail. It refused to budge. With clenched fists he punched as many numbers of random floors as his stamina allowed, trying to get through to the other side without opening a door. Ramming his head against the panel, he merely encountered the steely grid of unsympathetic buttons. The tantrum finally ended with the thrust of an angry leg.

Adam's chest tightened. A surge of anxiety possessed him. His mind alternated between control and chaos, trying to mediate the sudden emptiness. His eyes lost focus, as though forced to experience a new way of seeing. He wanted to die, but would that be enough? What had once been a reliably sharp and precise lawyer's mind rapidly became undone, replaced by something from another world, from another time, the imprinting of his legacy. Time lost all sensation; each second now palpable and deafening.

"Hel . . . p! Help!"

The sweat poured down his face in sheaths of salt, and the deepening furrows in his forehead assumed a most peculiar epidermal geometry. In abject surrender, with his back against the wall of the car, he slid down to his ankles and covered his face with his hands. Nerves had overtaken his sanity. He was now totally at the mercy of those demons that would deprive him of any rational thought. And he had no one but himself to blame; the psychic pranks of his deepest monstrous self had been summoned, reducing him to a prisoner within the locked walls of the elevator.

Suddenly a voice could be heard, glib scratches filtering through a metallic strainer built right into the panel.

"Hello, hello, are you all right in der, son?"

The voice of God? Adam wondered. So silent at Auschwitz, but here, shockingly, in the elevator—delivered with a surprisingly lilting pitch. An incomprehensible choosing of divine intervention.

"It's the night guard from the lobby. Can ya hear me?"

Adam looked up to the ceiling. He squinted, trying to make out the shapes and sounds of rescue amidst an evolving fog of subconscious turmoil.

"Can ya hear me?" an urgent male voice persisted in reaching him. The voice carried the melody of an Irishman from an outer borough, but Adam, unaccountably, heard only a strident German.

"Yes, I am here," Adam replied, absently, weakly, almost inaudibly.

"Are ya all right?"

"No."

"We 'ave a situation 'ere," the security guard said calmly. "The motor to the elevator is jam'd. I can't repair it from 'ere; so I've called the maint'nance people. There's a fire in another buildin' downtown; and they're busy wit' dat. They said they'll be here as soon as humanly possible. Will you be okay, son?"

Adam lifted himself to his feet, pressed his mouth against the intercom—a static current startled his face—and then screamed: "What do you mean by 'okay'? How can I be okay? This is not life— being trapped in a box made for animals! Is there no dignity for man?" After another pause, he wailed, "You are barbarians! Get me out!"

The guard's lips pursed with all due bewilderment, and his tone sank. "You 'aven't been inside der long, mister. I know ya want to get out and go home for de night, but let's not make this a bigger ordeal than it already 'tis."

Adam then volunteered the nature of this "ordeal."

"Why should we be forced to resettle? This is our home. We are Germans! We have done nothing wrong! Nazis! Murderers! Nazis!"

The lobby of the building was barren, the only sound the quiet gurgle of water dripping down the side of a Henry Moore fountain. The stark marble walls were spare. The interior lights dimmed for the evening.

The security guard pondered Adam's reply, and then muttered to himself: "It takes all kinds. The elevator gets stuck, and he calls *me* a Nazi. Who told him to labor so long? Goddamn yuppie, asshole."

Recovering, he picked up the receiver and said, "I'm sorry, sir. I don't get your meanin'. Say, ya got a German in der wit' ya?"

"We can't breathe in here! And the children, what will they eat? How can we dispose of our waste? We are not animals! We are not cattle! There are no windows in here, and the air is too thin for all of us to share. You have already taken our homes. What more do you want? Please give us some air to breathe."

By now the guard was joined by the driver of the limousine, who had been parked on Third Avenue waiting for Adam to arrive. The driver, a Russian émigré, had grown anxious and bored, staring out onto an endless stream of yellow cabs; honking fireflies passing into the night, heading uptown. By radio he called his dispatcher, trying to find out what had happened to his passenger, this Mr. Posner, this lawyer who needed the comforts of a plush sedan to travel thirty blocks back to his co-op. The dispatcher knew of no cancellation. Adam Posner was still expected downstairs to claim his ride. This was America after all, the driver mused. The elite take their time and leave others waiting.

So the driver left his car to stretch his legs. Electronically activated doors opened as he entered the building and shuffled over a burnished floor to a circular reception pedestal. The security guard was still struggling to communicate with Adam.

"I am looking for a Mr. Posner," the driver said, with Russian conviction. "I should pick him up outside, and to drive him to Twenty-ninth Street, East Side. Do you know this man?"

With a phone cradled under his chin, and a disturbed expression on his face, the guard said, "All I know is we have an elevator down, and at least one man stuck inside. But who knows who—or what—else he's got in der with 'im. I tink he's actin' out parts in a play. To tell you the truth, he sounds a bit daft to me."

With the aplomb of a police hostage negotiator, the Russian said, "Let me talk to him. I'll find out who he is." The guard shrugged as the phone changed hands. The Russian removed his angular chauffeur's cap and wiped his brow. A determined expression seized his face as he lifted the cradle to his mouth, and said, "Excuse me. Is a Mr. Posner in there?"

"What will become of the women and children?" Adam replied. "Why should we be resettled in Poland?" He did not wait for an answer. A brief interlude of silence was then followed by a chorus of moans and shrieks, as if a ward in a veterans' hospital had become an orchestra of human misery, tuning up for a concert. "I don't believe they are work camps! We won't be happy. We will die there! I can feel it!"

The Russian was himself a Jew and winced with all too much recognition. "Is this Mr. Posner?" he continued. "This is your limo. Don't worry, we will get you out. We will rescue you."

Adam now heard this man from Brighton Beach with his Russian accent, the intoned voice of liberation. Who better to free him from his bondage than a Bolshevik from the East—in this case from Minsk or Lvov—the army that could still defeat the Germans. "Liberate us! We are starving! We are skeletons, walking bones, ghosts! Get us out of this hell!"

"What's 'e sayin'?" the security guard asked.

"I'm not exactly sure, but I think it has something to do with the Holocaust, my friend."

"Ah, de Holycost; a terrible thing, dat."

The Russian nodded—the recognition of evil, a common language between them. "I'll talk to him again," he said, and grabbed the intercom once more. "Mr. Posner, don't worry. We will get you out. You are not in camps. You are not in cattle car. You are just inside elevator, in your office building. You are a lawyer; you've worked late. You are tired, and scared. You must calm down."

"Calm down, calm down, so easy for you Russians to say," Adam replied, abruptly. "We have been selected for extermination. We cannot survive. Who will believe what has happened to us? Who will be able to comprehend? Who will say kaddish for me?"

The lobby was crowding up. Two drowsy-looking repairmen, their sleep disturbed by the downtown fire and now this, entered the building and went up to the guard console. "What's the problem here?" one of them asked. "We're with the elevator company."

Fully exasperated, the guard replied indignantly, "Ya want to know what's wrong, do ya? Ya want to know what the *problem* is? I'll tell ya! It's supposed to be de graveyard shift. Piece o' cake, they say, nothin' ever happens, right? Not when I'm on duty. No, sir. When I'm 'ere, graveyard means all the ghosts come out, the mummies, the wackos! We 'ave a loony tune stuck in one o' the elevators!" Jauntily, winking at one of the maintenance men, he added, "I think de guy in de elevator thinks he's in some fuckin' World War Two movie."

"This man in elevator is not crazy," the Russian driver said in defense. "It is world that is crazy; he is only one of its victims. Who knows what made him like this?"

One of the repairmen dashed off to the control room. Moments later he returned, carrying a large mechanical device, an extraction that would bring the night to an end and allow everyone to go home. "I think I fixed the problem," he announced. "It was just a jammed crank."

As he was about to finish explaining the exploits behind the repair, the elevator began its appointment with gravity. The four men moved from the center of the lobby and gathered in front of the arriving elevator car.

"Should we ring an ambulance?" the security guard wondered. "I hope I don't lose me wages over this. I've done all anyone could. You know," he gestured toward the limousine driver, "you were here." The driver refused to take his eyes off the blinking lights, the overhead constellation that signaled the car's gradual descent.

The elevator glided to a safe stop. Like a performer on opening night, the car indulged in a brief hesitation—a momentary hiccup, of sorts—before the doors opened.

As the elevator doors separated like a curtain, the four men, in one tiny choreographed step, edged closer to the threshold, eager to glimpse the man inside. Suddenly there was a collective shudder, and then a retreat.

The unveiling of Adam Posner.

Light filtered into the car. The stench of amassed filth was evident. It had been a long journey. An unfathomable end.

Adam was sitting on the floor, dressed in soiled rags. Silvery flecks of stubble dappled his bearded face. Haltingly, he stared at those who greeted him. Were they liberators or tormentors? He did not yet know. His eyes slowly adjusted to the light, as though his confinement offered nothing but darkness. He presented the men of the transport with an empty stare, a vacancy of inner peace. As he lifted himself to his feet, he reached for a suitcase stuffed with a life's worth of possessions, held together by leather straps fastened like rope. Grabbing his hat and pressing it on his head, Adam emerged, each step the punctuation of an uncertain sentence. His eyes were wide open as he awaited the pronouncement: right or left, in which line was he required to stand?

from *Writing the Book of Esther*

BY HENRI RACZYMOV

Translated from the French by Dori Katz

THE PHOTOGRAPH

It's been decreed: Esther is the "brain" of the family. It's been decided; let's not bring it up again. Mathieu and Yanick must do the best they can. It doesn't matter. Esther is the only one who really counts, that's the way it is. It's in the nature of things. And, besides, the most important thing is to be well adjusted. Too much education, too much reading. Esther is "sick." It's settled, let's not bring it up again. She is "sick."

At home, the "library" is in the bathroom—basically, three small shelves. Some Communist and Soviet literature, a few Communist and Soviet novels. That's enough for the time spent going to bathrooms. The music corner is in the living room, next to the record-player: Red Army choruses, Yves Montand, 78-rpm tangos, paso dobles in Yiddish, scratched long-playing albums missing their jackets, all in careless piles.

Esther has her own books, her own records, no one's allowed to touch them. She is a gifted student. She wants to become a teacher, later on. "Sick" as she is, she will succeed. Gifted, yes. Yet Charles and Fanny don't brag about her, ever. Something in her remains closed to them, a total lack of understanding, a painful mystery, a punishment from the good Lord. What exactly did they do wrong? They wonder. The war, says Charles, it's the war's doing. Nothing can be done.

On the wall of her room Esther has pinned up the photograph of women fighters in the Warsaw Ghetto, young women in rags and wearing caps, lined up, probably facing a firing squad. You can't see the firing squad. But they are lined up. And it's the Germans who took this picture. Therefore they must be facing a firing squad. This photograph has always been up on the wall near Esther's bed. Still there today. No one thought of removing it, or thought of it and didn't dare. It is fitting that it stay there, after all. The picture is moving. And, besides, this photograph is really Esther. It evokes Esther. It's a little as if she were still there among them. Charles and Fanny didn't see the point of removing it, either after their daughter's marriage or her death.

BORN ON . . . IN . . .

Whenever Mathieu goes to visit his parents, he rushes to his sister's room without anyone knowing. He stands in front of the photograph. He tries to understand. He concentrates, but his mind grows confused, and it doesn't take long for his head to feel empty. But he stays in front of the picture as though collecting his thoughts. On Esther's desk, next to her notebooks and a few books, there sat, until Mathieu snatched it, the cap that Charles and Fanny kept of her, the cap that she bought herself and wore in the streets. She looked ridiculous; it was embarrassing to see her in it. She was trying to look like one of these young women in the picture. Each time he is in his sister's room, after making sure that he's alone, Mathieu tries on the cap. It is much too big for him, as it must have been for his sister. And he quickly puts it back in its place, as if he were committing a sacrilege. He would wonder about the photograph's date. By the time Esther was born, there hadn't been a ghetto in Warsaw for months. All that was left there was rubble, rubble. When Esther was born, the ghetto was little more than a field of rubble. Born too late, and on top of it, on the wrong meridian. How do you make up for two mistakes?

When Esther was born, the Jews of Warsaw had been exterminated, all of them. She had missed a train. So she set her watch back on time, to the time of that train's departure. One fine day in the spring of 1975, she stuck her head into her oven. When her husband came home from work, he found her dead. Not the least explanation, no note. At least, none were found. For Mathieu, Esther's goodbye letter was the photograph in her old room, and the oversized cap sitting on her desk. She probably bought it in some flea market. She loved browsing in flea markets, looking for unpromising old things, relics from the past, like evidence.

Charles and Fanny were quite repulsed by the cap but didn't dare throw it out. A letter of goodbye would have been superfluous. Her act did not really surprise anyone. As if it were expected, expected because it was so dreaded. Even Yanick must have understood the whole business.

Mathieu and Yanick had been offered life on a platter. Not Esther. It was as if she were guilty of being alive. She had to earn this "luck," this misfortune. Charles and Fanny felt guilty, in turn, responsible for their eldest daughter's unhappiness.

Esther used to stand in front of her mirror wearing this ridiculous and oversized cap. How many times did they surprise her in this pose, trying hard to suppress their smiles? A girl her age, look at her still playing like a child? And screaming insults, she would slam the door right in their faces. And, then and there, outside the door to her room, they would burst out laughing. Hunched over, face flushed, head between his shoulders, Charles would put his finger against his open mouth roaring like a tiger, *Shhhh!*

Esther frightens Mathieu. When he's near her, he's afraid of being contaminated. He feels he must protect himself. He protects himself with blindness and deafness, he sees no other way. Simon Pessakow-icz, her husband, isn't as complicated. You can talk to him. To Esther, you cannot. She's locked behind the ghetto wall, unattainable. And why not write a novel about the Warsaw Ghetto? Since it's her obsession. There's an idea! Bunch of morons, she says. Just morons. But why is the idea so crazy? Yes, why, let her explain. Bunch of morons, that's what they are. Fine.

Perhaps she's already writing this novel on the sly. And that's what disturbs her so much. Better not insist.

Mathieu has forgotten Esther since her death. They have all forgotten her. In any case, they never speak about her. She is taboo. Her old room remains untouched, like a memorial. Mathieu stands in front of the photograph. But it's not familiar to him. It doesn't ring a bell, doesn't remind him of anything. However hard he searches his memory, nothing. So he returns to the family circle.

What's there to say about Esther? What's there to add? Every-thing has been said. She herself has said everything. Even Simon doesn't speak of it. As Mathieu thinks it over, Simon took no time at all to remarry. . . . As if he had to rectify an error, correct a misun-derstanding, right away . . .

West Beirut = Warsaw Ghetto

In the beginning of the summer of 1982 the Israeli army went into Lebanon. The newspapers spoke of the Warsaw Ghetto. Well, the newspapers are very cultured! They know their history. Beirut, where the PLO army was entrenched, was *like* the Warsaw Ghetto. That's obvious, indeed. Soon they refined it: they stopped saying "like." They eliminated the "like." Beirut *was* the Warsaw Ghetto. Not like. Was. And the Palestinians? The Jews of the ghetto. And the Israelis? The Nazi army. It all fit well together, a marvelous conjuring trick. Were they lying in good faith or in ignorance? Were they lying by design? That summer Mathieu missed Esther. He wouldn't have hesitated to give her a call, and this time they could have talked. But she wasn't there anymore. She was dead. Esther was dead, and Mathieu realized it that summer when the Israeli army went into Lebanon. And when the newspapers spoke of the ghetto. There were even Jews who spoke of the ghetto. Who omitted the *like*. That was the most unbearable part, these Jews serving as handle for the steel ax, that same ax that would strike them, that already was striking them that summer, and meanwhile they yelled with the others, *Israel = Nazi!*

THE RATS

Mathieu's life flows like a river, widening, almost without meandering. He works for a government agency. He knows that his position is not really brilliant. You would have thought he had to apologize for it to his parents. Not at all, they say; as for "brilliant," we already gave. There's been enough "brilliant" in their life; that will do. They don't want any more "brilliant." What they aspire to, from now on, is some "normal," nothing but "normal." No "brilliant." No more "brilliant," thank you. At least with the government, says Charles, Mathieu won't have any slow season. Oh, does he think that there's a fast season in the office? That's it, let him complain! He doesn't realize how lucky he is. The life they knew in Poland is over, once and for all, a life of *pariahsites*. To be a civil servant in France, that's ideal!

Mathieu deploys his talents in a crammed office, a cramped nook on the seventh floor of a large building. It can be reached by one of four elevators. Mathieu doesn't always choose the same one; it depends on his mood, on whether or not he feels like exploring a new corner, or encountering new faces—feminine perhaps. He even had the strange idea that, one time or other, he would run into a rat scurrying around the corner of a hallway. Fear or wish, he couldn't say. Perhaps a wish. He dreamed that all of it would be gnawed away, little by little, this large building with tons of papers and files; but gnawed away slowly, imperceptibly, so that no one could tell. Only he would have noticed. He would guard this secret preciously in his heart of hearts; he would measure the infinitesimal progress of the damage every day, the faint, less and less faint, bite marks at the foot of a door, on top of a cabinet, chair, table. But he never saw the slightest rat. And no trace whatsoever of bites.

THE GRAVE

Mathieu is rather fond of the cemetery in Bagneux where his sister is buried. She's interred in the Jewish section, with the other family members, those who died normal deaths. On her tombstone there also appear the slightly old-fashioned medallion-portraits of the others, those whose bodies are not there, whose bodies lie elsewhere, whose bodies no longer exist, whose bodies are scattered, dissolved in rivers, the Bug, the Vistula, or are mixed with the earth, well mixed, as ash and earth can be mixed, then raked clean. Most of all, raked clean.

There are three portraits, one for the "other" Esther, Fanny's sister, one for Rivka Tenenbaum, one for Raisl Litvak. The first two died in Auschwitz, the third in Treblinka. It's all spelled out on the gravestone. All you have to do is read.

Mathieu always liked cemeteries. It's no easy thing to walk around in them. There are holes in the ground as numerous as the holes in Swiss cheese. You could fall in at any moment and become trapped. The Jewish cemeteries are especially moving, or rather, the Jewish sections of certain cemeteries. Perhaps because death seems less commonplace there. It's ridiculous, obviously. But Jewish death, even the ordinary kind, is never a small matter to him. He's tempted to respect it more than the other kind, to be more moved by it. The other kind, that is, the ordinary, everyday kind. Even ordinary Jewish death is never entirely ordinary in his eyes. It's always like the carbon copy, the duplicate of another death, not ordinary, a death that means that your corpse doesn't last long as a corpse. The immediate burning of the corpse—as if one didn't quite know what to do with it—is very burdensome, isn't it? As is the fact that the gathered ashes are never quite gathered but dispersed, mixing with the earth, the good, fertile, Polish earth, or thrown in the water of a river, an abundant and clear Polish river, like the Bug or the Vistula, or any kind of river. And these ashes also are mixed with tons of ashes coming from tons of other corpses, from tons of Jews. Burdensome. One can see that required "special measures." Well, by coincidence they called it simply "special handling"—*Sonderbehandlung*. Why look for complications where there are none? "Special handling" is simple and clear. And in the name of even greater simplicity they abbreviated it as *SB*. And those who carried out these very "special measures" were put into a special commando, a *Sonderkommando*. Which, in all their correspondence, they abbreviated as *SK*. And the *SK* were Jews. It was the Jews themselves who handled these "measures"; they were called, and saw themselves as, "dirty Jews."

Which is why Jewish death prompts him to remove his hat. Which is also ridiculous. And for two reasons. First, because in the presence of Jewish death it's customary to wear a hat, not remove it. Second, because Mathieu never wears a hat. At least not until recently. He borrowed Esther's cap. He asked his parents to lend it to him. What does he plan to do with it? He doesn't know. It was the summer of 1982.

Esther's Cap

Wearing this cap, Mathieu at first "plays at being Jewish." He wanders about, much as his sister used to do, in the streets, into stores, trying to gauge the impression he makes on people. Can they tell that he's Jewish? He catches the reflection of his face in store windows, in mirrors, and he sees in it a Jew. In any case, an SS man would have recognized him immediately. But there are no more SS. Perhaps Esther regretted it, that there are no more SS. No more SS to recognize Jews in the street, round them up, make them climb into trucks, tell them that they're being "relocated" to a better place, a place where they will be able to work, a place where their children will be able to go to school, and then gas them, then and there, right in those trucks, just like that, in the five minutes the ride takes—no need even to transport them to a place conceived for that purpose, bigger, more convenient, more efficient. Because at the time, places conceived for that purpose didn't yet exist. There were only trucks then, gas trailers. No, Esther couldn't have known that fate; for that, too, she was born too late. And besides, she was born in France, not in Poland. It's true that she could have been deported from Grenoble with Fanny, in 1943 or 1944. She even missed that by a hair. But as far as the gas trailers in Chelmno are concerned, or the SS trucks of the *Einsatzgruppen* in Poland, and in the Ukraine, no, that would not have been possible, sorry. Nor the Warsaw Ghetto. So many things that she couldn't have known. The ghetto she could only have imagined, read books, studied photographs—all so intensely that she succeeded in believing herself one of the fighters. Wearing a cap. And led to the *Umschlagplatz,* and brutally shoved into a wagon, very brutally. And setting out for the northeast. The Warsaw-Bialystok line with a stop midway. Treblinka they call this village. Pretty little train station. And flowers. Yes indeed, flowers. There's no doubt that we'll work here, and eat our fill. But why so much brutality to make us disembark? Maybe they're in a hurry. In a hurry to put us to work. And then the undressing, the shearing of hair, the path to heaven, why these brutalities? Receipt of soap, why these brutalities? And the lungs catching fire. The brutalities stopped. And so has life.

Walking in the streets wearing this cap, Mathieu looks people in the eye. He tries to meet their gaze. They, on the other hand, seem not to notice him. What blindness, what indifference! But the thing is, these people are not SS. They're people, simply people. Not only don't they detect a Jew in him, they don't even see him. It's like before, without the cap. He was a pure ghost, and pure ghost he remains. Commonplace. He's not threatened at all. He's not Esther after all.

Esther's great superiority, her incomparable superiority, lies in the fact that she'd been threatened. Born after the war, Mathieu can never catch up. Beat her on her own turf? She, who already had missed the "train." Who ate away at herself for having been neither victim nor fighter, cap or no cap, and for still being here, alive. It made her sick.

The truth is that he never loved Esther. He doesn't love her, period. All that he thinks, all that he imagines, all that he discovers, she had already thought, already imagined, already discovered. She'd completed the course a long time ago. She always walks ahead of him; it's unbearable. Today Mathieu writes in order to bear it. But even in this she precedes him, a shadow that he cannot overtake. He strives to follow it, to trample it. Trample her shadow. He's made up his mind: he'll have her die in Treblinka, he'll finally give her the death she wanted. With the others. But first he will bring her to life. That way, once and for all he'll trample the ever-present shadow of her corpse.

The first time Mathieu wore Esther's cap was at her burial in the Bagneux cemetery. Mathieu disguised himself for his sister. Since he had to cover his head, might as well be with her own cap, he told himself. Perhaps it gave her pleasure there, beyond the grave, to have close to her, on her death, this symbol of the ghetto, of a mythology that she alone could construe, a very secret and closed sect with its rituals, its cult objects, its ex voto—the whole shebang devoted to death, the death she did not have!

Mathieu kept the cap. He wears it as he writes. Yes, he's writing. And she, was she writing? Is he then taking her place? Like the other Esther, Aunt Esther, who took Fanny's "place," in July 1942 in Paris when the police came to 27, rue des Couronnes, Paris 20? Took the place of the dead woman, the place of a woman whom "they" had decreed would die? Is the place of a dead person vacant so that any-one can occupy it? Or is it the opposite, is it that you mustn't touch it, just as Charles and Fanny had the fundamental decency to leave Esther's room intact? All in all, Mathieu is disgusted with himself. He's writing in disgust. A disgusting sewer, that's what he is.

Madame Supervisor

Each morning at the agency, at precisely nine o'clock as some employee presses the elevator button, people greet each other with the eternal joke: "Well, Madame Dumas, Monsieur Lautremond, going up to seventh heaven?" A rather worn-out joke no one can resist smiling at, if somewhat mechanically.

Mathieu Litvak's supervisor is Mme Roubestan. What's great about being boss, she likes to repeat, is that you are your own boss. Mathieu always agrees with her. What she doesn't realize, he thinks to himself, is that she herself has a boss, M. Sallustre.

Mme Roubestan is the same age as Esther. The age that Esther would have been if. Fortyish. Also the same long black hair that she pulls up into a pseudo-medieval bun that makes her look older. Esther used to wear her hair loose down her back; it reached to her hips and made her look like a young girl. Mathieu never dared make the slightest remark to Mme Roubestan about her hairdo; she's always known how to keep her distance. After all, she's the boss, isn't she? She would have been a perfect Kapo. Mathieu sometimes tells himself that. Then he's suspicious of her for a while. But not for long because he quickly realizes that his mind is wandering.

Esther's Hair

It's summer. Yanick has been sent to summer camp in the mountains. Esther and Mathieu are to go together to a camp in Brittany. She must be fourteen, and Mathieu nine. In those days she didn't eat. Well, she ate very little. She couldn't have weighed much. Her cheeks grew more and more hollow so that she began to look frightening. Fanny blamed this whim on the women's magazines her daughter reads, with their emphasis on dieting. She's wrong: these aren't at all her reasons. Coming home from the store one evening, and as if he just noticed how she looks, Charles asks her if she hasn't lost her mind. She looks like she just got out of Auschwitz! And all three stare at her with compassion. Esther runs out and slams the door to her room. She comes back a few minutes later, dressed like a concentration camp inmate, head shaved. Fanny faints, falls like a dead weight to the floor. Charles runs to her, talks to her, slaps her. Mathieu starts crying. The next day he catches sight of his mother in the hall; she holds, rolled up in one arm, the striped pajamas Esther got who knows where, and in her other hand, the hair razor.

Afterward no one ever mentioned the incident. Esther gave up her "diet." She even put on weight.

Her Death

That his sister was buried in a Jewish grave pleased Mathieu. He found that rather fitting. Well, pleased is not exactly the word. And in what other kind of grave could she have been interred? She hadn't bothered to leave any instruction, or any message. For someone who loved to write, it's, at the very least, inexplicable. She left without a flourish, with no comment. Which adds to their grief. Granted, she was "sick," but even so, why? They questioned Simon for a long time, and, after a while, talked at length to him about her. He was also at sea; he knew no more than they did. Mathieu suspected otherwise. Why then was he so overwhelmed, so much so that his in-laws had to convince him, over and over again, that she was "sick," and that it was incurable. It wasn't his fault, he must never think that. He was in no way to blame, neither were they, no one was. Except perhaps the war. . . . She was sick because of the past, a past she hadn't known, but that pursued her.

Simon often saw her writing. He knew that she wrote. He'd seen the sheets of paper pile up on her desk. But he'd never read any of her work. She had forbidden it. Besides, no one had ever read anything she wrote. That's what Simon said in those days. Later he told Mathieu that she had a filmmaker friend of hers, Jacques Lipshitz, read some of her things. Which shows that Simon lied, that some details bothered him. In any case, before she died she destroyed everything. Yes she'll remain an enigma, one it would be foolish to try to penetrate. Might as well question this Lydia Polack she consulted the year before her suicide. But what could she have told them, and to what purpose?

After her death, life went on as usual, on the surface. But only on the surface. Because underneath the surface it was better not to look too close. Of course, they didn't forget Esther. How could they forget? But they never spoke about her. At least not until the summer of 1982. Then Mathieu thought about her again. Her death, which took place seven years earlier, really struck him only then. He questioned his parents. Saw Simon again. And Uncle Avrum. He bought a fat notebook. He invented another life for his sister, and another death. Perhaps the life and death she had imagined for herself. The life and death she couldn't live without.

Why, then, did Charles, his father, leave Warsaw before the war? What was it like on Nowolipie Street? What did it look like? And the streetcars, the synagogues, and the Vistula, and the Saxon Gardens, and Leszno, and the Danzig Station? Esther had never set foot in Warsaw but she knew it by heart. She must have spent hours, days, studying its topography from current maps and old ones. If she had been let loose in that city, she would have managed. Without hesitation. Wouldn't have had to ask for directions. "Sick" as she was. When she was little, dogs were her passion. When she grew up, it was Poland. And the war. Sick.

SILENCE

Maybe Mathieu will manage to write the book that Esther was to write and that no one has read. Because he's writing, isn't he? That's what he's doing now, isn't it? Esther will never know about it, thank

God. She wouldn't have allowed it. She would have asked him why he was butting in, what business was it of his, and Mathieu would have been speechless at that question, acquiescing—indeed, indeed, what business was it of his, acquiescing, admitting, acknowledging his guilt—he was guilty of giving up his rightful place, of having usurped another's place, another's role. Only survivors had a right to speak. The others, especially those born after the war, should keep quiet, be silent. Their words are obscene, impudent. That's what Esther would have said. But what about her? Even though Esther was born during the war, what did she know actually? What had she experienced that Mathieu had not? What had she witnessed still in the cradle? Yes, she had escaped the train and Drancy. But she had escaped it, which is the point. She and Fanny had escaped the convoy to the East. As for the rest, she had been told. Or she had read it. Or she had imagined it. Just like Mathieu, nothing more. What right does she have to talk about Warsaw? What has she to say that she actually experienced herself? Treblinka? Auschwitz? But even her parents are alive. *Nothing* happened to them. Nothing. Yes, Fanny saw the disappearance of her mother and sister, Rivka and Esther. Yes, Charles lost his mother, his sister, one of his brothers— Raisl, Guta, Bolek. But Esther? What suffering and what bereavement?

Do You Deserve to Live?

BY SONIA PILCER

Affliction stamps the soul to its very depths with the scorn, the disgust and even the self-hatred and sense of guilt that crime logically should produce but actually does not. —Simone Weil

"What crap," I grumbled, leafing through my Elizabeth Taylor file of clips. Diamonds, husbands and hysterectomies. She had converted to Judaism to marry Eddie Fisher, who called her his "Yiddena," his little Jewish woman.

"I'm proud to be a Jew," Liz had declared, pledging $100,000 in war bonds for Israel. *Life* ran the wedding pictures.

"I feel as if I've been a Jew all my life," she exulted, dark lashes sweeping over the famed violet eyes. Draped in Beverly Hills crepe, a deep Prussian blue, her head veiled Sarah-like, she was once again the beautiful Jewess Rebecca in *Ivanhoe*.

"I felt terribly sorry for the suffering of the Jews during the war. I was attracted to their heritage. I guess I identified with them as underdog."

"Makes her furious," Richard Burton quipped years later. "I tell her, 'You're not Jewish at all.' She turns white with rage."

1972. I was Managing Editor of *Movie Screen,* the magazine of the
stars. When I wasn't doing what I thought of as my real work, pen-
ning blood-eyed poems in a blue-lined notebook, I edited stories,
composed captions for the gossip pix, calling Celebrity Service several times a day to check facts like the names and ages of Michael
Caine and exotic wife, Shakira's children.

On my desk, there was a gold-framed photograph from Germany.
I am posed like a Spanish infanta painted by Goya or Velázquez,
crowned with a white satin bonnet, its sash tied in a white bow. The
dress is a marvel: white satin with lace on the collar and bodice,
puffed sleeves from which two plump arms unfold. But it's the eyes
that amaze my mother's friends in Landsberg, the displaced persons
camp, where I was born.

"Such eyes. The very *spitten* image of *Elisabet* Taylor," declared Gita
Blum, who had survived eight months of Auschwitz. Her numbers
flashed like blue neon on her bejeweled arm.

"Genia, when you get to America, you must take Zosha to Hollywood. Get her a *scream* test," insisted Mushka Scheine. She had lived
as a Christian maid for the family of an SS soldier. "I tell you, she
could be star."

⌇

SHOCKING COVER LINES sold *Movie Screen.* My editor, Flavia
O'Neal, a black Irish woman with thick black brows, intense eyes,
was NYU Journalism '57. She came up with the hard-hitting,
news*like* headlines and bought sleazy photographs from paparazzi.
Our sleight-of-hand was to "justify" the headline, the more deli-
ciously sinful the implication, the greater the triumph of the con:
i.e., my very own "Cher's Secret Hours in the Dark with Robert
Redford." (She attended a premiere of his latest film.) This was years
before *People* published real dirt. Someone had to create it.

In the back of the magazine was a panacea of ads that promised:
firm chin muscles; increase your bustline by five full inches; be taller
instantly; you can eat the foods you crave and love, yet lose lumpy,

fatty excess weight; cover up ugly veins; unwanted hair gone; remove blackheads in seconds; and the satin porn of Frederick's of Hollywood with its peek-a-boo nipple bras, "sinsuous" slinks and open fanny panties. And in the front, our galaxy of stars.

⟿

"I WANT TO discuss something with you," my mother stated, holding open the *Daily News* in two hands. "Serious." Her tone was grave, like when she was going to read me a story about a Holocaust survivor who was reunited with her sister or a Nazi found living in Floral Gardens. I was eight.

"Debbie Reynolds was America's sweetheart," Genia said, pointing to a small photograph of a pert young woman with a flip, inserted over a huge, four-color spread of Elizabeth Taylor. "The girl next-to-door. Debbie was married to Eddie Fisher. A Jew. The stars aren't religious so they intermarry. No matter. He sang 'My Yiddishe Mama.' Remember him on television?"

I turned to my mother, who had laid down the newspaper on the kitchen table, next to my multiplication tables, that I was trying to memorize. "Mom, I have to do my homework."

"Anyway, Liz is a beautiful woman," she continued, ignoring me. "The most beautiful in the world. What a shame."

My mother shook her head sadly. "I hate to say this. Especially because you have her eyes, everyone says so, even when you were a baby. That's why it breaks my heart to talk about this. But you have to know the truth."

I stared at my multiplication tables. *Nine times nine equals eighty-one.*

"You're too young to know what a housebreaker is. It's a woman who steals the husband of another woman, making him leave his children, his happy home. For what? A moment's pleasure? This is what Elizabeth Taylor has done. Sure, she was upset about Mike Todd dying. He was a good man, the only man she ever loved. She divorced that Nicky Hilton guy. He was a drunk. Such a thing? How can she do it? Debbie just had a baby and now there's another one on the way. Liz doesn't care about nobody but herself."

⌒

W HAT WE AT the magazine had to do was whip up a pastiche on the themes of money and misery, the curse of being beautiful and/or talented, and how success and fame can never be a substitute for love. The *Movie Screen* bible stated: "We give them courtship, weddings, babies, divorces, illness and sex. But the most important thing, remember: the stars are just like you and me, only more so."

Only a few stars, maybe half a dozen, actually sold movie fan magazines. There had to be something larger than life that transcended time and personal tragedy, inspiring the most passionate, undying loyalty or just simple adoration. And Elizabeth Taylor was still queen.

Mort Jacobs, legal counsel for Flame Publishing, checked out manuscripts, refusing to let copy through unless, point by point, the story delivered—without any real slander, which recent suits had proved costly. He had surprised us by rejecting a cover story by one of our regulars. So yours truly, Doctor Shlock, had to take over at zero hour, breathing life into one of the genre's oldest diddles, trying to reach the punch line with a minimum of moans and guffaws from her reader. I was not only reigning high priestess of low journalism, but also the fastest ER writer in movie fanzinedom. My specialty, vulnerability stories—movie stars have feelings too—taking on the occasional true confession or soap story, but nonpareil on Liz, my altered ego.

⌒

F EEDING A SHEET of bond into electric Olympia, black carbon flagging behind, I typed the headline: THE LOVE-CHILD LIZ TAYLOR WILL NOT ACKNOWLEDGE AS HER OWN. Dropping several lines, I added the heart-clenching subhead: *How It Has Destroyed Her Marriage! Liz Cries:"God, Can You Ever Forgive Me?"*

Lighting a cigarette, I summoned my shlock muse. Oh muse, so tacky, bless me with the silken tongue to touch the baby-sitting ghettos of the human heart. To bamboozle them with the promise of sin, titillate their yens, give succor to their delusions.

Come to me in your rhinestone harlequin glasses, cabana pants and spiked heels. Get started, Hedda Hophead. Go on! Suck into the metaphysick of star worship, its temples, corner drugstores and Laundromats, altars of the washer and dryer. I could feel it like an orgasm. Soon, I would be the voice of female longing in America, aching after the famous, the ass-sucked and arrogant, cannibalizing them to satisfy her reader's hunger.

"Do it, goddamn it!" I crushed my cigarette in the shell ashtray. Cover unsightly stretch marks; longer, thicker hair in ten minutes; appear twenty years younger.

> The sun streaked through a splinter of an opening in the royal blue drapes of Liz's opulent bedroom. She tried to shield her sleep-filled violet eyes, instinctively flinging her arm to reach out for her husband, but the pain of memory surfaced: he was gone. Richard had walked out on her. A shiver ran down her spine, chilling her though it was a balmy June morning. Memory was a tidal wave sweeping her in its whirlpool of images.

Suddenly, the stench of burning! I watched with fascination as a small transparent disc fried in the ashtray, folding into itself as it singed. Picking it up, I discovered it was human in its stickiness. It was my own fingernail, clipped some days ago, now fixed to the tip of my finger.

"Ugh!" I recoiled, trying to flick the singed nail off one finger, but it stuck to the other finger. That's how they burned. I grabbed my notebook.

> Like burnt crust in a frying pan
> you stuck to the edges

you had to be
scraped out
hair by tender hair

Stop it. Concentrate on Liz! The story was due at four. I stuck the notebook in my desk drawer. My fingers lined up on the typewriter keys like a firing squad. The cash register of words per dollar ringing at the end of each line.

Liz wished she could share her terrible secret with one of her friends. It might relieve the burden of her guilt. But she was not one to open her pain and anguish to others. She buried it deep within her soul.

"Fuck the art!" Richard Burton had raved. "I want to be rich, rich, rich."

⌒

WOULD I HAVE SURVIVED? How did a person live from day to day? Would I have traded my body for bread? Fucked Nazis? What would I do with my desire to die? With my impatience. My impulsiveness? What would I do with my fears? Do you deserve to live?

"Write!" I cried out. "Enuf with the introspection!"

At that moment, Christine peeked in from the doorway. "I heard that. You know, I read somewhere that people who live by themselves talk to themselves." She occupied the office next to *Movie Screen,* and had the exact same job, except her magazine was *MovieLand.*

"Okay, Chris. Twenty-four-thousand-dollar question. How would you write: 'The Love-Child Liz Taylor Will Not Acknowledge As Her Own'?"

"Her grandson, of course," Christine suggested, twisting her long red braid around her hand.

"We did that story with Jackie two months ago," I told her.

"How about 'the child within herself,' who was never allowed to grow up like a normal little girl . . ." Christine began.

"A star at eight, famous at such a tender age," I continued in my best Hollywood tragedy voice. "She had fans by the millions, rode in limousines."

"But what she didn't have—" Christine crooned.

"Was a sense of being loved for her self."

"—And she never had a childhood," Christine concluded. "So now she must go back and acknowledge that child who was never allowed to grow up." She grinned at me. "I wrote that story about Ann-Margret."

"Hey, no one ever accused us of originality."

Christine was an English major, like me, two years out of college. Shared contempt for fan magazines and shared mutual sense of each other's greater destinies united us. She lived with an Italian painter in a loft on Wooster Street.

The phone rang. I let it ring until a machine picked up. "Listen, Chris," I began.

Her eyes met mine. "*Ciao,* darling. Send Liz my best."

It started like a migraine. The blue haze before the assault. Silent, cruel, insidious accusations.

Did we survive the war for this? Sleaze? You think you're a real writer? Shlockmeister. Try standing in the freezing snow for two hours without shoes.

What about my years of scribbling in notebooks? I protested meekly. The poems. My files. The self-proclaimed poetess. What a hoot. I had found my calling with Liz & Dick, and like a wedding cake pair, they crowned my fondest aspirations. *Just write the damn story!*

What I wanted, why I yearned to be a writer was to tell stories. My parents' stories, which were mine too. Slowly, I slid open my desk drawer, pulling out a manila folder. I had printed one word on the cover. SURVIVORS.

First story. A young girl is taken from Czenstochowa to a work camp. Her parents are killed. Her brother killed. She's saved by a white scarf. Survives in the camp because her uncle shares his bread.

Second story: a religious boy is taken to Auschwitz. His parents and sisters are killed. He escapes while an officer pees in the woods. His brother suffocates in a cellar of potatoes four months before the liberation.

And I, their daughter, live in two time frames. Normal, shared reality, everyone stops at the red light. The other zone has no temporal sense. Burnt by a dog-eared yellow star, sign of the Jew, rising, hungry eyes, overripe crazylegs nerve. I live in the ghetto of the dead.

I pressed the red button on my phone machine. "Are you there? Are you there?" My mother's Polish-accented voice. "I von't talk to a machine. Zosha, call your Momma, right away."

Shut the folder. Return it to the drawer. I picked up the receiver. My mother's phone was busy. I tried again. Still busy. Always busy. A flibbertigibbet. I could see her sitting at the kitchen table, fruit and vegetable wallpaper whirling around her. She wound the phone cord around her wrist as she spoke her musical Polish. Now she was doing the dishes as she talked. It was dangerous to be idle, even for a moment. The yellow wall phone jerked as she moved around with the long cord following like a leash.

Finally, she picked up. On the first ring. "I knew it was you!" she rejoiced, then her voice became critical. "What took so long?"

"You were busy."

"It's true. I was talking to Fela Brumstein. You remember her?"

"Did you call for any reason?"

"I hate that *meshugge* machine! Do I have to have a reason to call my own daughter?" She paused, then began again. "I never hear from you. You don't call—"

"I'm calling you right now."

"Because I called you."

"Mother, let's stop this."

"I don't know anything about your life. Are you—uh—seeing"—she inquired hopefully—"someone?"

"No one special."

"Someone not so special then. He doesn't have to be Prince Charming. Though people always say how good-looking is your father. Do you go out on dates?"

There was Ludwig, of course. My own private Nazi. But what she didn't know didn't drive me crazy. "I'm at work," I insisted. "I can't have this conversation."

"Zosha, I don't see why you can't find someone. All my friends have already grandchildren and what do I have? *Bupkes.*"

"Mom, I'm hanging up!"

Seemingly chastened, her tone turned grave. "I called about something important."

"Okay."

"Next Sunday is *Yom Hashoa.*"

I didn't say anything.

"The day when we remember—"

"I know what *Yom Hashoa* is."

"We bought you a ticket. It's at Temple Emanuel on Fifth Avenue," she continued. "You know, that fancy shul with the rich people."

"Mom, I have plans—"

"And what could be more important than *Yom Hashoa?*" she demanded. "You must come. Everyone will be there. The Mayor always come. Senator Javits. Theodore Bikel. Lots of celebrities, too."

"I wish you had told me sooner," I said, trying to think of a worthy excuse. Something she'd accept. "I have to—"

"Zosha, for us." Her voice heavy. My stomach twisted, the gnarled torso of an ancient tree. "Please do it for us," she implored.

"I don't know," I said. "I'll try—"

"We've bought you a seat," she stated conclusively. "Twelve noon sharp." Then added, "Could you wear the dress I sewed for you? It so brings out your eyes."

"Sure," I surrendered weakly.

"Okay, I know you're a busy lady. But I've been thinking on a totally different subject. And you can tell me if you don't want to do it." Her voice trailed off. "Okay?"

"Yes?" I held the receiver from my ear.

"You know how you have to make up names for those stories you write for the magazine?"

"Mom," I resisted. "What do you want? I have to finish a story today."

"I know that. But I was just thinking about something. Why should you make the names up of the writers from the air?"

"We all use pseudonyms."

"It's a pity you don't use your name so everyone will know what a wonderful writer you are. I show my friends the magazine and say, 'This one, my Zosha wrote.' I'm so proud, but to be honest, I don't know if they even believe me. Who's this Louise Colet? It doesn't say anywhere—"

I broke in. "Mom, I don't want my name attached to this magazine."

"Such a big shot she's become! They're good stories about Elizabeth Taylor, Elvis Pretsley, Jackie O—with human feelings. Of course, I never bring such magazines in the house, but in America, everyone reads them at the beauty parlor."

"I don't want—"

She cut me off. "So, all right. You don't want. But I was talking to Fela Brumstein. You know her, with the daughter Bella, a little fat but with a pretty face, who goes to Queens College. And I don't know if you know, but before the war, she wrote very nice poems and stories."

"Yes, yes—" I said impatiently.

"Not even a moment for your mommy?"

"I've got to go—" my voice was becoming ugly, the one I hated. After all the resolutions: *what she went through, how she suffered. I could never have survived. I mustn't make my mother suffer more.*

"Anyway, I'll be Speedy Gonzalez since you've become such an important person. We were talking and she asked me if you wouldn't mind using her name for one of the stories. That way she could see her name in print. I mean, of course, if you use your name, that's something else. But if you're going to make up Louise Colet, why not Fela Brumstein? Or even, for that matter, why not Genia Radon?"

At first, Liz swore to herself that she would never tell him about her child, afraid that it would destroy her marriage. How she cried nights as he slept peacefully. "God, can you ever forgive me?" She prayed in the silence of the night. Finally, she could no longer keep it inside of herself. Richard had to know the truth. But would he ever come back to her?

Eventually all my stories were signed with the names of my mother's Polski platoon. But my most frequent pseudonym, once even receiving a note from a befuddled Glenn Ford, thanking her for a stimulating interview, which, of course, never happened except in my imagination: Genia Radon, my mother's maiden name.

"Half-There"
from *What God Wants*

BY LILY BRETT

"I feel mixed up," Golda Goldenfein said to Bella Fleker. Golda and Bella talked on the phone every day. They had been talking to each other for thirty years. They were both forty-two. They often repeated themselves. Sometimes, Golda thought, they had probably repeated entire conversations verbatim. "I feel mixed up and exhausted," she said to Bella. "I spent the whole morning at Rosa Cohen's house. Remember I told you that Rosa Cohen was interviewing children of survivors of concentration camps?"

"I remember," said Bella, "only I forgot that it was this morning. How did it go?"

"How did it go?" said Golda. "How did it go? I don't know. She asked me endless questions and I talked for three hours. But I don't think I said anything. I wanted to do it well. I feel that the fact that my father was in Auschwitz has always been a very important part of my life, but I don't know why and I don't know how. I think I thought that by talking to Rosa Cohen I might find out something."

"You've never talked to me about it," said Bella. "Did your mother know you were doing it?"

"My mother didn't want me to do it. My mother said it was a plot by Mr. Bloom. She said that Mr. Bloom knows Rosa Cohen's father and planted the idea in his head that I would be a good person for Rosa to interview. My mother said Mr. Bloom wants to show the world that our family has problems. I don't even know which problems she is thinking about, but Mr. Bloom didn't give Rosa Cohen my name. I volunteered. I heard about this book of interviews from Arnold Klepner, who was really upset that he didn't qualify because his parents were hidden in a cellar."

"So you don't think Mr. Bloom had anything to do with it?" said Bella.

"Of course he didn't," said Golda. "You're starting to sound just like my mother. I asked Rosa Cohen and she said that she didn't know Mr. Bloom and she didn't think her father did either. She said that the Mr. Bloom story sounded very far-fetched to her.

"I felt incredibly nervous before I went to her place. I almost canceled the appointment. I didn't know what I was so nervous about. Anyway, Rosa Cohen asked me all these questions, and I didn't really have many answers.

"Rosa Cohen told me after the interview that even the most articulate people have had terrible trouble talking about this subject. I'm not sure whether I was in the category of most articulate but I certainly had trouble. I felt so dumb. There were so many things I didn't know. When I started talking to Rosa Cohen I could see that I didn't know much about what my mother or my father had gone through during the war. It was strange, because the feeling of them being in camps was so strong to me. I thought about my girls and how they know every important thing that has happened to me. I felt a failure for knowing so little about my parents.

"When I was talking to Rosa, I couldn't really feel anything. I looked at her at one stage and thought how weird it was that here we both were, Rosa Cohen and I, comfortably off, living in Australia and sitting and talking in a very nice house about my father drinking another man's piss in Auschwitz."

"I didn't know about that," said Bella.

"Well it's not something you talk about, is it? I don't even think I've told Charlie. My dad told me when I was about eight. It was a hot day and I didn't want to drink this orange juice he had bought for me. I thought it tasted funny. He said to me that when you are thirsty nothing tastes funny. He said, 'In Auschwitz I had to drink pishy from another man.' That's all he said. I thought about it for years. How did he get the piss? Did he drink it from a container, or did he drink it directly from the man? I told Rosa Cohen about it, and she said that in the final days in Auschwitz, when the Nazis had fled, there was very little water and many of the prisoners, who were on the verge of death anyway, had to drink their own piss.

"I didn't cry when I told Rosa Cohen about my father, and she didn't cry when she was talking about Auschwitz. She seemed very sympathetic, but it was hard to know how she felt. She's got a very composed face. She's got such a composed face that sometimes I thought she might be thinking about other things while I was talking. Both her mother and her father were in Auschwitz."

"What did Dora think about you talking to Rosa Cohen?" asked Bella.

"Oh, Dora thought I was stupid," said Golda. "She knows everything better than I do. Dora said that what happened to our parents has had no effect on her life or on my life. She said that the Holocaust was over with, and what did I want to talk to a stranger about it for anyway? Dora said that she's got no problems and I've got no problems. I said to Dora that I didn't feel that I had more than a normal share of problems, and she said that she and I were more normal than normal, and that there was nothing to talk about from the past. Oh, I almost forgot, Dora said that she thought that there might be some truth in my mother's suggestion that my interview was a plot by Mr. Bloom."

"What did Rosa Cohen ask you?" said Bella.

"She asked me lots of things," said Golda, "but I can't really remember any specific questions. She told me that she had often had trouble separating her experience from her mother's experience. She said that she sometimes had not been sure that she too hadn't been in Auschwitz. It sounds crazy but I knew what she meant."

"It sounds really crazy to me," said Bella.

"It's not so crazy, Bella. Why is that any more crazy than going and sitting by a river and catching fish when there are plenty of fish in the fish shops?"

"I don't go fishing," said Bella.

"Bella, I think you don't really want to talk about my interview," said Golda.

"Yes I do," said Bella. "Tell me what else you talked about."

"I told Rosa Cohen that I used to dream that Nazis were chasing me," said Golda. "She told me that she dreamt about Nazis too. I never knew that other people dreamt about Nazis."

"I've never dreamt about Nazis," said Bella.

"Yes, but your father was only in a labor camp in Russia, and your mother wasn't even in the war, she was already in Australia," said Golda.

There was a silence. Golda thought that Bella probably didn't like the way she said "only" in a labor camp. She thought that Bella was probably bristling and contemplating saying that there was some-body at the door and she had to go. Well, she didn't care. Bella was being as thick as a brick today. Couldn't Bella see that this was a very sensitive issue? And couldn't Bella see that being in a labor camp couldn't be compared to being in Auschwitz?

"Rosie Berg's mother was in a labor camp in Russia, and Rosie is always talking about the Nazis," said Bella. "Rosie says that she has nightmares about the Nazis."

"Rosie Berg is another matter altogether," said Golda. "If Rosie Berg had been born to a mother who'd spent her whole life on holiday in the Bahamas she'd say she had nightmares about the Nazis. Rosie Berg just loves to be the center of attention."

"When I told my mother that you were doing the interview with Rosa Cohen," said Bella, "she said that it was disgusting that the children of survivors thought that the attention should be on them and not on their parents. She said that the survivors went through the suffering, not their children."

"Well, your mother certainly didn't suffer," said Golda.

She felt flat. She wondered whether this message about who experienced the suffering was from Bella or her mother. She half agreed anyway. Why should anyone spend time thinking about how she had been affected? She wasn't the one who had suffered. And maybe Dora was right, maybe there was nothing wrong with her. If there was nothing wrong with her, she thought, then there was also nothing that was spectacularly right with her.

There was nothing that was spectacularly wrong. She had two nice kids. Charlie was a good husband. He was a good accountant. They were well off. Charlie's mother had been in Bergen-Belsen, but Charlie didn't think it had affected his life. Golda thought that Charlie was frightened of his mother, and far too scared to ask her anything about the past. Charlie worried a lot about upsetting his mother.

Golda thought that Charlie didn't want to upset anybody. Everything was always fine with Charlie. In an argument he would always give in. If she said that she didn't feel like sex, that was fine. If she cooked fish it was fine and if she cooked tripe it was fine. If she was on an egg diet, Charlie ate eggs. People said that he was very good-natured. Golda appreciated his good nature, but sometimes she worried about his eagerness to please.

She was grateful to Charlie for never criticizing her, and for not making an issue out of the fact that she didn't work. When she said that she was tired at the end of the day, Charlie was sympathetic. He never asked her what it was that was tiring her. Danielle and Simone were seventeen and fifteen, and quite independent. Milka the cleaning lady came three times a week. Golda didn't have to do much around the house. Golda wasn't quite sure what it was that tired her. When people asked her what she did, she said, "I'm just Golda, I don't do anything in particular."

Most of the women that Golda knew worked. If they didn't have a job they worked at their figure, or their suntan, or they worked for charity. Golda had mostly been too plump to worry about her figure. She thought that if she'd only been a stone or so overweight, she might have felt more motivated to lose the extra weight. But Golda weighed eleven stone when she should have weighed eight.

Three months ago Ruthie Brot had asked her if she would like to come to the aerobics class at her house on Tuesday mornings. Golda had felt so grateful to be seen as a possible candidate for aerobics that she had said yes. She had bought purple lycra leotards and blue tights. She didn't look as awful in them as she thought she would.

Now the aerobics session was the highlight of Golda's week. She liked moving to music. She liked just moving. She liked being with Ruthie and Zoe and Ella. Last week she had begun a diet that Ruthie had given her. It was a black-eyed bean and rice diet.

Golda felt upset. Why did Bella have to say it was disgusting for children of survivors to look at how they had been affected? She'd asked Bella not to tell anyone about the interview. Bella's mother had the biggest mouth in Melbourne. If you wanted someone to know something, all you had to do is tell Bella's mother about it. Golda knew that Bella knew exactly what her mother was like, so why had she told her? There was so much that was right about Bella, Golda thought, but every now and then a mean thin sentence would streak out of her and skewer whoever was around her. She was glad that she hadn't asked Ruthie if Bella could come to the aerobics classes.

Golda was bewildered by why it was so hard to be good friends. Why did people feel the need to distress and disturb others? Golda remembered the day that she and Bella had worn their first straight skirts. They had been fourteen. Bella had looked at her and said, "That skirt looks fabulous on you. You can't see your knees at all. The fattest parts of your legs are covered up and nobody would even know you were fat."

Golda's mother had always said to her, "You can't trust anybody except your family." Golda wasn't sure that she could trust her family. She didn't feel all that close to her mother or Dora, and she felt winded and breathless from the punches that her father threw at her from time to time. Yesterday when she had dropped around to visit him he had looked at her affectionately and said, "It's a good thing, Golda my darling, that Danielle and Simone look like Charlie. I love you very much and you've got a good heart, but it is easier for a girl if she is pretty. You and I can speak plainly to each other, can't we, Golda? We don't have to have big politenesses between us?"

"No, we don't," said Golda.

Something that Rosa Cohen had said to her this morning had startled her. Rosa had been talking about her husband Allan. Allan was not Jewish. "Allan's father used to thump him," Rosa had said. "Sometimes he'd beat the shit out of Allan, but at least it was a very clear message and Allan knew exactly where he stood. The real problem for kids is when the message is ambiguous." What was her father's message? Golda wondered. Was it ambiguous or was it in another language?

"Did you ask Ruthie Brot if I could join the aerobics classes?" said Bella.

"Yes," said Golda, "I asked her and she said that she would have loved you to come, but Peter, the instructor, won't take more than four people in a class. So sorry, Bella, I did try."

Bella sounded disappointed. Golda felt pleased. "I'd better go now," she said to Bella. "I haven't prepared anything for dinner. Speak to you tomorrow."

"Speak to you tomorrow."

Golda reminded herself to mention the business of Bella not

being able to come to the aerobics class to Ruthie. Just in case Bella ever met Ruthie and brought it up. Melbourne was so small that you could never be sure that two people would not meet each other.

Golda prepared dinner. She put a chicken and some potatoes in the oven. Maybe she would forget the beans and rice tonight. Maybe she'd have chicken with the others. She was feeling too rattled to diet.

Charlie arrived home a bit earlier than usual. Golda was happy to see him. He walked in carrying two briefcases and a large folder of papers. He always brought work home with him. "Hello, darling," he said. "How are you? I thought of you this morning. How did it go with Rosa Cohen?"

"I guess it was OK," said Golda. "I don't know that anything that I said enlightened either of us. I talked for so long, but I can hardly remember a word I said. I don't think I was very intelligent. I felt absolutely wrung out by the time I left. I felt terrible, and I had no idea what it was that was making me feel so bad.

"It's all such a muddle, this business of our parents' suffering. I feel scared to think about it too much. But I feel scared of so many things. My parents are scared, but at least they have got a reason for being scared. You know, Charlie, I feel angry with my dad for always having such a good reason for what's gone wrong with his life, when I haven't got a good excuse for what's gone wrong with mine."

"But nothing is particularly wrong with your father's life," said Charlie, "and what is wrong with your life?"

"Well, my dad didn't make as much money as most of his friends," said Golda. "He feels inferior about that, even though he always scoffs at people who are really rich. He says money isn't what is important, but I know that he feels that he hasn't been as success-ful a human being as those of his friends who've made lots of money. Look at how my mother has to buy everyone more expensive pres-ents than they give her. She's very keen to show people that she can afford everything they can. And when she does buy a bargain my father gets really furious and says we've got enough money to pay full price, we don't need to buy bargains.

"Managing a knitwear factory wasn't what my father saw himself doing when he was a young boy. He said he dreamt of becoming a lawyer. His father and two uncles were lawyers. Haven't you noticed how often he manages to bring that up in a conversation? When I was little he used to say to me that it didn't matter if I wasn't too pretty because if I became a lawyer I would have the world at my feet."

"What a mean thing to say," said Charlie. "Your father says so many mean things to you. I don't know why. You're very pretty, and you look adorable in those photos of you when you were a little girl."

"Oh, Charlie, you're so biased," said Golda. "I'm sure my father would have been a much nicer person if he hadn't gone through the concentration camp. I don't think he would have been so angry. I think he was angry with me because I didn't have any hardships."

"Maybe that's why he gave you some hardships. Maybe that's why he convinced you you were awful looking, so that you would suffer too," said Charlie.

"I don't know," said Golda. "You know something creepy about Rosa Cohen? She's got all these books on the Holocaust. Hundreds of them. No, probably thousands of them. And you know where she keeps them? In her bedroom. Isn't that weird? I asked her, actually, why she has to have them in the bedroom. I mean, she could easily have them in bookshelves in another part of the house. She's got bookshelves everywhere."

"What did she say?"

"She said that she likes to see them. She said that they anchor her. They stop her from feeling sorry for herself, or getting things out of perspective. Isn't that strange? And she said something else that sounded a bit mad. She was talking about one of the reference books on the Holocaust which is out of print and very hard to get, and she said that when she went away for a couple of months last year, she put the book in a friend's safe. I asked her if she had put her own playscripts in the safe too. She said no."

"Is she a bit weird?"

"No, she's really very nice," said Golda. "I felt comfortable with her, but I felt a bit like we were two children who were doing something that we weren't supposed to be doing. I don't think she felt like that, I think it was just me. Although I noticed that every time she talked about her own family she reminded me that what she was saying was confidential.

"You know, by the end of the morning I could see that, even though she has read all those shelves of books, the whole business is as difficult and confusing for her as it is for me. She told me that she had been reading books on the Holocaust for over eight years. She said that she can't stop. That every time she thinks she's had enough and can't bear to read one more word on the subject she finds another book and starts reading again. It sounds to me like she's got a problem."

"Even if she didn't have a problem to begin with," said Charlie, "she'd sure as hell get a problem from reading all that depressing stuff all the time."

"I said that to her, Charlie," said Golda, "and she said to me that it wasn't at all depressing to face things. She told me to read *Survival in Auschwitz* by Primo Levi and *Night* by Elie Wiesel. She said they may be distressing books, but they were brilliant and uplifting as well. I think I might go to Balberyszski's and buy them."

"Are you sure, Golda? I think it may be asking for trouble to go looking into the past."

"But I feel as though it's my past and your past, not just our parents' past," said Golda.

"It's not my past," Charlie said, and went into his study.

Charlie sat in his study. He was agitated by all this talk about the Holocaust. It was the 1990s, not the 1930s. What good could it do to think about it now? He could see that it was important for other people to know about what had happened, so that it couldn't happen again, but Jews already knew about it. Golda said that even Jews didn't know too much about it. But how much did they need to know? Maybe it would be harmful to know too much? It could be very distressing. Golda had been hysterical last week when Miriam Pincas had said that she couldn't possibly read anything about the Holocaust because it would upset her too much. "Look at her," Golda had raged, "in her expensive clothes and her Victorian mansion. She's air-conditioned and heated and demisted and totally coated with her wealth. But it's not enough for her to be protected from the weather or from burglars, she wants to be protected from feeling anything." Sometimes Charlie was so full of admiration for the way that Golda put things. She really did have a talent for words. It was a pity she had been determined not to do law. She would have been a good lawyer. Instead, she was a good mother. Who was to say that that wasn't more important? thought Charlie.

Still, he felt upset. Why had Golda become preoccupied with the past? It had only happened in the last year or two. Recently in the *Jewish News,* he had read an interview with Elie Wiesel. Elie Wiesel had said that it was important not to trivialize the Holocaust. Well, maybe to think that the Holocaust had affected the children of survivors was trivializing it. He didn't know.

Last night he and Golda had had dinner at Scheherezade with Bella and her husband David. They were talking about how the food in Australia had changed, how now you could buy so many different varieties of food. "My father," Bella had said, "said that when he came here after the war, the food was shocking. He said that the cheese tasted like wax. It must have been awful because my father was fresh out of labor camp and he can't have been too fussy about his food." Charlie wondered if that was what Elie Wiesel had meant by trivializing.

The phone rang. Charlie knew it would be his mother. "Hello, Charlie darling," she said. "How are you? I've got a shocking cold, darling. I didn't have it yesterday, and today I am sick like a dog. And, of course, do I get some sympathy from your father? Not one bit. You know your father, he doesn't like to see any problems. He likes to pretend that everything is all right all the time. He said to me, 'It's not such a bad cold. Take an aspirin and you'll feel better.' Probably when I drop dead he will look at me and say, 'Take an aspirin and you'll feel better.'"

Charlie usually sympathized with his mother. He usually spent most of the phone call listening. His mother called at this time every night. She knew that he would be home but that he wouldn't have started his dinner yet. Sometimes Charlie worked on a client's accounts while his mother talked.

Charlie took a deep breath. His stomach knotted slightly. Before his mother could get on to the next subject, Charlie asked her a question. "Mum," he said, "do you think you are still affected from being in Bergen-Belsen?"

"Charlie, are you stupid?" she said. "Of course I am. Not one day goes by when I don't think about what happened to me. Not one day goes by when I don't think about what happened to my mother and father and my sister. Of course I know that they died, but how did they die? I didn't bury them. No one buried them. Charlie, I thought you were clever enough to know that something like this never leaves you. Why do you think I have so much trouble with my stomach? Because of the camp, of course. I don't know why I'm explaining so much to you. Nobody who wasn't there could understand anything about it at all."

"Do you think I was affected by you having been there?" asked Charlie.

"Of course not," said his mother.

Charlie and his mother chatted for another ten minutes. As soon as he hung up from his mother, Golda's mother was on the line. "Charlie," she said, "get me Golda. I know she's busy in the kitchen but I won't keep her long." Charlie got Golda.

"Hello, my dear daughter," Golda's mother shouted. "I did hear already that you did go to Rosa Cohen's house this morning."

"Who told you?" said Golda.

"What does it matter who told me? Did you enjoy telling the family secrets to a stranger? Did it make you feel better?" she shouted.

"Couldn't you calm down, Mum? I don't want to upset you," said Golda.

"Golda, it's a little bit late for you to be so concerned with upsetting me," she answered. "If you didn't want to upset me or your father you should have thought about it before you went to talk to this Rosa Cohen. I think I am going to ring Mr. Bloom and congratulate him. I'll tell him his plot worked. My loyal daughter couldn't wait to talk about her family."

"Mum," said Golda, "what is it that you thought I'd be talking about? What are the secrets that I'm supposed to have given away? How can I give them away when I don't know what they are?"

"In a family there are always things that you don't talk to other people about."

"But what are they in our family? What are you so worried about?"

"Golda," said her mother, "you were not in Auschwitz, and that is why you can so easily decide that this is a subject to discuss with a stranger. If you had been there you would understand what is wrong with what you are doing. Your father wants to speak to you."

"Hello," said Golda's father, "is this the traitor in the family? I suppose that you feel better after your long talk to Rosa Cohen. I am glad that you talked to her. It is good that a poor child like you, who grew up with plenty of food and her family around her, should be able to talk about her suffering. Was Rosa Cohen interested in your suffering?" Golda tried to answer but her father wouldn't stop.

"Did she ask you if I was a Kapo?" he said. "I suppose she thought that I must have been a Kapo. Probably you think the same. Well, you can tell her that I wasn't a Kapo. Most of the people who survived were for sure Kapos. I don't trust anyone who was in Auschwitz who says they were not a Kapo. How did they survive?"

"How can you say that, Dad?" said Golda. "If Jews can speak like that what hope is there for anybody else?"

"I can see that you have already become an expert about Auschwitz," said her father. "It didn't take you long. My dear daughter, you are not an expert. I am an expert. I was there. I am saying goodbye now. I am too upset to talk anymore." He hung up.

Golda sat down at the kitchen table. Tears ran down her face. What had she done? What was so bad about talking to Rosa Cohen? It had felt harmless. Hadn't all the harm been done a long time ago? She wiped her eyes with her apron. Maybe she would ring Dora. Maybe her sister would be sympathetic.

"What the hell are you doing?" was Dora's first question. "Don't you know how much you've upset Mum and Dad? Haven't they suffered enough already? What's wrong with you? Were you feeling a bit bored? If you were that bored you should have joined a club, or come and worked with me once a week in the Rosenthal Homes kitchen. What is wrong with you, Golda? You've got a good husband and two nice girls. What do you want to stir up so much trouble for? You'll kill Mum and Dad with all this trouble." Golda didn't have an answer. She said goodbye and hung up.

Two days later Golda said to Charlie, "I think I might ring Rosa Cohen and tell her that I have to drop out of this project."

"Are you sure?" said Charlie.

"I'm not sure that I don't want to do it, but I am sure that I don't want to cause my parents any more pain. They've had enough pain," she said.

"Yes," said Charlie, "they are the victims, and why should they be victims again?"

"But I'm not victimizing them," said Golda.

"But they feel as though you are," said Charlie.

"Charlie, I feel so fucked up," said Golda. "I've never done anything much. And I've never known why I haven't done anything much. I didn't do law because my father wanted me to do it. The feeling of not wanting to do law was much stronger than any feeling I had of wanting to do anything else. I feel like I'm a half-person. I'm half-there. I'm half a mother. I'm half a wife. I'm half-pretty. I'm half-clever."

"Maybe you should go ahead and do the interviews," said Charlie.

Golda decided that she would ring Rosa Cohen on Monday and tell her that she wouldn't be able to come on Wednesday, and in fact she wouldn't be able to continue with the interviews. She felt flat and depressed. She wasn't sure how she was going to explain it to Rosa Cohen.

On Monday, Rosa Cohen rang Golda. "Golda," she said, "I'm sorry, but I've got some bad news. Don't worry, it's not a catastrophe, well at least not for you. I've decided to scrap my book of interviews with children of survivors. In over thirty-five interviews I had two really good ones and a couple of others that might have worked. Well, my two best interviews both rang this week to say that they couldn't continue with the project. So I thought about it a lot and I decided that this book is too difficult to do. Maybe someone else could do it, but I can't. I'm going to file away my four hundred kilos of transcripts and go back to my normal life."

"I'm really sorry about that," said Golda. "I enjoyed talking to you. It made me feel better."

"Would you like a copy of your interview?" said Rosa Cohen.

"Yes, I would," said Golda.

Golda put down the phone. She didn't know how she felt. She decided to go to Balberyszski's and buy Primo Levi and Elie Wiesel. She looked for her car keys. She thought she might stop at Krauss's, on the way, and buy herself a block of that new Swiss bittersweet chocolate.

The Deposit

BY VAL VINOKUROV

I have proof.

A year ago I got my hands on a video taped in 1981 by Dr. Alfred Kahn, M.D., a distant relative from Skokie. About two years after we arrived in Miami Beach from Moscow, Kahn, an amateur oral historian, decided to use this epic delivery of the lost remnant as an excuse to convene a family reunion in South Florida. So he interviewed my mother, grandmother, and me, as well as the older American relatives who fled Russia in the teens and twenties of this century.

I was nine and my English was already unaccented, a feat of automatic learning for which I can't take credit. As for ambitions, I said I wanted to be a singer. And a doctor like my father, a radiologist who remained in Moscow. A singing radiologist. ("Any cyst you can see I can see better! I can see any cyst better than you!")

My mother grimaced through the whole interview: "Vot? Vot? I don' understand vot you ask." But he kept at it, like Charlie Rose interviewing Anatoly Sharansky: "What does it feel like to be a Jew in a free country now?" As if this question meant anything to a single parent who took two buses to work. Besides, Dr. Kahn failed to understand that my mother never gives up anything asked of her. Demands puzzle her.

Babushka Lyuba is also grimacing on the tape. A fright mask set since the war. She's sitting in a foldout chair, testifying in Yiddish about the Germans and what they did, how they murdered her sister in Byelorussia while they starved her in Leningrad. I can tell because of her gestures. Discreetly violent, thick-fingered gestures, incongruous against the backdrop of her pastel green and pink floral dress. Gestures that indicate planes, spiraling bombs, explosions, nothing (as in, no food, no help, no respite, no mercy). And periodically, she lifts her head and crosses her throat with her index finger.

But I have proof. Proof on tape that my fresh-cut b'rith hadn't really taken, even in the eyes of the perpetrating American relatives. There's the indefatigable Judy Levin—my grandma's steel-fisted cousin and former President of the Greater Miami Jewish Federation—who does not seem completely satisfied: "Oh yeaah, little Valery, cousin Faina's son from Russia, he looks just Spanish, just like a little boy from the Mariel."

What can I say if the other kids back at my Moscow kindergarten used to call me *njegger,* along with the venerable *zhyd?* My best friend there was, perhaps by default, Armenian; he and his family left for California a year before we left for Florida. Maybe it's just the shared melanin, but Russian Jews and Armenians have always had a peculiar goodwill toward each other. There's an old joke about the dying Armenian patriarch imploring his bewildered heir to save the Jews: "Because after the Jews, my brave son, it'll be *our* necks!"

By now, the Jews of the former Soviet Union have more or less saved themselves: most of them left for Israel, Canada, the States, even Germany. And in the process they've become Russians, just like that. I, however, have been mistaken for a Turk, a Greek, an Italian, an Arab, a Vietnamese. And of course, a Cuban.

Miami is about half-Cuban, and the non-Cubans are steadily becoming Cubans through osmosis. Anyone who spends enough time in Miami will be overcome by the urge to wear guayaberas and drink amphetamine espresso out of paper thimbles. I have tried my best to resist this urge, if only because there isn't one Cuban in the Greater Miami area who believes me when I say I don't speak Spanish. Generally, Miamians reply to my English in Spanish, I keep speaking English, they keep speaking Spanish, each pretending to understand the other, reluctant to force a linguistic confrontation.

I would have had it made if I'd spoken Spanish as a kid. In the Jewish day school where I spent the third through eighth grades, all of the popular kids were Jubans (cousins, all of them). When I went away to college up North I was shocked to learn that Jubans are rather exotic outside Miami, where they are as regular as the afternoon rains that glide east from the Everglades.

The specifications that make someone Juban are not all that stringent. And a Juban may be many other things besides. For instance, Sam Rodkin: patriarch, real estate tyrant, many-time Miami Beach City Commissioner, Auschwitz survivor, bit of a crook, Juban. He was born in Russia (really Poland), deported to a death camp as a teenager, survived, found refuge in Cuba, and less than fifteen years later fled Castro for South Florida.

There are around 20,000 Holocaust survivors in Miami Beach— less every day—and there are as many ways that they cope with their survival. Some kill themselves, unable to bear the guilt of dying in their sleep. Most others are too broken to do that much.

A few become exemplary moral figures, witnesses, philanthropists, living testaments to the generosity and endurance of the human spirit, and so forth. Sam Rodkin could often be seen on TV jauntily wearing one of these noble hats, making his contribution on

Larry King. But truth be told, Rodkin acquired two basic dicta as he escaped the chimneys of Birkenau: 1) fuck them before they fuck you, and 2) use it or lose it. So he used it—his uncanny business sense, his sympathetic tone, his soft-spoken fluency in Russian, Yiddish, Polish, Hebrew, Spanish, and English, and most of all, he used the poignant numerical tattoo on his arm—to fuck everybody before they fucked him, whether they wanted to fuck him or not.

My mother and I were in no position to fuck him. We just wanted our fucking security deposit back. During my first year in college, my mother moved out of the apartment of my late childhood and adolescence, the Meridian Manor, two mirror-image sixties-built twin-storied structures sprouting catwalks like rotten onions, with a large keep-off-the-grass lawn and palm grove between them. One of Rodkin's sons co-owned the property, and it seems that he couldn't do without his share of our $600 deposit. Now, the reason he almost got away with it has to do with our manager, Mr. Cofino, as well as another freak of naturalization, my friend, Sagi Kfir.

Mr. Cofino was a decent Cuban gentleman with whom we had excellent relations up until the time my mother couldn't find her checkbook on rent day. That was when she stuffed $600 in tens and twenties into my hand and told me take it over to Mrs. Cofino, whose husband was out of town.

"Did she give you a receipt, where's the receipt?" my mother staccatoed.

"But Ma, you didn't tell me anything about a receipt."

"Maybe I should send you back? Never mind, I trust Mrs. Cofino."

A week later, Mr. Cofino came asking for the rent. His wife, it seems, plain forgot the whole transaction had ever taken place. After some polite mutual recrimination, Mr. and Mrs. Cofino agreed to "pretend" that we had paid the rent. The first transfusion of bad blood had taken.

But it was really Sagi—a true freak of naturalization—who finished things off between us and Mr. Cofino two years later. Sagi Kfir is a blond beast of an Israeli who came to Miami Beach with his family when he was four. He was extravagantly contemptuous of all things American and vividly mythic about all things Near Eastern. And there was one habit—which I will come to in a moment—that enabled him to express these two divergent streams as one unified current.

Throughout all of high school, Sagi and I would give each other identical mushroom haircuts with my electric clipper. Since I lived near school, usually this was done at my place in the afternoon, out on the catwalk veranda so that the hair could be swept off the second floor and become the wind's responsibility. By our senior year, our operation had such word-of-mouth that we agreed to cut the hair of the uninitiated in what became known as Biff & Roy's Hair Emporium. At the end of each shift at Biff & Roy's, Biff (that was Sagi) had a particular custom: rather than use my more-than-adequate facilities, he would walk downstairs and relieve himself like a Bedouin in the shade of the oasis between the two buildings of the Meridian Manor.

Finally, one day an elderly Columbian tenant, leaning on the railing of the building across, decided that he was witnessing this ritual for the last time: "Oyez, maricon! Perro! Everyday jyou pissing like a dog here!"

Sagi looked up at him with curiosity and goodwill. Without zipping up, he turned to him and said, "How are you, sir? What's your name? Can I ask you something?"

"Hijo-de-puta! I call the police!"

"But sir, don't you think that if God had meant for us to use toilets He would have said so in the Bible? You're a good Catholic, you read the Bible, sir?"

"I'm going to tell the manager," the neighbor muttered as he went back inside his apartment.

"There's nothing like pissing in nature, old man! It's how God wanted things to be! Ach, I hate this fucking country . . ."

The next day, Mr. Cofino knocked on our door. He told me that if he ever saw my friend's face here again he would evict us. This was

June of my senior year, and I knew I'd be out of Miami in the fall, so I didn't much care. By November, soon after my mother had moved out, he was helping Rodkin's son invent pretexts to hold onto our security deposit.

I came down from college that Thanksgiving, and my mother decided that we should go and wrest our money back. First, we went to the junior Rodkin's office on Alton Road. After my mother muscled our way in, he threw up his hands saying, "Talk to my partner! Nothing I can do!" So then my mother determines: "We go to his fahzer now . . ."

We drive to City Hall, where we are told we just missed Commissioner Rodkin. As we walk out, we see him pull out in his white Continental. We attempt pursuit in our burnt sienna '79 Ford Fairmont, but we lose him. We drive around the neighborhood for about half-an-hour, until we spot his car in front of the Epicure Market: "The devil's buying caviar with my six hundred dollars," Mother observes in Russian, conflating all Rodkins.

"Watch his car," she tells me. "They have the best peaches across the street, I have to get some peaches for you, you don't have peaches up North, I don't understand what you're doing there." Ignoring my automatic protests, she walks a block down to the Publix. I sit in the car, gently sweating, fiddling with the AM radio. All I get is WKAT, a station shared by Creole and Spanish-language broadcast. It's a Creole program: *Chak ma'di cé fet ou nan Super 'Appy Club, 55 South Dixie Eyeooway!* I smile recalling the dark-blue neon feline grinning slyly from WKAT's location at a dry dock on Biscayne Boulevard.

When I look up, the white sedan is gone. "Listen, what were you doing anyway!?" my mother yells as she returns with two plastic bags full of fruit.

Finally, we decide to wait near the Sun Bank Building at the end of Lincoln Road, where Sam Rodkin has another office. Forty minutes later, he drives up, emerges from his sedan, and darts upstairs. We follow. We announce ourselves to his secretary. We are admitted.

"*Kak dela,* Faina?" he greets my mother.

"Fine, havayou," she replies.

"Old, but not so bad. Valera has gotten big. You finish with high school, sonny?"

"Heis eighteen. Heis in callege now. He has schalarship, but I still pay like sree souzand, you know?"

"Congratulations, *zeit gezundt!* You know what it means *zeit gezundt?*"

"Yes, thank you, but, you know, your san Bruuce, he has my deposit. I didn't damage apartment, and he won't give me back deposit, I donno what to do."

"Give me a second."

He turns on the speaker-phone and pushes a speed dial button. After two rings, a voice answers and Rodkin picks up the receiver.

"Hi, Brucie. Good. I have Faina, Faina Vinokurov, and her son in my office. From the Meridian. Okay . Why you don't give the deposit? *Pero, que es eso, mira?* Look, I know you have partner, you don't need to tell me you have partner. Okay. . . . But tell me something, who is your father? That's right, so you will . . . so you will do this for me. No, you will do this for me, okay? Okay. Thank you very much, Mister Bruce Rodkin."

Sam Rodkin told us to go to his son's accountant on Collins Avenue. By day's end, and after four solid hours of gruntwork, my mother was issued a check in the amount of $600.

$\sim$

I HAVE PROOF.

The tape, a different tape, arrived from the Shoah Survivors Foundation last week. I ordered it after my mother saw it aired on the public access channel in Miami Beach. Sam Rodkin's video testimony.

So great was her shock that she described it to me in English.

"I almost had hardattack. He was talking about how he surwive in Russia after the war. How there was Russian officer, Russian tank cornel who looked Jewish. And how this cornel adopted him and took care of him and made sure he was sent in west to Germany so he wouldn' go in gulag. And then so Rodkin is saying all this. And! He says the name of this man who saved his life was Cornel Vinokurov! It was your grandfahzer Leonid, my fahzer-in-low, who else? I almost had hardattack. I donno what happen with me, but I was crying."

My mother saw the broadcast seven years after our deposit crusade. The next morning she found Sam Rodkin's number in the White Pages.

It was some other Sam Rodkin (no relation), who informed her that the Rodkin she wanted had been dead two years. My mother said the fake Sam Rodkin didn't seem annoyed, though. He was rather flattered by all the misplaced calls. He tried to chat it up with her. Cute accent, he said.

I believed my mother's account, but I wanted to see Rodkin's testimony for myself. An auntly voice at the Shoah Foundation told me that the Rodkin family owned the rights and that the heir had to sign a release for me to get my own copy. Through a series of Rodkins, I ultimately reached our former landlord Bruce.

Bruce, Sam Rodkin's firstborn, was curious and obliging, and felt a bit guilty too. Not about the deposit—I don't think he remembered having tenants named Vinokurov. As far as he knew I was just "doing research for a family history." He felt bad that he himself never had time to do anything with his father's stories.

A month and $35 later, I got the tape in the mail. There was no mistake: Rodkin's Colonel was my grandfather Leonid. Sam Rodkin, smiling and wearing a baby-blue long-sleeved guayabera, was sitting in front of an ivory backdrop, his pale head glowing, a friendly ghost. All the details matched everything I knew about my grandpa.

He was a dark man, a little bit on the Oriental side, if you know what I mean. High forehead, full lips. Very unusual-looking for a Russian. Could have been Jewish, probably, but he never let you know one way or the other. A lot of Communist Jews were like that, especially in the army. But he was a prince. He didn't have to do nothing for me. He could have let me get sent to the factories or the gulags along with the rest of the refugees liberated by the Red Army on the Byelorussian front. But he made me an interpreter, a lieutenant in his tank squad. He would call me bratik, little brother. And when they were sending everybody to Vladivostok or some place like that because they said they were going to open a second front against the Japanese, Colonel Vinokurov pulled a few strings to get me transferred to occupied Berlin instead. In Berlin, I dumped my Soviet uniform and crossed over to the American side, where the agency told me I had people in Cuba. So I went to Cuba, and the rest everybody in Miami Beach knows about the rest.

But what I didn't tell nobody, almost nobody, was about this Colonel. You see, when the war was ended, I felt like ending myself. My parents, my brothers and sisters (we were eleven brothers and sisters, you understand), everybody was gone. My life was over. But this Colonel, he looked at me and saw a smart handsome kid with everything in front of him. He knew he could make something out of me, so he picked me up out of the grave, cleaned me off, gave me a uniform and stripes, and sent me in the right direction.

I'm not a religious man so much, not now and not then. But it makes you think. I saw my father go to the gas. And now it was like somebody sending me a new father.

A year after the end of the war, my grandfather got a real son of his own. A decidedly unheroic offspring. Selfish, irresponsible, and eventually old enough to use youth as an excuse. That was my father, the singing radiologist who stayed behind in Moscow as my mother and I made our way to America.

My mother's own father, Ilya, died when I was a few months old. Her father-in-law, Leonid, filled Ilya's shoes admirably, stepping in whenever my father neglected his obligations.

Leonid died of lung cancer when I was four. He had a strange all-consuming passion for me, ready to do anything. On his deathbed, he confided to my uncle that "if Valerik wanted to pee" in his mouth he'd drink it. When my cousin Dima recently passed along this bit of family lore to me, he sounded both jealous and ominous. As if to say, this is what has already been invested in you: I can be a fuck-up, but you, Valera . . .

In my desk drawer, I have a black-and-white photograph of the two of us, Dedushka Lyonia and myself. I'm a two-year-old Mongolian bundle of sweaters, scarf, and cap. And he's holding me aloft, my feet perched on his shoulder. Planted there, his chubby trophy.

from *Lessons of Darkness*

BY HELENA JANACZEK

Translated from the Italian by Stephen Sartarelli

The other evening on television some woman claimed she was the reincarnation of a Jewish girl killed in a death camp. My friend Olek phoned me from Rome to tell me this, and as he spoke he kept following the stages, reconstructed God knows how, of that prior life, the precise recollection of prenatal memories, and kept repeating: "How bizarre." So I hung up at once, saying I too was interested in the program, though it wasn't true, and turned on the TV. I saw a woman of about thirty, a psychologist according to the caption that appeared chest-high on the screen, who now was no longer talking about her other self named Anna or Hannah Baumann or Naumann, but explaining to the studio audience and the vast, invisible viewing audience the meaning and conclusions she had drawn from this experience. Then they turned to the experts: psychologists, parapsychologists, priests, Buddhist lamas with monks as their interpreters, as well as a Jewish psychiatrist who took the side of science, but also that of what he defined "non-dogmatic" religion, admitting that, yes, the Jewish mystical tradition did consider the idea of metempsychosis, but it involved a reincarnation of an anonymous, unfathomable sort. I doubt he knew anything more about it or understood the subject very well at all. Then an elderly lady, also Jewish, spoke of the concentration camp as a sublime experience—that's exactly how she put it: "Look, the concentration camp was also a sublime experience"—and at that moment her pure white dress and wooden necklace visibly stood out, as she went on about some man, the favorite pupil (does one say pupil? follower? adept?) of the Indian guru Sri Aurobindo, anyway a man with an Indian name who became holy from his stay in a Nazi camp, offering him as an example to the young woman psychologist, who welcomed the advice and confirmed this by saying: "What you are telling me is very beautiful," a smile on her lips. I continued watching that program on reincarnation for a little while, repeating to myself, just to lessen the irritation and a vague sense of desecration, "Who are you to laugh at the good faith of these people? What do you know about it, really?"

I, actually, have been wanting for some time to know about something else. I would like to know if it is possible to pass on knowledge and experience not through a mother's milk, but even earlier, through the fluids of the placenta and I don't know how else, since I wasn't breast-fed by my mother and actually have an atavistic hunger, a desperate, starvation hunger, which she no longer has. It's all I ever talk about, this particular and obviously neurotic hunger that rises up at certain moments in front of a piece of bread, any kind of bread, good, bad, fresh, chewy, dry. I even sometimes maul hard crusts of bread and never throw any away, not even a little, even going so far as to collect crumbs from the tablecloth to eat them. I suffer from a kind of mild bread bulimia, the main reason, or perhaps the only reason, for my physical heft, which my mother often criticizes. But even absent these uncontrollable outbursts, I always have to eat the entire roll I get at the cafeteria. It was she who taught me that bread is sacred, and that when she sees a piece of bread on the street, she picks it up and places it somewhere higher up, just so as not to leave it there, on the ground. I learned my lesson all too well, maybe that's it.

As a little girl, my mother was not a big eater like me. She never liked anything. She has told the story many times, just to criticize those modern parents who comply with their children's whims by cooking only their favorite dishes, specially for them. She says her lack of appetite was cured only by the war and elicits complicitous looks from those of her generation who remember the heroism of hunger. She doesn't say what sort of hunger she suffered from, but that there are many meanings to the statement, "There was nothing to eat." She doesn't say that it was purely by chance, or by some miracle, that she didn't die of hunger or, which would have been more likely, wasn't killed by malnutritional asthenia or gas.

After the war, my mother got hungry; she ate, and ate seriously. Her clothes from that time fit me well, even though I'm four inches taller and twenty-two pounds heavier than she. I don't understand how this is possible, since in photographs of the period she looks only slightly plump. I actually have to put them on—to wear, for example, the waist-fitted white polka-dotted silk dress—to experience her different appetite, to get an idea of the hunger that finally abated with the passing years.

Now that she's old, and has left behind the caprices of adolescence, she has resumed a strict control of her own nutrition and displays a certain mistrust of foods she hasn't known all her life, a habit she keeps in check so as not to seem like a difficult person or, worse, an ignorant plebeian who, like the peasant in the German proverb, "eats only what he knows."

Now she claims to eat "with her head" and reproaches me for not doing the same, for not weighing myself each day to do something about the half-pounds before they become a whole one and then two and then a misshapen physical mass offensive to good taste and aesthetic ideals and who knows what else. She chides me for stuffing myself with bread and deposits only half of her own portion on my plate, because she absolutely cannot eat more than this, while I nurse resentment for an old woman's mania for watching her own waist-line so severely and talking so often about it as if it were a moral question. She notices I'm a bit bulimic, while I, with my half-baked notions of psychology, think that she, since childhood, has had a ten-dency toward anorexia that has reemerged with increasing force over the years. We are at opposite poles, I think with satisfaction and shame for my body and my hunger. Perhaps this is why I would like to know if it might be she who stuck me with that hunger, if she passed her own hunger on to me, the same way that today, even while calling me "her chubby girl," she passes me her half-cutlets, potatoes, half-dishes of pasta, I would like to know if she passed on to me her near-death starvation in order to overcome that near death and recapture the character, personality, and individual psy-chology she had before the hunger. This is what I ask myself. And I ask myself this so I won't have to think that not only was the concen-tration camp experience not "sublime," but it wasn't even an experi-ence, that one learns nothing from it, that one becomes neither better nor worse, and once it's over it's over, withdrawn into the remotest recesses of the soul where it undermines, oppresses, per-sists. And perhaps it undermines, oppresses, and persists because it doesn't want to vanish entirely, but, formless as it is, formless as it will always be, it does not bear upon the behavior and personality of one who has returned to the norm, returned to the social fabric, returned to the world of the living and the sated who have the right to be alive and sated.

My mother, a little girl who didn't eat, a girl who stole silk stock-ings and lipstick, to beautify herself without her mother's knowing, who was always "more charming than you and paid more attention to my appearance," my mother who used to read Scandinavian novels to the very last page even though she found them extremely boring, because you were supposed to read them and "I was a bit of a snob back then," my mother who never tolerated fat or ugly people, who had always been an "aesthete," is the same one I know, the one who irritates me, the one who seems the opposite of me because I want to be the opposite of her. But the one who fled the ghetto with two coins in her pocket, knowing it was about to be liquidated and knowing the meaning of those words, and saying to her mother, "I'm leaving, I don't want to be burned up in the ovens!" who was she?

She weeps, fifty years later, in Poland, shouts that she abandoned "my mother, my mother." She shrieks like an eagle in the museum established at Auschwitz I, that solid hotel complex where neither she nor any of those Jews had ever been, in front of a showcase displaying a sample of Zyklon B, she cries, "mama, mama," like a baby. I loved her with a full, proud love for that "public" scene she made. I love the surviving mother who picks up bread in the street, and much less the other mother who climbs onto the scale every morning, and I am unable to put them together and know that I am up against an unsolvable mystery, I know that I will never succeed in knowing my mother and I also know that I know her all too well and that all our quarrels are only—no more, no less—the usual, common conflicts and follies of family life.

⌒

My mother in a brown hotel room in Warsaw, large, ugly and dark as all upper-level and not terribly new hotel rooms are, except that it is a bit gloomier, a bit darker, a bit browner than similar rooms in the West. It's the first thing we saw calmly since arriving in this country, exactly fifty years later, for her. I didn't know it was exactly fifty years, just as there were many other things I didn't know: for example, I didn't know—since even before leaving, and later on the airplane, she had been so tense and taciturn (I might have imagined it, of course, since I too had been agitated for days by fear, fear of this very journey)—that for her, more than a journey, it was a return. This I could have understood.

Instead, I understood almost nothing, nothing, until she, in that hotel room, burst into tears, crying hard, shouting, "It's fifty years today," repeating it each time she managed to catch her breath and speak, while I kept asking, "What is?" and trying to embrace her and caress her like a child to whom something terrible has happened, like losing a doll or finding some small animal dead, and I said, "It's all right, Mama, it's all right," or something similar, because it's possible I'm making up some of these details. "It's exactly fifty years from that day," she finally said, and in my embrace, or pulling away from my embrace, she told me about the time she told her mother she didn't want to go off with them to die.

It was the evening of that same day, at supper with her mother, father and brother, who, much braver than she—"He was much braver than I," my mother shouts, "Jerzy was much braver"—had put the potatoes on the stove, very few I imagine, or done something of the sort, I don't remember, when she had shouted, "It's not true that they're taking us somewhere else, I know where they're taking us, I don't want to burn in the ovens!" That's how she said it to me, shouting these words, I can't forget them. Then she started crying, "mama, mama," and once again I tried to calm my mother down the way a mother tries to calm a small child screaming and crying, "mama, mama," but it was no use. A little later, however, she managed to stop and shout: "It was the worst day of my life"—for it was worse than the rest, the day she decided to run away and leave her mother, who was so good, to the fate she knew awaited her.

Only once did I open an enormous book entitled *Calendar of Events in the Auschwitz-Birkenau Concentration Camp, 1939–1945.* For the date of August 27, 1943—fifty years before and one and a half days after our arrival in Warsaw—a paragraph notes:

> About 1500 Jewish men, women and children arrived from the Zawiercie ghetto on an RSHA transport. After selection, 387 men, to whom were assigned the numbers 140334 to 140720, and 418 women, given numbers 56520 to 56937, were interned in the camp. The roughly 700 remaining people were killed in the gas chambers.

It is the only page commemorating those whom, during my trip to Poland with my mother, I forced myself for the first time to call grandparents and aunts and uncles. Zawiercie is about twenty miles away from Auschwitz, and even an overloaded freight or livestock train doesn't take long to get there. No point in imagining in which half they ended up after "selection." I know that my grandfather wasn't immediately gassed, that he went through strange and various vicissitudes. I've heard rumors about Jerzy's shoes—Jerzy, my mother's younger brother—shoes which he no longer had in the camp, but I don't know where or when. I no longer know anything about my grandmother.

Those railroad cars also deported my paternal grandparents and aunts and uncles. I know even less about them. I can no longer ask my father anything, and I've never mentioned it to my mother. I can't ask her about the others unless it is she who first indicates she wants to tell me something. But she, too, knows almost nothing about them: and "almost" means some rumor like that about the shoes, some rumor that is impossible to verify, but then what's the difference, since the result remains the same.

↗

WRITE, SAYS MY *mother as she reads this page, write that they were Wehrmacht boots, that they took them from him before putting him on the railroad car.—What?—Before the deportation, he had worn them for work. He was left barefoot, on the train.*

On the night of August 25–26, 1943, my mother escaped from the Zawiercie ghetto with ten *zloti* in her pocket. Or maybe it was five or seven or twenty, I can never remember figures, especially when they concern currencies I'm unfamiliar with. She was about twenty years old.

At her age, it cost me great effort to do anything I thought would be unpleasant for her. I would never openly oppose her. I succumbed to her attacks, which were aimed at punishing some sin of mine,

usually of omission, and always ended with an accusation of dispro-
portionate egotism, for which I atoned by crying and apologizing.
But I never thereby achieved forgiveness or an end to the quarrel; in
fact, very often the violence would increase, seeming to augment
with my words, especially with my weeping. And so she would keep
yelling at me, and I would keep crying. At twenty, with saving my
own life as my only reason for leaving, I would never have had the
strength to abandon my mother; I would have accompanied her. I
cannot know this with any certainty, but the contrary seems incon-
ceivable to me. Perhaps this is also why—that is, to win this absolute
loyalty—she always attacked me with such passion at every little
slipup on my part.

from *Joemi's Table*

BY ESTHER DISCHEREIT

Translated from the German by Krishna Winston

Here I am, sitting on this stupid swivel chair. After twenty years of being a non-Jew I want to be a Jew again. I've spent ten years thinking it over. What does the man behind the desk have to say? "Tax evasion," he says, and smiles. I have to do penance for four years and pay the back taxes. I tell him: Mother dead, Papa a goy—fourteen years old, shipped off to the country, no letter, no nothing from the community—and I come back after twenty years, want to be a Jew again, and the Jew tells me, "Approximately eight hundred marks—or should I let you do the calculation yourself?"

Must one be a Jew? I've asked myself that long enough. The congenital mark of Cain, forgotten under the waters of socialism, is shining through on my skin.

History's dead caught up with me, and drew me in. I didn't want to be drawn in, was determined to be a perfectly normal leftist—

oppressed in the standard repertory of classes, class struggle, of rulers and ruled.

My attempt proved a complete failure. I'm on the street recruiting, class struggle, and someone asks me my nationality. Neither proud nor self-confident, certainly not indifferent . . . should I say German? German is what one probably should say. BUT then . . . BUT what? But Jewish. There it is, bold and heavy, the word that was pinned to my lapel, that hung on a string around my neck. The string is cutting into my neck. My comrade on the rug we've spread on the sidewalk, piled high with propaganda brochures, leaflets, and our canister for contributions—he doesn't know. And why should he? Rome wasn't built by history's chronic losers.

I'll forget this question about being German, I decide. In the evening the news comes on. In some connection a clip of Nuremberg flashes across the screen, and again I'm upset, like this morning. Why does the news upset me so? There's enough terrible news as it is—isn't there? Of course I know that . . . and am all the more upset. Stupid question, is that allowed? Distribute feelings of injustice properly. Has reason gone mad?

What a feeling—when I don't even like them, the rich, evil, building-larded Jews, and also those who take other people's water for themselves and joyfully plant saplings on the houses of other peoples, as though it had to be that way and were decreed by Providence. I, too, danced around the tree, far away in a German city. We had bought it—thinking aloud in song of thrusting the spade into foreign soil. A distant land, which would always be a place of refuge, always? Perhaps that's why we didn't go there? No, we never went there, never. To go there was like undertaking a pilgrimage to Rome, or the Haj to Mecca. We didn't make a pilgrimage. We might have seen the children of the Haj. We might have seen the ruins of their destroyed houses. We might have seen parents without their children. Or we might not have seen all that—and the Dead Sea, it holds you up. It holds you up so wonderfully that no one can drown. Even so, it's dead, and perhaps no one can live who cannot drown. . . .

⚯

Wʜᴀᴛ ᴅᴏ ʏᴏᴜ want, Jew, soap or heat? The Jew says, I want heat. So the chimneys smoke, and soap is extra.—The blond, short-cropped hair leans way back with laughter. He's been in this job for six years, was trained here, has stayed here. Three evenings a week he goes to practice. Soccer. He's already getting fat, drinks too much beer.

He wants to talk, especially about last night. And how things just flowed. And the whole thing again from the beginning. He breaks off uneasily when the boss's son comes in. "Here's your, um—appoint-ment at 3:00 ᴘ.ᴍ." The door closes. That business last night went until the early hours of the morning. Quite something, you should see how red my eyes are, colleague. He picks up the paperwork; everything's in there. He can't read it, again. Breathes mint fumes on his superior's vest and then slowly turns away to his typesetting machine. One time he went away for a summer course. The boss couldn't believe it. Then he got back and had a lot to tell, as usual. Thought there would be soccer, but there was also stuff about soci-ety and so forth. The guy really impressed him, said some things about the Jews. Say, I don't think I've ever really seen one. What do they look like?

⚯

I sᴛᴀɴᴅ ᴛʜᴇʀᴇ and listen to him. What do these Jews look like? In the past one had to show one's ear for passport photos and at the border. Hey, colleague, you want to see my ear? Finally I say it.

He's all excited. He'll have to tell his instructor. He actually met one; probably he's the only one in the course. The next time he tells a joke, he pulls himself up short. "Sorry." At lunch we have hamburg-ers. Are you even allowed to eat this?

Maybe next time I can go along for the summer course. Then they'd have me right there in the flesh and could actually touch history.

"Nowadays we're more enlightened about these things, you know . . . actually I don't know any . . . Jews, I mean. They were somehow, you know, at the time they were already in a separate school, well, sometimes in the courtyard, yes . . . pale . . . different-looking, I don't know how to put it. Simply no opportunity to get to know them."

His wife told me over the telephone that he was going to Israel—his second time already. It really appealed to him there, she said—maybe not the right way to put it. Oh—this Promised Land. In his day the Promised People were pale and tubercular.

He feels deeply moved by this people and its fate, especially in Germany.

. . .

"Your identity, couldn't your identity—somehow interfere with your performance of your duties . . ."—he didn't mean to say that, "but you understand—a case where in connection with your identity you might have—a conflict of interest . . ."Aha, a genuine, pure, racially healthy Jewish conflict of interest—you see, the man's making an effort—or isn't he? One could have refused at the beginning, after all . . . Somehow this Judaism is archaic—the Antichrist is abroad in the land, is not abroad in the land. Of course, the Sermon on the Mount. Nevertheless, Paul indubitably implies the possibility of working with Jews. God, how grateful I am to St. Paul.

Eyes behind glasses smile noncommittally. He can't help that, to be sure.

Now and then he glances up. The tasteful tabletop mirrors an angel, probably an archangel. In the annunciation lives Jesus.

"Would you like another cup of coffee? You know, these long meetings—actually too much coffee. Of course my wife has already adjusted to low-calorie cooking—we're not used to this anymore. Yes, earlier one was really grateful for every piece of bread. You know, recently we were invited to dinner, my wife and I, it was really a lavish meal, more than lavish . . ." Before my inner eye appears salmon filet, coq au vin, vanilla ice cream with raspberry sauce, cream truffles . . .

"I said to my wife—you know, it's grotesque, in a way—back then everything in our town revolved around bread, dry bread. My first memory of the railroad station back then. In September 1945. A military policeman: he pulls this piece of bread out of his pocket.

"Well—back to you. Thank you for going to the trouble. I've been able to get a pretty good idea. Please don't get me wrong." "Good-bye." "Good-bye."

A light drizzle is falling on the paths outside the large house. Educational facilities usually offer drizzle in the evening—or Ping-Pong. Did you know that he's really well preserved—I mean for his age.

"What I have to ask you, just between you and me: do you know anything specific about . . . that Jew who was just here—I mean, how should I put it, his conscience . . ."

What's this about a Jew's conscience?

"Please don't get me wrong, that's not what I meant to say . . ."

What didn't he mean to say?

"How do you think?"

I think Dreyfus and thank Emile Zola. The whole business took place so long ago, and yet it's caught up with me. What's special about this story? Really? My friends don't understand.

Haven't we all been kicked out somewhere and somehow. We're always being kicked out somewhere, my friends and I, since we pick up stones. But this time—this time I don't have a stone in my hand. The stone around my neck the others can't throw.

꞊

"I HAVE A CONFESSION to make to you. You don't know me. I'm approaching you, how should I say, with embarrassment. You know, you look like Ruth Deretz. She was in my class back then. And somehow also a little—well, as attractive as you, a big girl, pretty, you understand. Then she . . . I was born in 1921. Was in the Hitler Youth—of my own free will. I'd volunteered. Then I was on a U-boat off the coasts of Africa and Spain. Please don't get me wrong, I regret it today. I had to watch shootings—some of my fellow soldiers didn't want to participate anymore . . . And I'll tell you straight out: Heddernheim, VDM, there was a concentration camp annex there. Anyone who says today he didn't know anything about it. That's not true at all—we knew. Not the full dimensions; of course not. But still—we knew. Recently we had a class reunion. I suggested all of us should go to Auschwitz together. You should have seen how they came down on me—I was shook up. No, to think they still haven't learned anything. I can't begin to tell you.

"I know, you actually came just to apply for admission. Yes, we'll get to that right away. Please excuse me. Could you repeat your name again, I mean spell it. Your address, please, oh yes—up here at the top, I already have it, of course. All right: we don't have your age: thirty years. I really wouldn't have guessed to look at you. All right, I'll read the whole thing back to you to make sure we have it all right. Misspelled? I don't understand."

First rays of sun sparkle through the dusty office window and catch a corner of my application. I, Ruth Deretz—I'm hungry.

THE LANDLORD IS a Sudeten German. Sudeten German—it's all right to say that, isn't it? Of course it's all right to say that. The landlord from the Sudetenland now has two buildings—acquired thanks to the work of his hands and the equalization-of-burdens program, as I hear later. In our family are none with the work of their hands, because my mother's hands shake. They shake quite without reason. They really could stop shaking now. But they shake. For this shake she receives reparations. In return she can say that she has no profession, no school diploma, no parents, no brothers or sisters—just her life and this shake.

When she applies for a housing subsidy, they deduct this shake from the extra allowance. Yet she went very early in the morning, so as to have the shake still under control.

If the landlord knew he'd rented an apartment to us. It isn't known.

Above us lives an older man. We hear he's a minister, and his wife was very angry when the children played their flutes after school. Jews always want to be better than other people. Playing the violin, pianists, that doesn't happen by accident.

—

Ｈｏｗ ｔｏ ｅｘｐｌａｉｎ this flute? I didn't ask for anything for Christmas. What would one of those trees with candles be doing in the home of a Yid anyway?

When Hannah from the village comes into the city and is divorced from her husband, the goy, she dares to wear the Mogen David again, though only under her dress, of course. But still.

I see the candle-decked trees of the people we encounter on the street, of the other girls at school. Don't I at least have some decorated greenery at home, they ask; what am I supposed to tell them? That my mother doesn't love me? Christmas is a custom at least. Hannah has a second one, and that's Hanukkah—but in the community. So Hannah asks her daughter what she wants for Christmas. And now back to this business with the flute.

Hannah's daughter says: Nothing. And nothing the following year, and nothing for her birthday, only a beautiful flute of her own, a shining silver concert flute. Two years earlier she also said Nothing when asked, and Nothing again the following year. Hannah should make up with her divorced husband, her father. Hannah didn't answer. Now that's two years ago, and now her daughter asks for the flute. The heavy ebony flute was the first instrument she was allowed to learn, borrowed from the music school. She herself is the great exception, Hannah says, the only one who doesn't understand anything about music, has no ear and can't carry a tune. That's why Hannah's daughter wants the flute.

And since Hannah didn't marry her father again, Hannah's daughter plays the flute. And plays, till her raised arms are ready to drop off.

—

FRAU RAU PAUSES on the landing when our door opens. She and her husband, she says, did belong to the Confessing Church back then. I look at her. Bitterness has twisted her mouth. It's stretched down to her neck. Sensible shoes, a wool suit flecked with gray, like her hair. I didn't understand that, the business about the flute and the church.

—

THE NEIGHBORS NEXT door to us, I don't know anything about them. And because I don't know anything, I take in our laundry in the evening. I suspect them of being from the same region as our landlord. They will certainly turn out to be equally hardworking.

—

"WE COME FROM Wullachen in the Bohemian Forest. All the Germans were expelled, so to speak. We got word that by ten in the morning the next day we had to be in Gilowitz. With fifty kilos of baggage. No more. We were in a transit camp there, and then we were taken to Hohenfurt, Kaplitz, to the station, and there we were loaded into cattle cars."

My ears repeat: Hannah loaded into cattle cars.

"I was twelve years old at the time, I should add. At that age we still had a sense of adventure."

She was six years old.

"Until cold reality struck, and we had to stand in line for food in the camp."

. . .

"The only thing I haven't forgotten. It was a magnificent day in May. We had a big dog at home, and he ran after us."

Her sister ran after her . . . and stumbled and fell.

" . . . when we had to get onto that truck."

. . .

"We had to leave everything behind. In Butzbach we were assigned to families. There were people there who took in refugees."

Where were there people who took in refugees? In England? In Germany? Where?

"We were given an unbelievably warm welcome . . . Then in 1956–57 the parish church gave us this piece of land. Then everyone helped out. Yes—and there was also an equalization-of-burdens program."

Reparations, right?

"Most of us were in agriculture at home, large-scale agriculture. We were remunerated accordingly."

Terrible pain, numbers tattooed into our arms, the sums were calculated accordingly.

"Somehow I've really come to feel at home here."

Have I come to feel at home here?

"We can tell the children all sorts of things about home. But they don't really feel connected."

She's told me nothing, almost nothing. Oh—if only I didn't feel connected!

"Somehow all that's in the past."

⌐⌐

SOMEHOW, THAT'S TRUE, it's in the past.

⌐⌐

ASKING WHAT IT all means . . . yes, a mixture of pimples and a too-short skirt. A good thing all that passes. When things have to be taken care of, purchased, removed, called up, brought up. Imagine this unsolved question as to what it all means, an adolescent girl with hair falling to her shoulders in dark braids. When she passes the building site, a young construction worker whistles at her—he seems to be buried in the earth up to his hips. His eyes bore into her knees. St. Bernadette—is passing. If an angel blushes. She isn't fair-skinned. No blood rushes to her cheeks.

World or non-world—a god who has abandoned us. Why did this god-damned god allow this? Who broke the laws, that you should punish us this way? Is God an exterminating angel from the land of the Mizrayim? Do you even exist, since you abandoned us? If penance is to be done, then preferably the way the Catholics do it, no? To be allowed to be a victim, the fascination of renunciation. If eternal life is more beautiful, why not right away? . . . A bit of death, perhaps? Bernadette began to love this unknown death, which the fatherless child thought of as masculine. In any case, death is doubt-less something typical of men. Otherwise men would die feminine deaths.

In any case, Bernadette caressed her unknown death. Among her relatives there were no deaths. Not any longer. That was all long before her birth. The dead don't die. For death she feels the pulse in her wrist, runs her hand over knife blades.

A brightly patterned apron. Later on, wearing aprons went out of style. That must have something to do with washing machines. She knots the strings of the apron together, winds them around the rail of a bunkbed—for the sake of drama I have to say: low-income hous-ing. The strings are not attached high enough. Her feet brush the ground. For a while her neck carries the marks of these strings. From the psychiatric point of view: an entirely normal suicide attempt.

~

Can't an empty heart find comfort in God the Father, the Son, and the Holy Spirit? By all means, says Pastor Becker, though not immediately. In four or five years, at the latest. But what's this busi-ness with the Holy Spirit? The spirit is closed to her, and in any case Jesus just wants her to be a human being. Nevertheless Pastor

Becker wants her to swear, even if her soul won't go along with it. Do you know the picture of pious Helen in the book by Wilhelm Busch? The final scene, where her spirit flies away?

The wafer tastes like paper. She never tried it again. This is the second time she's failed to escape being a Jew.

from *Maus II: And Here My Troubles Began*

BY ART SPIEGELMAN

Part III

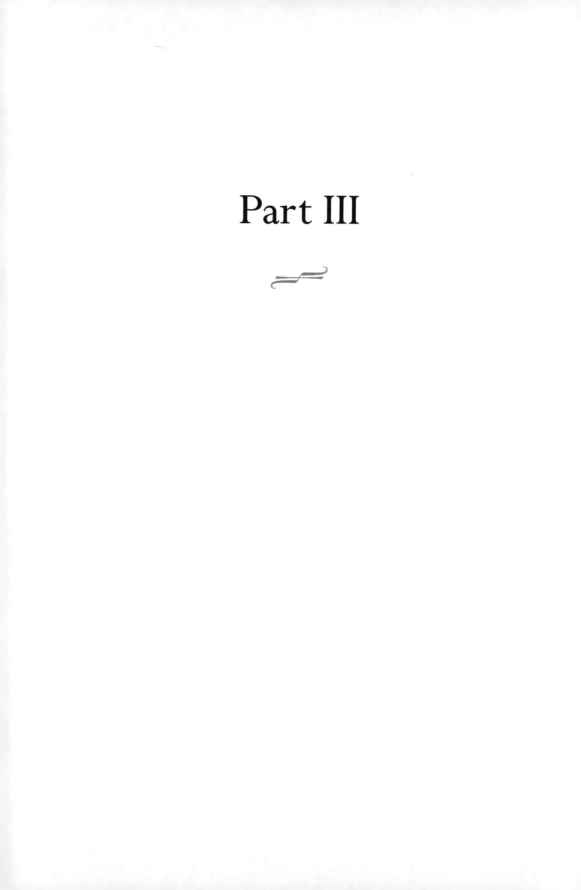

from *The War After*

BY ANNE KARPF

The Holocaust was our fairy tale. Other children were presumably told stories about goblins, monsters, and wicked witches; we learned about the Nazis. And while their heroes and heroines (I realize now) must have fled from castles and dungeons, the few I remember had escaped from ghettoes, concentration camps, and forced labor camps. Not that our parents' war recollections excluded other stories: we also had our Noddy, Hans Christian Andersen, La Fontaine, Hansel and Gretel, and the rest of the junior canon (I can vaguely recall), along with our father's own delightful invented tales. But no fictional evil could have possibly rivaled the documentary version so often recounted to us and our visitors.

How does a child cope with information about the past brutalization of its parents? What does it do with such knowledge? How does she process it, render it halfway tolerable? Perhaps it becomes another story. You mythicize it, structure it round the rhetorical devices and narrative features of the other fables you know.

I turned my mother's war into a story I could tell. All families make stories of their lives, at times sharing narratives, at others struggling over whose account will prevail. In my case I used my mother's life to enthrall and appall, milking it for drama by underplaying it. And it repaid the compliment by endowing me (in other people's eyes) with a kind of reflected martyrdom. I managed, through my retelling of my mother's Holocaust experience, to secure for myself a secondhand compassion. But it always left me with a slightly sour aftertaste.

Through constant recounting, my mother's story also acquired a kind of mythical quality. It was as if the narrative had taken on a life of its own, detached from the original events to which it referred. I found, curiously, that I could never remember those details of either of my parents' wartime experiences which fell outside my usual account. Right up until I transcribed the taped interviews with them for this book, I knew only the abbreviated drama I regularly told, and if anyone quizzed me, or tried to match it to historical chronology, I could never supply them with further information, and had the awful feeling that what I told might be untrue. It was as if my certainty about the story derived from my own repeated retelling rather than from the events themselves.

This may be because I hadn't experienced it firsthand and was still telling as an adult the version I'd first learned as a young child. Yet even after I'd recorded the taped interviews with my parents in my early and mid-thirties and pinned down precisely the whats, whys, whens, and how-did-it-feels, I soon reverted to the familiar, less detailed version I'd recited down the years. I probably remembered to the degree I found tolerable. But I was also clearly wedded to its storyness. It was as if I knew, somewhere, that the full account wouldn't quite support the version we proffered.

My family's working version of my mother's war was partial. We'd vacuumed everything intolerable from it (all sense of vulnerability and uncontrollable grief), we'd sheared it of helplessness and sorrow. She never depicted herself as abject (perhaps she never allowed herself to be), and admirably refused to be a victim.

Instead she—and so we—described the horror as though it were finite, denying that the war had any consequences beyond its immediate, obvious ones. It was as if we believed that the war could be cheated of its insistence that those who went through it should keep on paying. My mother's extraordinary resilience and exuberance made this seem plausible, with her new, postwar life as the putative happy ending.

My mother's story as told by us was triumphal; its organizing principles were heroism and survival. Through the narrative process, we made the Holocaust bearable: we used dramaturgic skills to anesthetize her trauma.

Whenever, over the past few years, I've gone to conferences and lectures on Holocaust survivors and their families, I've been maddened by the way they so often fetishize talk, as if the key factor determining the psychological health of both parents and children was whether the parents had spoken about their experiences to their children. But there are different ways of talking.

What made it all the harder was the historicity of the Holocaust, the most documented atrocity of the twentieth century (and perhaps all time). Already, by the early 1960s, it was to some—albeit still limited—extent lodged in public consciousness through iconic newsreels and photographs as well as print. But for us it was also biography. The Holocaust had become enmeshed in our parents' personal subjectivity and was part of the family tissue. Verbally or non-verbally it was recruited into arguments, enlisted as a rationale, brought out in admonition. And so it lost its otherness, its status as objective fact: it joined the living matter of our family, where powerful, often wayward feelings inevitably resided. The Holocaust was epic, but for us it was also domestic, and this confusion of the two made any commonplace adolescent cussedness seem monumental, as if we were cocking a snook at anguish.

I lied to my parents when I first met P. The fact that I'd met an attractive and interesting man would be as nothing, I knew, next to the fact that he wasn't Jewish. I was twenty-seven, but felt as if I were leaching poison into the family milk, or like a law-abiding citizen committing a first burglary—heady but utterly culpable. What increased the sense of danger was that P, though divorced, was available, unlike the married men I'd tended to have affairs with before, whose attachment had relieved me of any need to divorce my parents.

I was nauseous for two days after our first meeting, sick with excitement but also something else. My sister and I had always known that something awful had befallen our parents before we were born, and our unstated mission was to assuage its impact—we were somehow charged with their redemption. But it seemed that I was now about to renege on this duty, to rend instead of mend, and I was certain that it would excite an enormous anger.

So it did, when I told my parents about P, three months later. My mother, apprehending (among what seemed to her a job lot of defects) his worst, told me I was doing what Hitler hadn't managed to—finishing off the Jewish race. And this only confirmed the desecratory feel of the relationship.

An intense conflict developed, both in me and between me and my parents. I felt as though I was racked between them (whom I was desperate to sustain) in one corner, and in the other the possibility of unprecedented intimacy.

I chafed at my mother's stony disapproval, at her repeated barbs and homilies. My parents often told a cautionary (and possibly apocryphal) tale about a non-Jewish husband, quite happy to go along with his Jewish wife's desire to bring the children up as Jews until one of the kids has a life-threatening fever, whereupon the husband whisks him out of bed and takes him off to a priest to be baptized. When the chips were down, they told us, you couldn't trust them.

At the same time there was my own experience of P, charming, kind, funny, and apparently trustworthy.

I tried repeatedly to reconcile these warring views until, eventually, it all extruded through my hands, unerring somatic proof (the body being an incorrigible punster) that I couldn't in fact handle it. Beads of moisture appeared, trapped beneath the skin, on the palm of one hand, and with them came a compelling urge to scratch. Then I started to claw at my left hand with the nails of my right until the blood ran. This mania of scratching continued until the whole surface of the hand turned raging, stinging scarlet and there came, despite the wound (or perhaps because of it), a sense of release, followed almost immediately by guilt.

This sequence was repeated many times until the palm was florid with yellow and green crests of pus. The other hand also became infected. They seemed like self-inflicted stigmata, visible and so particularly shaming. I hid my hands in public and dreaded social situations, using the healthier hand as far as possible, even if it seemed clumsy and unnatural. And when I resorted to a gauze bandage, I lied about the reason. (But why did people feel entitled to ask? Why did every little plaster need to be publicly accounted for?)

With my parents and P I brooked no talk about my hands or the scratching, insisting (like an alcoholic or drug addict) that soon I'd be able to control it. Eventually, after months of misery, I reached crisis point. I was at a conference, and the effort of avoiding my hands being seen became so overwhelming that I went home and cried and thought that maybe it wasn't all my fault after all, and perhaps in any case I might be helped.

So I went to the dermatologist my parents had been urging me to see, and he looked at my infected hands with horror, and ignored my protestations of guilt, and treated it just like some mechanical failure, and when I tried to draw attention to the underlying distress, he pooh-poohed it, saying, "How could an attractive young woman have reason to be stressed?"

And I went away with his potions and emollients which did the trick, and I was cured. (I had to soak my hands in purple liquid twice a day, then coat them with greasy ointment and wear white cotton gloves. I couldn't even wash my hair myself, so P did it, gently and without complaint.)

As time passed, my parents' hostility to P diminished. His commitment to me, and his interest in Jewish culture, were apparent. He became assimilated into the family, invited to family events and reunions. My mother even gave him a yarmulke for Christmas. Eventually we decided to live together; we made a home.

But the eczema revisited. This time it couldn't be attributed to parental disapproval. And this time the scratching and subsequent infection of my hands were even more virulent. Once again I tried to hide it. Once more, after a long delay, I visited the dermatologist who prescribed his nostrums. And again he eliminated my every symptom.

Apart from the hands business I relished cohabitation, despite the new problems it ushered in. In the past I'd managed my fear of loss preventively, by not having: you couldn't lose something you'd never had in the first place. But now that I'd admitted an other into my life, I did have something to lose and was convinced that its removal was imminent. If P didn't return at the precise hour that he'd said he would, I'd immediately pace the flat, constructing tableaux of catastrophes. And many times, between the first ring of the telephone and the picking up of the receiver, I buried him, just as I'd buried my parents so often down the years. I dealt with the fear of loss by anticipating it, as if preemptive grief might somehow exempt me from the real thing, or perhaps you could accumulate credit in mourning, to be cashed in in the event of future bereavement. Since I was convinced that, when it came, the pain of losing someone would be intolerable—I assumed all deaths were epic, tragic, and aberrant— I hoped that down payments might diminish its eventual force.

Winning over my parents to accept P had in some way proved easier than winning over myself. Despite the external changes in my life, there'd been no abating of the sense of exclusion and insufficiency which I'd felt so powerfully in adolescence. I nursed such an unfailing belief that I couldn't have or join that it was almost as if I couldn't tolerate plenitude should it choose to visit, which it now appeared to be doing. After any really good experience I immediately expected a bad one—a swift retributive blow. (If it didn't arrive, I usually supplied it myself.) And long after my parents' initial disapproval of P had evaporated, I often stared at him while he sat reading or watching television, and felt him to be utterly unavailable: he wasn't allowed.

Indeed, whenever too much pleasure threatened, I felt guilty. P was astounded at my capacity for tolerating discomfort, for sitting in unheated rooms or under glaring central lights, perching on the end of the bed for hours on end without back support, and commandeering myself to do things—almost as if I found something reassuring in self-denial, a certain comfort in discomfort. He, by contrast, was a playful person, and exceptionally attuned to his physical needs.

I burdened myself to the limit by embarking on a two-year part-time postgraduate degree, to be done alongside my full-time work. In the summer of the second year when it was almost completed, we took a month's holiday in Italy, but I needed a liter of wine for every few hours of enjoyment. Otherwise, all was inexplicable anxiety, especially first thing in the morning. I also reexperienced the out-of-the-body sensations of my schooldays. These reactions seemed so unwarranted that I harangued myself with "How can you feel bad on holiday?" (a faint, but unwitting echo of "How could you feel bad if you weren't in a concentration camp?").

We returned and I finished my dissertation with the conviction that life thereafter would finally be perfect. But two things happened instead. One was a growing conflict with my parents. This time there was no obvious cause. My life from the outside seemed far more like that of my contemporaries than at any previous period. I was now in my thirties, living with my lover who was accepted by my family (although, like my sister, I was still phoning home every day). I had my work, my friends. Yet I would get into adolescent disagreements with my parents that left me enraged. The slightest thing would set me off: I ranted, I seethed, and finally I begged forgiveness. The pattern was repeated almost daily, and I was usually the aggressor, exuding belligerence, steaming with bile, as if out to pick fights in the misguided hope that I might, now, at last, win them.

The second thing preventing nirvana came from that eloquent spokesperson, my body, whose protests were once again epidermal. They started off as modest dry patches of skin on the inside of my elbows. But my response was brutal: the venom which had been loosed on my hands was now vented on to the larger canvas of my arms, and I began to attack my body. Paradise was proving elusive.

One day after yet another bruising telephone row with my mother I made an appointment to see a psychotherapist. It seemed an enormously bold step—it was not part of our culture. My parents and their friends prized self-reliance and regarded seeking help as an admission of failure. Plenty of people I knew were in therapy (eventually, in my part of North London, almost everyone I met turned out to be either analyst or analysand) but my fantasies of psychotherapy were wholly punitive—a forbidding, aging, paternalistic man hovering out of sight behind the couch, exposing undreamt-of badness.

The initial few weeks were a revelation. It had never occurred to me that there could be two different perspectives—my parents' and mine—coexisting in the world and that mine might be perfectly legitimate. I had no inkling of the possibility of, let alone necessity for, psychological boundaries, places beyond which others couldn't enter without invitation, and so naturally it had never dawned on me that I might be entitled to them. To me, private had always been equivalent to secret: my parents were coterminous with me—we were unicellular, an atom. Now fission was being proposed.

But alongside these discoveries, the scratching intensified. It was now turning into some private, shameful, almost erotic release. I tried desperately to police the urge to scratch but it was always stronger. Then, heart throbbing, I would tear at my arms until the blood ran and the carpet was stippled with skin. In its violence it was like the shower scene in *Psycho,* and as it subsided I felt like a murderer after a frenzied, uncontrolled attack. But as yet I had no clear sense of whom I was trying to kill.

Soon, other parts of my body joined my arms as targets, and these sessions of self-injury were taking place every day. As I moved further and further from my previous sense of equilibrium (however precarious and illusory), I tried to coerce myself back to physical and mental health. To no avail.

The therapist talked about anger directed inwards, and tried to get me to empty it over her, even inviting me—symbolically—to scratch her. But while I had some intellectual understanding of the concept of transference, I couldn't recognize any anger in my feelings towards her, nor even in the scratching. In fact I had no idea what frankly faced anger felt like at all; it was a flavor I had never knowingly tasted.

I began to feel uncomfortable almost all the time. My body became a prickly thing, constantly drawing attention to itself. I wanted to divest myself of my skin, slip out of it like a starched dress left standing, while my self crept away to hide. The therapist, arguing that skin marked the frontier between I and not-I, suggested that perhaps for me that frontier had never really existed, and now I was trying to scratch what little there was of it away. Indeed, my skin no longer seemed able to keep what was inside in. I struggled to present an unagitated, unblemished face to the world, but my body mutinied. At night I had dreams of pulling away peeling wallpaper from the walls, exposing cracked and uneven plaster beneath.

My rage towards my parents, interned for decades, began to venture out, and it felt utterly consuming and murderous. The scratching extended upwards, into view, on to my neck. Sometimes even my eyelids and the skin under my eyes turned red and scurfy too, and had to be scoured furiously. But if my unconscious self was trying to articulate its distress, it spoke in a language my conscious self couldn't comprehend, much less converse in. Indeed I invested a lot of energy in hiding what was going on, simulating normalcy despite wearing dark glasses in winter and long sleeves in hot summer. I was usually scarved to the chin, sometimes with my head so immobile because of my now permanently sore neck that I must have looked as if I were frightened of it falling off.

Though convinced of the utter iniquity of my self-mutilation, at the same time I was almost disinterestedly fascinated by the serum and scabs which formed daily and which I daily destroyed. It seemed vaguely fitting that my outside was now beginning to look as scabrous as my inside must have felt for so long, though I was far more aware of the need to prevent any of the inside badness seeping out. Yet it never occurred to me to reduce my work or social activities in any way. On the contrary they intensified: at one time during this period I was writing three weekly columns, as well as doing other freelance work and broadcasting, all between regular bouts of scratching and while feeling almost constantly abject. A runner up to a journalism award (for work done in Year Two of misery), I attended the awards ceremony with thick pats of makeup to conceal my scarlet, flaky eyes. I permitted myself no respite from going and doing.

But at the same time none of my former palliatives seemed any longer to work. Quite soon after starting therapy I learned that I'd gained a distinction in my M.Sc. In the old days this kind of achievement would have pumped me with confidence and vitality; now it barely registered. I focused entirely on my symptoms—all I wanted was for them to go away. It was as if I'd pressed the piano pedal which shifts the keyboard, and nothing any longer was in the right place.

Yet I was never tempted to return to the dermatologist. I knew that if I did so without facing the underlying reasons for the problem, the symptoms might disappear for a few years but then they would surely reappear. So I went instead to a homeopath. I also realized that, beyond the symptoms, there was no returning to my former self: it would not be able to contain my insistent, dissonant new emotions. Through all my despair (which was considerable, often overwhelming), I maintained some sort of small, vague, but palpable long-term hope that I would eventually emerge healthier.

Although close friends knew what was going on, I managed to conceal it from colleagues and professional contacts. Occasionally, to acquaintances I thought might be sympathetic, I referred obliquely to an "emotional crisis." A colleague at a party, after getting me to elaborate, told me that I was the only person she knew who could relay such a tale with a broad beam on her face. (That, of course, was part of the problem.)

In my search for the instant solution I tried a bioenergetics weekend. I'd never had much time for touchy-feely therapies—partly through fear, but also because I was drawn to the more orthodox one-to-one psychotherapy I was now in. Gestalt cushion-bashing and primal screaming in the company of ten other neurotics seemed to me far too embarrassing and parodiable (as well as intolerably ununique).

But, early on the first morning, when the therapist invited anyone who wanted to work on something particular to step inside the circle, I found myself volunteering. And through carrying out some simple but tiring physical gesture again and again, I began to sob and cry so uninhibitedly about being bad that it must have seemed as if I were an old hand in the self-exposure business. Secretly I was a little proud of myself, and it was genuinely cathartic. Yet it also left me with absurd fantasies of an instantaneous "cure." I'd seen so many Hollywood movies about repressed traumas solved after a single dramatic therapeutic revelation that I really believed that my problems too might immediately right themselves. It worked in Hitchcock's *Spellbound,* so why not with me? But it wasn't to be.

My parents, meanwhile, were bewildered by my growing disintegration, and dealt with it by ignoring it. On one occasion we arranged to have lunch in a Czech club in West Hampstead, I arrived grim-faced after a scratching session, bundled in scarves barely hiding a bloodied neck, my arms stiff and purulent. But my parents acted as if everything were quite normal, even trying to quip their way through the lunch, though this only served to inflame my rage, because by now I desperately wanted them to acknowledge my distress.

Yet I craved something they were in no position to give. We were so undifferentiated, so merged that what one felt, all felt: it was as if we held shares in each other's dejection and delight. If they admitted my despair, they would in some sense be experiencing it themselves. And they'd had quite enough of their own.

(Indeed, when, a few years earlier, my sister had lain in a hospital bed, miscarrying her first child at twenty-four weeks her overriding preoccupation had been not her own distress, but how she was going to tell our parents and how devastated *they* would be.)

In some inadmissible way I think I gained a grim satisfaction from my wretchedness. If children always try to compete with their parents, in this case it had been no contest: we knew, from the first, that our mother's suffering would always exceed, and be more legitimate than, ours—her experience rendered everything else petty. But now I had some misery of my own, and I wanted to force them to acknowledge its existence and authenticity.

After years of my scratching, a close friend asked whether the place on my inside forearm that I was repeatedly injuring wasn't the same place, indeed the very same arm, where my mother's concentration camp number was inked. I was astonished—it had never occurred to me. But I couldn't believe that the unconscious could go in for such crude symbolism, the kind you find in made-for-TV movies—it seemed like a base attempt to endow my own flimsy desolation with historical gravitas and dignify it by reference to my mother's. (I remain unconvinced.)

On the other hand, years later, when my daughter was in nursery and my arms long past healed, a little friend of hers gave her mother a transfer. As we were leaving the nursery the next day, the mother pulled up her left sleeve to reveal laughingly the transfer in that same place on the inner elbow. I gasped, shocked that such a part of the

body could be thought innocent, and that a tattoo—however temporary and childish—could be applied in jest.

While the therapy was starting to validate all kinds of states and
emotions, it was also freeing a terrible sense of anxiety, which
struck most forcibly first thing in the morning when my defenses
were probably still slumbering. It was a primitive, terrible feeling of
unsafeness. I tried to scratch it away.

By now I could scarcely get out of bed, let alone out of the house;
I was caught in a spiral of distress. Despite all my attempts to control
myself, the scratching came to stand for the recalcitrant part of
myself, those particles which refused to comply and which I was no
longer able to extirpate. At the same time my attempts to expel my
parents from a zone where they had no place to be seemed like a
giant act of aggression, which would surely be punished. I was all
anger, and simultaneously frantic to protect my parents from my
rage. I felt bad about feeling bad, which made me feel even worse.

I had two recurring fantasies. In one I was like a jelly which
hadn't set: if you took away the mold I just dribbled away. The jelly
mold seemed to embody the rigid, prescriptive side of me—the
unyielding bully who kept me in check, myself as Nazi. But without
it I felt utterly uncontained, as though I wouldn't cohere. The other
fantasy was of being in a vast, dark vat, on to whose sides I was clinging for dear life. If I let go, I would surely drown.

The therapist identified a life-and-death struggle. In some way
this was gratifying—it *did* feel as if my crisis was somehow about my
ability to survive, and to have her acknowledge this without derision
or disapproval (I wasn't in a concentration camp, so how could I possibly be struggling to survive?) was itself extraordinary, and pro-
foundly legitimating. Yet I couldn't help believing that such thoughts
were blasphemous. There were no real threats to my life, at least not
external, but my mother's life had been full of them.

I became increasingly inert. My posture, which had never been
great, deteriorated. My shoulders were now permanently hunched
over, as if I wanted to fold myself up into a ball and roll away. Since

most of the sensations I was experiencing were so ghastly, I longed to be insensate. It seemed as though I'd receded into a small corner of myself.

I also discovered in myself great sumps of despair, and began to comprehend my old excessive jollity: it must have served as protection against a flood of anxiety and depression.

My parents and I were now mostly locked in combat. My father dismissed any kind of self-scrutiny as "philosophy," my mother refused to allow that my difficulties might in any way be connected with her experience, as if such a link would constitute some criticism of her. "I survived the war and I didn't have to see a therapist," she would sometimes say, sending me delirious with rage.

But very occasionally I saw another side of my mother, what I thought of as her adult mode. It was so unreachably sad that I actually preferred the taunting, battling side, however bad it made me feel.

I also began to see what a talky lot we were, how much we busied ourselves with words and feats, how intolerably empty we found silence.

And I had the odd, astonishing, drunken glimpse of some possible future time when my behavior might match my feelings, where what I showed was what I thought, not what I thought I should think. I even fantasized about being rude.

Already I was getting slightly bolder in my relationships. I'd always been an affirmer: if somebody in conversation said something foolish, I'd readily join them in their foolishness—I could tolerate my own concealed embarrassment better than open disagreement or the unsupportive role. But about six months into my therapy, at a planning meeting of a TV series for which I was a consultant, a producer came out with the kind of half-baked comment which she made regularly and with absolute confidence. And this time, instead of endorsing her platitude, I found myself feeling detached: she rambled on and I let her travel alone. Of course no one else noticed, but observing my own reaction and fearing that I might lose my nerve, I silently cheered my decision not to accompany her. It was a totally novel feeling and an exhilarating one.

A year later I was at a dinner party with some young people whom I'd met on holiday and hardly knew. I realized instantly that one of the other guests was Jewish. Halfway through the evening another man, who lived in Golders Green, made a comment about the oily people he saw around him on Saturday mornings. My eye caught that of the other Jew, who then looked away. The conversation, after a short embarrassed silence (our hosts knew there was at least one Jew present), started up again, but I felt my heart palpitating and knew that I must speak. I turned to the man directly and asked him what he meant. Before he had a chance to reply I told him that I was Jewish and that his comments had made me feel uncomfortable.

I hardly heard his answer, as he tried to extricate himself; I only knew that I'd confronted someone directly. Later on in the evening, sluiced with drink and dope, I had a panic attack: feeling sick and anxious I glanced round for someone to look after me, but no one seemed suitable. I think my modest little action had terrified me.

But such changes were slow, and overshadowed by something devastating which happened in the meantime: P and I split up, seemingly over an affair he was having.

The real reason, I was convinced, was that what he saw when I finally allowed him close was too terrible—I imagined him like someone in a Ralph Bateman cartoon running for the exit, crying, "One glimpse of what's in there is enough." In fact our split, though overdetermined, certainly wasn't due to an excess of intimacy. The opposite in fact: mired as I was in my own misery, I was now no longer emotionally accessible in any way.

After the breakup I felt worse than ever. It was as though someone had pulled away a vital, plump internal organ and left a desiccated hole. My parents, having denounced him for causing me pain, refused to mention his name again. But I wouldn't acquiesce in this symbolic annihilation and, for the first time, allowed myself to feel misery in all its variety. Like a grieving Arab widow, I keened.

Until the Entire Guard
Has Passed

Translated from the Hebrew by Philip Simpson

From time to time he couldn't resist leaning over the rail of the balcony to peer at the path leading to his house. He still had some twenty minutes to wait, and the men didn't usually arrive early, although Dr. Mashiah, the dentist, was capable of popping up suddenly a quarter of an hour before the rest, eager as ever, his hat crumpled in his hands.

He smiled to himself nervously, and turned to inspect the living room once more. The two heavy armchairs had been moved against the wall, and the round table brought into the middle of the room, where the imitation-crystal hanging lamp cast a slight shadow on the navel of the room. A woollen army blanket, old but freshly laundered, was spread on the table meticulously. In the center, a new pack of cards stood to attention together with writing paper and a fountain pen carefully filled with ink. On the footstool stood the old fan, poised and ready to rattle the air. He glanced at the blanket once again and then left the rail and hurried to the sideboard. His gaze darted among the ornaments until he found what he was looking for. He placed a polished glass ashtray on the table and then returned to the balcony, swallowing his excitement.

Passersby walked down the street with hands clasped behind their backs, and children scampered among them. They sauntered down the street and back again. The intense heat of the Sabbath eve was still exhibiting lavish signs of dying, and most of the men were clad only in white vests and shorts. The children jumped about barefoot. Old women sat on rickety chairs outside their houses, flapping in vain at the fetid, steamy air with flowery sweat-soaked handkerchiefs.

His wife came in and he turned again to inspect the room. Sophie, who was in the final months of her pregnancy, dragged the four tall chairs to the table and smoothed the blanket from time to time. He didn't rush to help her. Instead, he leaned his elbows against the blazing rail and watched her with concern. Now she had only one housedress left—all the others were too small and stifled her stomach. He glanced at her belly, which stood out before her like a strange hill teeming with life, and a tiny thrill of delight ran about at the base of his spine, like an animal with multiple slender legs. They had been married about three years, but had decided not to have the child until they were properly established in the little carpentry workshop. And indeed, only when the old women who spent the summer days glued to the walls of their houses began to greet the meticulous and prompt carpenter and his delicate wife, hurrying to take him his meals even in the broiling midday heat—it was only then that Sophie had wanted to conceive, and he willingly consented. But the peak of social acceptance was when Baruch the upholsterer, to whom he sometimes brought furniture frames for covering, suggested that he become the fourth hand in the traditional card game, which was an established routine among several groups of players in the southern neighborhood. He remembered how his fingernail reddened with excitement on the frame of the bare chair, and he couldn't help wiping away his sweat with the back of a hand powdered with itchy sawdust.

He was already sufficiently versed in the ways of the neighborhood to know that the upholsterer's group, which should really be called the dentist's group, was the oldest and most respected. After Dario, the old porter at the electrical appliances shop, succumbed to a fatal heart attack—there had been much gossip as to who would be the fourth hand. The other member of the club was Samson the butcher, owner not only of his big shop with its modern and sophisticated cold-storage facilities, and the empty lot near the school, but also of the grocery store attached to the shop, which was leased to the tiny shopkeeper. Baruch the upholsterer was also known for spending his spare time repairing vehicles that had been written off as wrecks. With admirable determination, he often worked wonders, sending some rusty and wheezing old banger, bought with the limited savings of a soldier, racing down the road like a wild colt, with hooves flailing and nostrils steaming.

But presiding over the club was none other than Dr. Mashiah, the widower dentist, who lived above his little surgery and was widely respected for his gentle hands and modest fees. In particular, he earned the gratitude of mothers, because at the start of the school year he would lecture the schoolchildren on proper brushing and deficient nutrition. Not only that, but afterwards he would examine the mouths of the urchins free of charge.

Now Levi rubbed his callused hands with pleasure, and smoothed down his light shirt. Sophie had gone to work in the kitchen and he again turned his back on the room, scanning the street anxiously. Suddenly, a great fear crept, like a chilling blast of wind, onto his face, stiffening his sprouting stubble. The heat was unbearable, but that wasn't the problem. The game, which took place every Sabbath at the home of one of the players, was to be held for the first time in his house, and he wondered how he would manage to get past eleven o'clock. Usually the game finished at midnight, since all were early risers, but the critical time could be expected to come an hour before this, and suddenly he was no longer confident of the fortune that had seemed to smile on him till now.

Light taps on the door roused him, and he hurried to the entrance, greeting the old dentist with evident pleasure. Gradually the others appeared, scrubbed and perfumed and wearing neat white shirts, rubbing their broad hands together in keen anticipation, as if scenting a victorious run of cards. Sophie came in too, wearily smiling, moving ponderously, to greet the guests and to pour cold water with lemon slices into glasses. Her neck flushed at the compliments of the men on seeing her full stomach, infused with new life, and she made an effort not to spill water on the tray in her delight, hurrying away to hide in the kitchen.

The host pressed the button of the fan which hummed softly, and they all took their places round the table. The cards were distributed at first with slow deliberation, and then with growing momentum from round to round. The dentist, who loved to sing to himself, soon began humming softly while he deftly sorted his cards, and the butcher, though used to the distracting crooning, tried to set his fleshy face in a frown.

Levi smiled thinly and swiveled, in the intervals between his turns, to write down the names of the participants in the order they were sitting. From time to time he stared at his hand, at the accordion of cards alternately opening and closing, his heart singing the fourth verse. For two and a half hours the game proceeded smoothly, as the small sums of money piled up alternately in front of the host and the butcher. The dentist, who was used to losing because he was a poor player, didn't seem unduly perturbed, and he continued with his soft humming, although the upholsterer was visibly tense during the deal, and was often enraged at the sight of a desirable card tossed casually to one of the others. At around ten o'clock Sophie appeared again, bearing a silver-plated tray which exuded the smell of fresh baking, went away and returned with slices of moist cucumber, hard-boiled eggs freckled with paprika, and red cubes of sweet watermelon. As one, the four men threw their cards on the table, moved their chairs back in anticipation, and hastily set about the food. Levi glanced at his wife with satisfaction, seeing her sinking gently into one of the armchairs, her hands clasped contentedly around her stomach, reveling in Dr. Mashiah's sighs. The dentist was licking his thin and oily fingers like a child, before seizing another helping of juicy watermelon.

"Well done, Sophie!" The plump butcher was complimenting her now, sugary saliva running down his solid chin, his eyes moist with desire.

Only Baruch the upholsterer was bolting his food, as if eager to return to the table as quickly as possible and recoup his losses.

When the refreshments had been consumed, Levi helped his wife rise from the armchair, a line of worry etched between his eyes. Sophie ignored his look and approached with hands clasped to gather the dishes. When she returned for the third time—now with cups of fragrant coffee on a little tray which had muddy pools gathering at its edges—she was already fingering the tightly stretched button on her belly, and her movements were jerky.

"Perhaps you should go and rest, you look very tired!" suggested Dr. Mashiah, and she responded to his kindly eyes with awkward gratitude. "Yes, you should go and lie down," said Levi, a cautious threat in his voice. Then he glanced knowingly at the rectangular clock on the sideboard, expecting his wife, in extreme nervousness, to follow suit.

A soft pallor spread over Sophie's face, and her lips were clenched. Now she thrust her hands into the big pockets of her smock, stretching the tight cloth across her belly, which seemed to have swelled appreciably in the last hour. She shrugged her shoulders, in vain ignoring the penetrating looks of her husband, until she blurted a hasty "Goodnight" and all but fled from the room. The butcher, whose turn it was to deal, gathered the cards towards him very slowly, his worried eyes still preoccupied with the strange disappearance of the hostess. As he began shuffling the pack, he turned cautiously to the dentist, whose delicate fingers were tapping smoothly on the blanket.

"Maybe her time has come?" he asked hesitantly, with a meaningful glance at the carpenter.

The dentist shook his head, smiled, and gathered up his cards eagerly. Impatient to start the game and annoyed by the interruption, the upholsterer urged the carpenter, who was still a little stunned, to make up his mind and throw down a card.

"Come on! Come on! Let's get back to the game!" he urged, and Levi, startled, threw down one of his cards without even noticing its value.

He wiped away his sweat and looked fearfully at the butcher, but the latter was already ordering his cards, arranging his best sets, as usual, in the upper story, and, looking pleased with himself, he turned to seize the card thrown down for him in telling haste.

"What's true is true. A poker face you don't have . . ." the dentist teased, enjoying the sight of the butcher's childish face, while humming melodiously.

The butcher's hairy eyebrows rose for a moment in disdain, then he angrily ignored the words.

Levi took his eyes from them, but while still debating whether to peer at the clock again or to throw down another card distractedly, he was forestalled by the first handclap, sharp and loud. He swallowed his saliva and froze in midthrow, even though it wasn't his turn. A series of loud and harsh handclaps came rolling down in the wake of the first: a repetitive, staccato avalanche, assaulting the ears of the players. Trembling, he discarded a red queen, and peered at the others, startled.

For the moment they weren't troubled by it, with the exception of Baruch the upholsterer, who moved uncomfortably in his chair, his lips pursed. After a few minutes he couldn't restrain himself and he cried, "That's your crazy neighbor, right? Damn it! You can't even play a quiet game of cards round here!"

"What crazy neighbor?" hummed the dentist in amusement.

The upholsterer threw down his superfluous card angrily and explained. "My wife told me. The deaf old woman who lives upstairs, who hardly ever goes out. Three times a day she claps her hands for half an hour—without stopping! I don't understand how you can live here!" he uttered resentfully, the newly drawn card conciliating his voice a little.

Levi struggled with his vocal chords, until he heard his metallic mumble creeping out somehow—"You get used to it . . ." and then glanced sideways at the butcher, seeing the green number under the thick hair of his arm, lit up for a moment in the light of the lamp as he reached to snatch up the card thrown down for him. Taking courage he added, "It's because of the Germans. That's what she told someone . . . told me." He didn't know where his voice was coming from, but his lips continued to form the words. "The convent where she hid during the war was close to the SS headquarters. Every time the guard on patrol passed near the place, the nuns taught the frightened children to clap their hands until the entire guard had passed . . ." he whispered, flushed with shame. He looked again at the butcher, desperate for his understanding, but he only lifted dull eyes to the lamp, shrugged his powerful shoulders and said dismissively: "Nobody came out in one piece."

He hurriedly lowered his eyes in time, making an effort to decide which of his cards to throw down, but not one of his cards matched the others. For a moment he stared at the jumbled sets, and then closed the colored fan, as if by doing so he could stop his ears as well.

The dentist hummed sadly and laid a short set of clubs on the table. "It isn't so bad," he said. "I have a patient, an Auschwitz survivor, who's completely round the bend." He launched into a lengthy story, but Levi could hear only the beating of his heart, pursuing in vain the tempo of the handclaps, as stiff and as rhythmic as boots thudding on a parade ground. The upholsterer, whose luck had improved somewhat, waved aside the distraction impatiently, again urging the others to concentrate on the game.

Gradually the clapping subsided and faded, as it had begun—out of nothing. The clock ticked on to midnight, and the dentist rose from his chair, stretching gracefully, despite the considerable sum he had lost. The upholsterer, gratified by his victory, was still poring over the score. When he found that the butcher was in fact the over-all winner, he glowered, but began to share out the profits fairly. Now they all rose and went out to the balcony. The butcher stuffed the banknotes into his pocket with obvious impatience, and hung back a little from the others. The heat had subsided now, but the air was still humid and leaden, barely stirred by the lazy, intermittent gusts of wind rising from the sea. The dentist tried to take a few deep breaths, but the experiment only elicited a sour grimace from the upholsterer, who was wiping the sweat from the nape of his neck with a handkerchief.

At last the guests began to take their leave of the host, and the last to shake his rather tense hand was the dentist. His handshake was soft and consoling, like a woman's, and his eyes were kind.

"Tell Sophie that we enjoyed the meal very much, and many thanks. Next week—at my house, don't forget," he warned, taking his pale blue hat from the hook and softly closing the door behind him.

Levi's polite smile disappeared at once. Slowly he shuffled towards the living room, seeing the heap of cards on the table, the blanket which had slipped slightly, and the ashtray, black with water-melon pips. The coffee cups were encrusted with muddy grounds, and the lamp glared tastelessly. He switched off the light and the fan, and stepped dejectedly to the kitchen. Like an automaton he took two ice cubes from the freezer, found the little kitchen towel, wrapped the ice in the soft material, and turned to the bedroom.

Sophie was sprawled on the bed, her pallor melted into cold sweat, her hands hanging limp at her sides. Her large belly towered above her, concealing most of her neck from him. He approached the bed, trying in vain to dispel the wave of nausea that had assailed him, and turned over his wife's hands.

Sophie let him do this, as if she were a doll. The palms of her hands were red and hot, her flesh tingling like roasted meat. He enclosed a dripping ice cube in each of her tormented fists, and wrapped them both in the towel. Then he moved away from her and sat on the end of his bed, his back turned to her. From behind him he heard the whisper of the ice in her hands, and the rasping of the towel in turns.

Sophie's voice was hoarse.

"Did they say anything?"

Long minutes passed before he found an answer, deep in his seared throat:

"What do you think . . ." he began harshly. Then he withdrew a little, trying to sound casual as he added. "They talked about the neighbor. I think they believe it . . ."

Sophie didn't answer, and he knew from the sound of her frantic breathing that tears were streaming down her cheeks. Still he didn't turn round.

"I've asked you before," she began again in turmoil, "I've asked you before to tie me up, bind my hands with rope, with steel wire . . . at least when there are people here . . ."

He uttered a scornful sigh and half-turned towards her. "And what will you do instead? Beat your head against the wall?" His shoulders rose and fell wearily. "No, we've discussed it before. You're better off clapping your hands, that way at least you're not doing yourself any harm, they can think what they like . . ." Sophie began to wail like an abandoned cub, the towel making its way from her chilled hands to her wet face.

"Stop it! Stop it, that's enough!" he pleaded in despair.

"But it was so, so important to you . . . to be the fourth hand and . . ." she choked.

"I don't give a damn," he snorted, but his eyes were wandering.

"And what's going to happen, what's going to happen when the baby is born," she panted, gasping for breath. "How will he sleep? I'm a madwoman, a mad mother. I'd be better off dead!" She was groaning now, harried by spasms of weeping.

He rose stiffly, wrenched the damp towel from her face, and then, without any intending to, his hand shot out like an arrow and slapped her cheek.

Sophie's head slumped forward at once, lifeless, but a powerful shudder racked her stomach, and then her weeping resumed, soft and moaning.

"Quiet now, be quiet."

He straightened her trembling legs, raising the light blanket from her dominant, overweening belly, which was all-consuming.

Sophie curled up in the bed, her hands limp on her chest, her breathing still irregular.

"Go to sleep. That's enough for today. We'll sort it out," he concluded angrily.

He returned to his bed and continued sitting with his back to her for some time, until he realized she was asleep. He turned cautiously, and began to undress.

When he slipped into bed, he momentarily clutched her hand, soft as a cotton-wool cloud, intending to put it to his mouth. But he changed his mind, and the hand sank back sleepily and powerlessly onto the bed. He laid his aching head on the pillow, listening to her faint breathing. A yellow moon shone at the window, and by its light he could see the mighty belly, teeming with life. Suddenly it seemed to him he could hear the breathing of the embryo too, tiny and rapid. He smiled to himself, remembering what Dr. Mashiah had told him once.

"At this stage," the dentist had told him, "he's already smiling and frowning—even sucking a thumb! There's no doubt," he concluded pleasantly, "he's going to be a fine, healthy boy!"

A thrill of thin pleasure tickled him, its thousand feet wandering along his spine. Calmly he closed his eyes, slowly dreaming of his baby, and he is already as he himself was in his infancy. Plump and soft-haired, laughter rolling from his mouth, with two pearly teeth blocking a pink and greedy tongue. Sophie, close by him, distracted and sweating, clapping her hands to death. Fear reigns in her face, in the stamping black boots and the claws of the Alsatians. But look at the child, he too is clapping a soft, unsteady hand against its partner, clumsily, without coordination, and starting to dance around in his new white shoes. His mother is very far from him, but he—his tongue hanging from his mouth in a bold and spirited laugh, his head giddy and spinning—for a long time he turns and turns, clapping and clapping, until the entire guard has passed.

"Statement of the Officer for Accounts" from *The Inventory*

BY GILA LUSTIGER

Translated from the French by Rebecca Morrison

The Stamp Collection

On our day of arrival, toward one o'clock—I had just taken up my quarters and had almost finished unpacking—Vogt, a member of our unit, came into the room and announced that a convoy of Jews was approaching.

"They have come from Wilna," he said and added that we would be able to see them pass through if we left that minute.

We had chosen the school for our living quarters, since it had central heating and space enough.

Although the civil population certainly would not have objected—their impeccable attitude had been picked out for special praise several times in the circular that we received once a week—I did not believe that the Jews would be driven into the village.

Vogt, well known for his opinion, asked me if I wanted to watch the convoy.

His exact words were: "We should not miss this piece of theater."

Since I didn't have any urge to write the letter I owed my mother, I took my jacket down from its hook and went with him. Corporal Zink joined us.

We took a shortcut over the field, crossed a stream that was already freezing at the banks, and thanks to Vogt's spurring us on we reached the country road after a good quarter of an hour. They would have to come by this way, approaching, as they were, from the north.

We got there in the nick of time. We only just managed to group loosely around the boundary stone that marked the field when we already saw the convoy in the distance, rapidly approaching.

Roughly estimating, there were around three hundred people. They walked in rows of four. On every coat and jacket the yellow star was attached.

"A model convoy of Jews," said Vogt.

I nodded, for he was right. The convoy, comprising only Jews, was divided up conventionally, children at the front, then women, some with small children in their arms, their husbands of all ages taking up the rear. Almost all the Jews were reasonably well dressed, had shoes and coats, and carried small suitcases or bundles.

The convoy was supervised by SS men who walked in intervals of four, five, or perhaps six rows alongside the group. I can remember it distinctly, since there was undeniably a certain competence that would have saved me much work had it appeared in our unit.

At the rear of the convoy were four SS men who greeted us with a nod of the head, and Vogt shouted over a risqué joke about the BDM,* whom he referred to as the "Baby Distract Me," and they guffawed with laughter.

That was just Vogt's way. His big mouth had gotten him into trouble in the past and he would have long since been sent packing if he were not considered an excellent soldier in every other way.

Out of curiosity, and to discover whether there was a camp in the

* *Bund Deutscher Mädel*: League of German Girls.

vicinity—we had not heard of any but were aware that they were popping up like mushrooms all over the place—we followed them at a distance of thirty meters. After ten minutes they swung off the country road and turned left onto a small path.

Before we had gone a full kilometer we reached a deciduous forest. Vogt said it could not have anything to do with a camp: the escape possibilities were too great in this terrain, where it was hard to see what was going on and therefore impossible to control.

"You can't go putting ideas in their heads."

This sort of terrain, Vogt continued, would be asking for trouble. That was why a camp should be set up only on even ground, and then only if the area had been cleared of trees.

"If one of them rebels," said Vogt, "you'll soon have the whole rabble at your throat, and then you can kiss it all good-bye."

We came to a clearing, which resembled a building site. A companion from the SS standing over to one side and smoking a cigarette told us it was a petrol storage area that the Russians had built and kindly handed over. We laughed. He held out a package of cigarettes. We refused: we knew how difficult it was to get hold of cigarettes. The SS man told us not to be shy.

"Like the 'Baby Distract Me,'" he said to Vogt, and told us to help ourselves. He got a special ration for the job he was about to perform.

Corporal Zink asked what was going on here.

"Feel free to look around," encouraged the SS man, which we immediately did.

We crossed over the area. In the middle of the clearing a ditch had been dug. The convoy of Jews stood somewhat to the side of it. They had been ordered to drop their luggage and stand in groups of ten. The Jewish women and children were led into the forest. This resulted in some shouting from the families who were split up in this way—the men remained, as I said, standing in groups of ten.

"If they don't see it," the SS man confided to us, "it all goes more smoothly."

He was referring to the women and children.

Vogt, who had taken a camera with him, went to the edge of the hole and took a photograph looking into it at the corpses already there, and joining us again asked the SS man when they completed that lot.

"We shot them just yesterday," he said, adding that it had gone without a hitch and that he hoped today would continue without any unexpected incidents. He thought this was unlikely, however.

"Today there are also children and women," he said. "They turn wild as soon as they hear the first shot and start screaming. The mothers in particular," he went on, "can turn quite aggressive."

That's why, the SS man explained, having smoked his cigarette to the end, as he went to the ditch, they were led into the forest, so that they did not see it happening. The first ten men were led to the edge of the ditch. As they had tied their shirts around their heads and could not see anything, they advanced slowly. The first man held onto the truncheon held out to him by an SS man. The other nine—old ones were mixed in with younger ones—held on to the man in front of them.

When the first one reached the edge, the chain stopped. The SS man pushed the second Jew next to the first one. And so it went until they were all lined up next to one another.

Vogt said he thought this method was a time-waster—by the second lineup at the very latest the Jews would realize they were going to be bumped off, so they could forget that blindfolding business.

"You may be right," responded Corporal Zink, "but a glimmer of hope always remains. That's human nature. They think it can't happen to them, so the method is not unrefined."

I didn't have an opinion on all this, and listened attentively.

The first group of Jews was shot. The shots came in a volley of fire from ten SS men standing about twenty meters behind the row. The Jews fell into the pit. An SS man stepped forward, checked if there was anyone still moving in the pit, and in some cases gave an extra shot in the head.

The second row was set up at the edge of the pit. Vogt took a photograph of them, taking a step backward so that he could fit in all ten Jews. Five minutes later that group was shot dead and the third row stepped forward.

I was starting to get cold, and as I thought we had seen enough now, I asked if we shouldn't be getting back. Vogt replied that I could go if I wanted to, Zink too, but that he wanted to watch the women and was thinking of photographing them. Since Zink wanted to stay too, I stayed with my companions and lit my cigarette.

It must have the fourth or fifth group, when a man broke out of the line, tearing the shirt from his head, and ran toward us. It was an elderly Jew. He stood in front of us. In immaculate German, he rolled his *r* a little but that was it, he asked us what we wanted from them.

"I am just a watchmaker," said the Jew. He was trembling all over.

Vogt took a photograph of him.

"Jew facing death," he said, and took another photograph of the SS man beating him with his truncheon to the pit.

The Jew fell headfirst into the pit. Vogt asked if he could take a photograph.

"Yes," someone told him. "If you are quick."

They were already behind time, and wanted to do the whole convoy, including women and children, before it got dark. They did not have any searchlights to keep watch or to aim.

"Now I have him dead too," said Vogt when he came back.

Naturally things did not proceed as smoothly as the SS man had hoped. Some Jews had to be beaten up to get them to the pit. Others tried to escape and were shot on the spot. Lots of Jews hung white cloths around their shoulders and went praying to the pit. Those that were praying refused to blindfold themselves. The officer in charge permitted this, for they went without a peep to the edge of the pit. This was a sign of his ability to adapt to situations, invaluable in such an operation.

A middle-aged Jew threw himself at an SS man who, after the

Jew had been beaten back into his row by two other SS men with truncheons, shot him in the arms and legs that had touched the officer: when he collapsed he was shot in the stomach and thrown into the pit alive.

"Now he will die a wretched death," said Vogt.

Corporal Zink agreed with him and added that he had been a fool, as he had to die anyway.

"Surely it is smarter to die as quickly and as painlessly as possible, which can be the case only if the men have a chance to aim."

"Logic," answered Vogt, who had also photographed this incident, "is not their strength."

We stayed at the place of execution for two hours in all. I could no longer say how many groups were led to the pit's rim. In any case, the pit was filled almost to the top with piles of corpses.

The children had their turn before the women. They were allowed to stay dressed and also did not have to be blindfolded.

"There is no point," said the SS man, who was taking a break and had joined them. "They are afraid of the dark. We've tried it before, but it had the exact opposite of the desired effect. The children sank to the ground crying, and we had to polish them off there. A messy business."

Corporal Zink said that he felt sorry for the children. You could see the fear in their eyes as they cautiously stepped to the edge of the pit.

"Jews' children," responded Vogt. He was renowned for his candid opinions.

A boy around age eleven or twelve clung to a stamp album so tightly with both hands that it looked as though it was helping him stand up. He did not want to go and was prodded forward by an SS man holding a stick. The boy kept looking around him and shouting something I did not understand. Probably his special name for his mother, as the letter *M* was in it.

Lots of small children between the ages of five and ten had dolls or cuddly animals with them that they pressed to their thin bodies.

"They are simply allowed to take them with them?" asked Vogt.

"You try getting them to let go," replied the SS man.

"That is their obsession with possessions," said Vogt, thereby earning a disapproving look from Corporal Zink and myself.

The children really flew into the pit, the impact of the shot throwing their light bodies in the air. I had had enough and said I didn't want to wait for the Jewish women. Corporal Zink joined me. Vogt would not have found his way back by himself, so he had to leave too.

An hour later we reached the school. The way back had been longer, since we had lost our way several times. Night had fallen unexpectedly quickly.

I took leave of my comrades and found a restaurant where I was served right away and sat myself next to four fellow soldiers, who were just back from home leave. They had lots to tell. I drank two glasses of a brown bitter-tasting beer that was brewed in the area. After three hours or thereabouts, I returned to my room and hung up the rest of my clothing in the steel cupboard that I had been allocated.

from *A Blessing on the Moon*

BY JOSEPH SKIBELL

I

It all happened so quickly. They rounded us up, took us out to the forests. We stood there, shivering, like trees in uneven rows, and one by one we fell. No one was brave enough to turn and look. Guns kept cracking in the air. Something pushed into my head. It was hard, like a rock. I fell. But I was secretly giddy. I thought they had missed me. When they put me in the ground, I didn't understand. I was still strong and healthy. But it was useless to protest. No one seemed to hear the sounds I made or see my thrashings, and anyway, I didn't want to draw attention to myself, because then they would have shot me.

I was lying in a pit with all my neighbors, true, but I was ecstatic. I felt lighter than ever before in my life. It was all I could do not to giggle.

And later, as dusk gathered, I climbed out of the grave, it was so shallow, and I ran through the forests. Nobody saw me. I ran with the dirt still in my mouth. I had to spit it out as I ran.

When I got to our village, everything was gone. A dozen work-men were lifting all the memories into carts and driving off. "Hey! Hey!" I shouted after them. "Where are you going with those?" But they wouldn't stop. In front of every house were piles of vows and promises, all in broken pieces. How I could see such things, I cannot tell you.

A villager and his family were moving into our house on Nonie-wicza Street. Crouching behind a low wall, I watched them, a man and his sons, sweating through their vests. They packed and unpacked their crates, their shirtsleeves rolled up high, carting fur-niture in and out of our courtyard. Now and then, one would leave off to smoke, only to be derided by the others for his idleness.

I was afraid if they saw me, they would come after me. Still, I couldn't stand to see what they were doing. I called to them, my voice escaping on its own. I was shouting. I shouted their names. I couldn't help it. But they said nothing, merely continued with their hauling and their crates.

So I touched them. I grabbed onto their shoulders, I pleaded with them. At that, they crossed themselves and shuddered. They mut-tered their oaths. They were peasants. Superstitious. But otherwise, there was no response. And I realized I was dead. I was dead. But why was I not in the World to Come?

"Perhaps this is the World to Come."

The words came from a black crow sitting in an empty tree.

"Rebbe," I said. I recognized the voice as belonging to our beloved Rabbi. "How can that be?" I said. "Strangers are moving into my house. You yourself are a crow. How is it possible this is the World to Come?"

"Be grateful," he squawked. "Rejoice in your portion."

And he flew away.

I felt worse than before. I had nowhere to go. Still, nobody could see me, what would it matter if I went home, if I entered my own house? Why not sleep in my own bed? So back to our court on Noniewicza Street I go. In through the front door. They didn't even bother to lock it. I stand in the foyer, peering into the various rooms. I clear my throat to announce myself, but there's no doubting I'm as invisible as air.

The family is sitting around the dining-room table. They are people I know, people I have traded with. Eggs sometimes, bread, linens, goods of this sort. "Look how nice everything is," the Mama says to her sons, clapping her hands in delight. "So beautiful, Mamuśku, so beautiful," a daughter says, but she is the one they never pay attention to, and the eldest son says over her, "A toast! To our home and to our table!" The father's face beams with pride.

Upstairs are three more sons, big snoring lummoxes, asleep in Ester's and my bed. Fully clothed they are, with even their boots on.

It's like a fairy tale from the Mayseh Book!

The rooms are filling up. And where can I sleep? They've invited all their relatives to come and settle in. No one is in the nursery and so I sleep in Sabina's little bed with my feet sticking over the edges. The bed we've kept from when her own mama, our daughter Edzia, was little and slept in the nursery as well.

Outside the window, the Rebbe pecks on the shutters to be let in. I open the sill as quietly as possible. "What was that?" a groggy voice from Lepke's old room echoes down the hall. "Mamuśku, the bed is so big, I'm swimming in it," one daughter cries. "Everyone to bed, to bed!" the Mama calls out, cross. The Rebbe circles the room, walking from side to side, his wings behind his back. "Chaim," he says. "Your legs, they stick out over the edges." I sigh. He settles onto a pillow near me. He tucks his head into his breast.

I wake up and the sun is black beneath a reddened sky. My head is pounding and my eyes hurt against the light.

Downstairs, the Serafinskis are exchanging gifts over breakfast, various things they have found in their rooms during the night. The table is festive with ribbons and all the colored packages. "Papa, oh Papa, thank you so much," the plump daughter says, leaning over the table to kiss her father. The shift she has slept in opens and her small breasts are momentarily revealed. "Don't disturb your father while he eats!" her Mama scolds. But she herself is made so gay by Ester's pearls, which gleam around her neck, that she cannot stay mad for long.

There are pigs now in the shul, and goats. They mill about, discussing methods of underground resistance. I'm amazed I can understand their language. "Can we rely on the villagers for protection?" one of the pigs says, his voice quavering with rage. "Think again, my friends," a goat warns, shaking his grey beard, although none of them seems convinced.

I recite the morning prayers outside in the town square, then sit on a bench and throw bread crumbs to the Rebbe.

"Hamotzi lechem min ha-aretz," he squawks out the blessing before pouncing on the little I have been able to find for him. He hops onto my shoulder and cackles reassurances into my ear. He turns his head, squinting through a hard yellow eye, to judge the effect his words have on me.

I nod, I listen, but only from habit. I'm too numb to really hear.

"And will you migrate, Rebbe?" I finally ask. "Do crows migrate?" The question has been burdening my heart.

"God willing," he caws. "With God's help. If it's God's will."

And he flies up to perch on the ledge of a high roof, spitting a shrill cry from his throat.

2

The Rebbe is not his usual self, that much is clear. Before, you could always see him, dashing through our narrow streets, his black coat flapping behind him, a holy book clutched against his spindly chest. He was everywhere at once, counseling, joking, wheedling, pressing Talmudic points into our children's stubborn skulls. Now, I crane my neck to look at him hopping about the roof of the Hotel Krakowski, his bonelike feet curling and uncurling around its rusted gutter pipe. How distracted he looks, how ruffled and how weary. He doesn't understand our new condition, I fear, or its dangers. Were it not for

a small collection of pebbles I've taken to flinging at them, for
instance, the Rebbe might easily have been devoured by any number
of neighborhood cats. "Shoo! Go away! Scat!" I cry. "Are you crazy?" I
shout at them. "Do you want to *eat* the Rebbe!" And they slink off,
chastened, licking their wounded paws.

The soldiers seem to like our town, with its sleepy squares and
the many bridges crossing its rivers. The worst of their work is over
and they can finally relax and enjoy their stay. I stroll among them
with my cane, searching for the ones who shot us, but their faces are
unrecognizable. Gone are the tight grimaces, the tensed piano wires
that stood up in their necks when they barked out their commands.
Now they are all sunniness and light, and even when they catch
someone hiding in a garret or a cellar, they are able to beat and kick
the poor wretch happily and shoot at him as though it were all a tri-
fling canard, without unpleasant yelling.

This is how it was with Lipski the butcher. The woman he had
traded his house to for a hiding place reported him at once. And who
can blame her? With Lipski curled into a circle below her staircase,
she was in danger and her family as well. But the soldiers danced him
out in that jolly way of theirs, flushing him so merrily from his hutch
and into the bright streets that even Lipski had to laugh, as they beat
his head into the curb.

In the late afternoon, a thin man in a homburg stands upon a
hastily erected platform to give a ringing speech. He congratulates
our town on its spirit of heroic cooperation.

"Never before . . ." he pounds his delicate fist against the podium.

"So often in . . ." he cries.

"Young men giving . . ." he thunders.

I try to listen, but the words are lost on me. The crowd pushes
forward eagerly. Men from the region's newspapers jot down notes
in little books, to print in their papers the following day. So busy is
everyone listening to the speech that no one notices a large black
bird swooping down, like a shadow, from the trees to peck at the
speechmaker's eyes. A purplish iridescent whirl descends about the

poor man's hat and he raises two bloodied fists to protect his shred-
ded cheeks. Those near to him laugh, once, as people will, before
realizing the true extent of his distress. Recovering their somber-
ness, they move in from all sides, offering their help. The mayor,
various townspeople, more than a dozen soldiers swat at the Rebbe,
but no one is able to stop him as he tears the man's finger from his
hand and flies towards the forests, a golden wedding band glinting in
his beak.

3

"Rebbe! Rebbe!" I run through the crowd after him, the guns shooting over my head. Away he flies, deep into the forests, far from our
little town. That I am able to run so fast, a man of my age, it's difficult to believe, even with the aid of my stick. The trees, black against
the darkening sky, scratch at my collar and tear at my neck. I keep
tripping over roots and stones, the forest is tangled and so dense.

"Rebbe," I shout up at him. "You have stolen something that
doesn't belong to you, something that must be returned! This isn't
proper!"

But on he sails, high above the treetops, ignoring my every word.

I follow him into a small clearing, where he begins gliding in circles, his wings long and stiff. He lands unsteadily near a small pond
and struts on his wiry legs to the water's edge. A twitch of his head
and the ring is tossed in with a gentle liquid *plink!*

"Rebbe," I say, laughing, "What a terrible thief you are! If you had
wanted to conceal your crimes, you should have dropped it from the
air above the middle of the pond. But now, let me see what have you
stolen."

I reach into the water.

The blues and the pinks of twilight stain the surface of the pond,
and through them I see, for the first time since I was shot, a reflection of my face. One side is entirely missing, except for an eye,
which has turned completely white. Barely hanging in its socket, it

stares at itself in an astonished wonder. My grey beard is matted thick with blood, and broken bits of bone protrude here and there through the raw patches of my flesh.

I look like a mangled dog carcass.

The Rebbe squawks.

"Why have you shown me this?"

"Chaim, Chaim, Chaim," he shrills in a piping tone. "Never in my life have I behaved like such an animal! What has happened to me? And look at you! Look what they have done to your face!"

"Rebbe," I say, "Rebbe," comforting him.

He caws softly. I suppose he is unable to cry. I nuzzle the top of his black head against my partial cheek.

Inside the ring, I see, is a small inscription. *To Johannes From His Margarite, Undying Love.* I slip it onto my finger so that I will not lose or misplace it before it can be returned.

Shadows gather in from behind the trees, inking the forests, until everything is black. Wolves snicker somewhere not far off. Together, the Rebbe and I offer up our evening prayers. He sits upon my shoulder and we walk home beneath a bright canopy of stars. . . .

8

The day is clear and crisp. The chilled smells of autumn fill the air. Lonely and with nothing else to do, nothing to keep myself occupied, I have come for a stroll in the forest. The sun pours its thickened light, like honey, through the trees. It must be nearing the month of Cheshvan, but without the moon, who can tell for sure?

I'm not certain what draws me here, to the mound the soldiers made when they covered our pit. I had worried the place might be difficult to find, but the ground virtually rolls and buckles from the bluish gases erupting in balloons beneath my feet.

Leaning on my cane, I lower myself and sit upon the mound. I haven't been here since I climbed out, scrambling over the edge, looking back only once, and quickly at that. Their bodies, still writhing, lay twisted in great heaps like so many pieces of a jigsaw puzzle, unassembled, on a parlor table.

The wind blows carelessly through the trees, tearing the leaves from their branches. I dig with my fingers, softly, into the dirt.

My lumber business used to bring me to all parts of the forest, but looking about now, I can't recall if I was ever here.

It's not a long walk from our house and yet it must have been more strenuous than I had at first thought, for suddenly, I find I have no strength at all and can barely remain sitting up. I lean over, lowering my ear to the ground, resting my head against it.

Faintly at first, but then more and more distinctly, I'm able to make out the sounds of Yiddish being spoken. How is this possible? I crawl about the mound, keeping my ear flat against it. Directly below me, mothers are clacking out tart instructions to their daughters. I nearly weep to hear it! To my left, there must be a cheder, for a class is clearly going on. The teacher remonstrates with his students, spitting out the alef-bais for the hundredth time. Below me, to my right, two men argue passionately. About what, at first it's difficult to hear. But so persistent are they, each one repeating his entrenched position over and over again, that soon I understand their disagreement concerns the price of trolley fares in Warsaw. I laugh, holding my sides with joy. I can't believe it. In a far corner, a deep voice drones a portion of the Mishnah in a lilting cantillation. How long has it been since I've heard the mother tongue!

"Landsmen! Landsmen!" I cry out to them.

"Who's that?" "Who is that up there?" "Reb Chaim, is that you?" The voices come at once.

"It's me! It's Chaim Skibelski!" I shout. "Is that you, Reb Motche? Who is that?"

"Reb Chaim, what are you doing out there?" Reb Motche asks me, amazed.

"I thought I'd visit you!" I say, laughing.

"You're alive then? Yes? You survived?"

"Not really, no."

"And the Rebbe?" another voice asks.

"One at a time, one at a time!" someone shouts thickly.

"He's well. He's alive, God be praised! He's well."

"Chaim?" Yet another voice.

"Yes, who is it?"

"This is Reb Elchonon."

"Elchonon! Praise God! How are you?"

"Reb Mendele and I have a question for you concerning trolley fares."

"And your family, Reb Chaim," his daughter Tsila Rochel interrupts him bluntly. "Where are they? We don't see them here."

"In Warsaw. Ester and my daughters are in Warsaw and in Lodz, and also my two sons. The others, of course, are in America, thank God."

After the Molotov-Ribbentrop treaty, I bundled Ester up and, together, we boarded the train for Warsaw. A city is safer, we thought, bigger, a Jew less conspicuous there. We'll be with our daughters, and besides, people are more civilized in a city, even the Poles. Unfortunately, we arrived only to discover that she had gone to Suwalk, our Mirki, in search of us! Our trains must have crossed paths, each on separate tracks. Immediately, I reboarded the train to bring her back, only to arrive in Suwalk on the night that the police went round, knocking on the doors where the soldiers slept, telling them where to go in the morning with their guns.

"Reb Chaim," someone calls up. "Why are we not in the World to Come?"

"The Rebbe will explain it when he returns," I say. "The important thing is to be of good cheer."

"Where *is* the Rebbe, Reb Chaim?"

I shout into the ground, "The Rebbe will explain everything, everything, when he returns."

How can I tell them that the Rebbe became a crow and flew away?

Letter from a Dogcatcher

BY LEON DE WINTER

Translated from the Dutch by Scott Rollins

G ood day.
It is cold outside. When I stand on my toes I can barely see out the small window and all I see is something grey. Is the window dirty or is the sky cloudy? For the last month now, at least when I stand on my toes, I've seen a grey surface interrupted only by iron bars. Just because I wrote *it is cold outside* doesn't mean that it is warm here inside, the exact opposite is true and I could have used the words *it is cold here inside* to begin. I must also note that I have actually misused the word *begin,* for in reality I began with the words good day, that is, the words good day were the first ones I wrote down on this paper. So, good day. Good day, Gentlemen. Good day to you all.

It is very hard writing with a numb hand. My left hand is lying flat on the paper and my right hand is holding the pen that scratches and makes splotches and which I'd rather put down on the table than keep holding with a cold thumb and forefinger. Yet I will not give up.

Now someone might get the idea (Gentlemen!) that the pen reminds me of a club but this is not true. Only the bad reader would arrive at that conclusion—seeing as I am a dogcatcher sitting here without a club and thus longing for such a piece of wood. Ha ha, but the bad reader does not know the first thing about dogcatching and what a dogcatcher feels and thinks. I'm not about to describe what happens during the course of a dogcatcher's day since I am directing myself to the good reader (Gentlemen!) who realized from the very outset of this letter that it is a dogcatcher who speaks and who devotes himself to evoking the atmosphere and local surroundings of dogcatching. Very good, Gentlemen! Good day!

It is cold outside. Here inside, in any case, it is not warm. As far as I can recall it has either been cold or warm, but not once have I not noticed the weather. Georg was different, Georg never once let on about the weather even though he was outside all the time—he was a dogcatcher and therefore dependent on the weather, I mean, it's no fun trudging around in the snow with a club in your hand tracking the prints of dog paws. So I could have begun this letter with *Georg was not bothered about the weather* and as a second sentence I could have written, *Georg was an old man whose profession was dogcatching, though the older he got the more he neglected his work.* The bad reader might construe from this sentence that Georg was a competitor of mine or a thorn in my side. The good reader, on the other hand, will understand and quickly intuit that Georg lived in Friedrichgasse, where I live too, and that Georg was my teacher. You (Gentlemen!) understand that I wish to address you concerning Georg; besides, concerning what else could I address myself to you, for the only other thing I can tell you is that when I stand on the tips of my toes and look through the window I see something grey but indistinct. But you must take it from me that when I was young I deeply admired Georg and would have loved to have ridden shotgun with him through the alleyways and streets. He set an example for me, so to speak. I must admit that I did follow him on his rounds a couple of times, but that was strictly to learn about dogcatching and not, as had been insinuated at the time, to spy on him as he stood urinating against a fence somewhere. (If I wanted to spy on someone urinating against a fence, I'd do better following Seipe whose bladder is always ready to burst and who is blind as well.) It was truly to find out more about Georg's technique, for he had a powerful stroke. Of late, however, his ability to react has proven insufficient. This is because of his eyes which have deteriorated rapidly and several times I have seen him hit and miss, which for a dogcatcher is the same thing as losing a ship is to a sea captain (I don't know how I came up with this analogy, I've never even seen the sea and have never spoken to a sea captain. You should just ignore this sentence). I'll state it clearly: I admired Georg but knew his shortcomings and thought it my unshakeable duty to write a letter to the City Council in which I pointed out that our municipality had need of a youthful dogcatcher better able to remove pestilent, abandoned strays from our streets, better able than a myopic old man who, however valuable and skillful he may once have been, had on a single occasion even struck a child with his club. Other than that I have nothing but compliments concerning Georg, may he rest in peace.

My offer was reasonable, wasn't it? I would have been satisfied with the same salary Georg had received and Georg could have been put on retirement. The rents are low in Friedrichgasse and the old man could get by on beans, potatoes and every once in a while an egg. You (Dear Sirs!) can rest assured that my only concern was for the sanitation of the city when I mailed the letter to the City Council. Sitting on the buckboard of a wagon with the reins and whip in your hands, the club within reach would merely have been a fringe benefit. You read it well: fringe benefit. I had already drawn up a plan which, had it been put into effect, would have rid the city of sickly stray dogs within a month. In the time I am standing here on tiptoe trying to determine just what the grey is (cloud cover, dirty window, grey surface), the city could once again become the jewel it once was before Georg's demise.

I saw his dying day approaching weeks in advance. I had indeed known his end was coming some time before his death. The bad reader (No, not you, Gentlemen!) is probably asking himself now why I didn't say anything to Georg about this. No, bad reader, you don't understand—I kept nothing from Georg and Georg himself knew his hour of death was near. Even after the initial blows I could immediately point to the howling of a dog that could be heard coming from his apartment one night, wrenching the stars from the sky, as an omen of his impending death. The question he put to me the following morning was just as unnecessary to him as it was to me. This question went as follows: (I do not wish to keep anything from you, Gentlemen) Did you hear a dog howling last night who, judging by his moans, must have been severely wounded? You read it, this question is pointless and Georg was well aware of this himself, but the question's significance and its eventual answer were wholly subordinate to the look in his eyes. And this look, as the good reader understands, is indescribable. Every now and then a comparison does a good job, though not a single comparison could do proper justice to this look; at any rate, in this case it is impossible to find words that could aptly describe what Georg's eyes were saying then. Like a weasel's? No. Like a drowned man's? No. Like a man who realizes his hour of death has revealed itself to him but who fearfully tries to ignore it? Almost yes, but not quite. It's a pity that in the meantime Georg is dead and buried, otherwise I'd have invited you to come over to Friedrichgasse one night to listen to the dog howling and see the look in his eyes on the morning he asked me that question. "Did you hear a dog howling last night who, judging by his moans, must have been severely wounded?" was the question which I repeat for the bad reader's sake (not for yours, Gentlemen!).

What I expected would happen happened: the howl of a dog could be heard regularly coming from Georg's apartment which kept the whole alley awake at night. Blind old Seipe, who also lives in Friedrichgasse and whose power of hearing is quite acute, said the sound that kept him awake at night had the quality of barking but it was also conceivable that the barking was produced by a human and was not canine. I would like to point out to both the good and the bad readers in this connection that not only could Seipe distinguish the barks of each of his six dogs, he could also imitate each one to a T.

I'm writing the night before Georg's death. Six nights passed which terrorized the alley with the howl of a dog who, judging by his moans, was severely wounded, and I lay waiting for the seventh and, as we know, fatal moment in my little . . . Ok, ok, it was a cold night. If I had looked outside I most certainly would have seen the stars falling from the sky. That I did not must have been because I lay tensely waiting for the sound that would come from Georg's apartment. Please excuse the expression but at a *given moment* I heard a sound totally different from the one I had expected to hear: I grabbed my club (a gorgeous, iron-plated model I had already acquired while awaiting your reply) and went outside where to my *utter amazement* I saw how Georg was pummeling his bed with his club, the bed he had dragged out of his apartment. When he noticed me he stopped and I saw his sweating face even though it was as cold then as it is now—now I must rub my hands together for a minute since all feeling has left them and I am only able, therefore, to complete sentences with the greatest difficulty, ending up with anemic constructions such as *given moment* and *utter amazement*.

⌐⌐

THE WORDS I exchanged with him shall certainly be of interest to you. I asked him what he was doing, to which he replied that he was looking for a severely wounded dog, judging by the dog's moans, one he had been tracking down for weeks. "This dog roams through our alley," he said. As to the question of where the dog stayed during the day he could make no answer; that is, his lips did not move and all I could hear was his panting. You will of course understand what I'm going to write (the bad reader won't, but then I don't have to explain everything to him): the look in his eyes said infinitely more than the panting from his mouth or the sweat from his brow. I took his club away from him and led him inside. Then I brought him the remains of his bed and said: "Now get some sleep." Seipe, who lives below Brodky the grocer, must have heard this.

When I got back to bed I heard the terrible howl of the dog for the last time. In all honesty, Gentlemen, I must report that chills ran up and down my spine; at the instant when the howl turned into a kind of gurgling I even (perhaps you'll find this detail of interest) stuck my fingers in my ears. It was clear the dog would never disturb the alley's sleep again.

The next morning I found Georg lying in a pool of blood. His hands were clenched around the club that had smashed in his skull. I had to break his finger to get my club—I had put my club down somewhere in his apartment when I had taken him back to bed and had inadvertently left it there. Gentlemen! Georg was ice cold. The bad reader is informed that his fingers were as cold as mine are now, the only difference being that my hand is now holding a pen while his held a club.

It is cold here, good reader; it has never been this cold before and that is saying a great deal for someone who always pays close attention to weather conditions. It is always too cold or too warm. For me, I hasten to add, since this of course does not have to hold true for others. Georg, for example, paid no mind to the weather, even though it really is no fun trudging around in the snow with a club in your hand tracking the prints of dog paws. I write: no fun, but the trustworthy dogcatcher even when noticing the weather will fulfill his duty come rain or shine. There is no fun for a dogcatcher. The only thing there is for a dogcatcher is the yapping, moaning mutts, the befoulers of our city. It comes as no surprise at all that Georg spent the last week of his life feverishly hunting down the howling dog. It was in his blood. And in my blood, good reader, Good Gentlemen.

Now you can imagine how it is for me to walk around an area of a few square yards and to feel my hands itch. I long for my club, my bludgeon. Our city is what motivates me, Gentlemen, to purge our city of the bastard race of mutts and strays. And so deliver me from this room with the single window high up in the wall and behind which I stand on tiptoe seeing something grey. It is a misunderstanding. Georg struck himself with *my* club which I had left in his apartment. He smashed his skull in with his own hands when he realized the howl of the dog came from his own mouth. He could no longer ignore the fact that it was he who was howling at night. *Georg, the old dogcatcher, smashed in his own skull with another man's club on a cold night when he discovered as he lay in bed that it was he who was making the sounds of a howling dog,* could be the third and likewise final sentence.

Now you know. I am innocent. The cold, to which I am sensitive, is creeping through my bones. My hands have gone numb. I do not blame you, Good Gentlemen, you have nothing to do with this deplorable misunderstanding. I greet you humbly, good reader. Good day. Good day, Gentlemen, Good day, Dear Council, Good day to you all. Good day.

Ur

BY ALCINA LUBITCH DOMECQ

Translated from the Spanish by Ilan Stavans

"In Ur I kept my little secret."

Father never wanted to talk about Ur. Yet he appeared forever lost in it.

In Spanish, he pronounced the word uneasily but with meticulous care: OOh-rrh. Inquisitive as I was, I relentlessly asked myself: Where is the place? And is it really a place? Has anyone else ever lived in it?

At one point, Father evasively described Ur: it was, I was told, a location, *un lugar,* complete with buildings, a hospital, a collective bath, and a huge fence. But he refused to go any further. Instead, he recurred, as always, to silence.

Long, deep, sepulchral silences.

Silence, I dare to say, was his way of communication. Indeed, for years I tried to define, for myself and for no one else, what his silences were about: the absence of words? Not quite . . . Perhaps the interstice between words. Or better: the reverse of words, in the same way that a shadow is not the absence of light but only a different tonality.

Father envied Mother. He talked about her Mixtec ancestry with a mix of admiration and jealously, about the myth of creation among Guatemalans, and about One Deer, also known as Lion Serpent, an omnipotent and wise deity. "For the Mixtecs," he once told me, "the heavens are merciful. Humans are respectful of other humans." He complained of Judaism not offering him the key to endure the pervasiveness of Ur.

Still, he refused to talk about such pervasiveness. His refusal did not imply calmness. Inside his heart Father had a burning fire. I remember him anxious, intolerant, an insomniac.

"Your daughter needs to know," I said to him in my adolescence. "Mother talks to me but you won't. She talks to me about her mestizo background. And about you, about your experience in . . ."

"Ur?" he asked.

"Yes," I responded, "about the land of Ur."

ONE AFTERNOON HE finally opened up.

No, *opened up* is the wrong phrase: he simply forced silences into a corner, domesticated them, and let the tongue loose.

Not too many words, though. In fact, there were only a few. But my imagination, for decades hungry for data, has filled in the blanks. Father talked about a single individual in Ur around whom everyone—and everything—rotated: Das Kommandant. "I was at his mercy, his employee, his servant, his slave. I was a specimen for research. Or better, a *collaborator.*" He uttered the last sentence without hiding his shame. "I helped him spread the terror. I fell into disgrace: people in Ur realized I was his right hand. They hated me. They shouldn't be blamed, though. They loved me once, but their love became venomous." Father had obviously crossed the party line.

Father's family had been separated early on in the war. He was deported to a concentration camp in a railway transport. He lasted over a year as prisoner. Eventually, in winter, he escaped into the forest, where he joined the resistance until the end of the conflict.

I have no more details about his journey. Mother filled me in after Father died of a heart attack, in his mid-sixties. She too knew little else. So I've left it to my imagination to fill in the lacunae—the silences. I've visualized, for myself, his overall odyssey in Ur, and his liaison to Das Kommandant.

The Nazi was a bureaucrat in his thirties. His uniform was invariably neat, his hair always in the right place. He was handsome yet arrogant, wore a mustache, and displayed an infectious sense of humor. Father was selected by him to perform domestic duties: clean floors, cut wood, dust the chimney.

Did they empathize? Was there something between them beyond their relationship as master and servant? In any case, he carried his responsibilities as caretaker dutifully.

Ur was dark, sinister. The sun hardly went out. The air was dry.

Father was the subject of special treatment: he ate better than others, his diet always at the mercy of his provider, was allowed on occasion to sleep in a basement, away from the barracks . . . He pondered the benefits, the special treatment, against the life he had before Das Kommandant paid attention to him. His response was plagued by ambivalence.

He told himself: "At least under his service I might be able to help others by . . ." It was known that his *employer*—is that the right term?—suffered from a terminal disease, which manifested itself first as progressive loss of sight, then as muscular atrophy, and ultimately as a complete form of paralysis. Father might be able to take advantage of his provider's precarious condition to improve on the status of other prisoners.

"In Ur I kept my little secret."

Das Kommandant tried different sorts of medicines, brought to him from Berlin, but none helped. The hospital in Ur was a laboratory wherein Nazi doctors experimented with children. No German ever dared to seek help in it. So my father's provider traveled long distances (to Leipzig and beyond) to receive attention.

Still, his blindness accelerated, and mobility was increasingly reduced.

This, fortunately, made him more and more dependent on Father. "I was his nurse." Every type of service—cooking, laundry, bookkeeping, reading out loud even—was expected of him. The rest of the German officers in the camp were unhappy with the comfortable treatment the Jew received, but their dislike for Das Kommandant, the king of arrogance in an arrogant kingdom, kept them uninvolved in his affairs.

Probably they simply wanted to let him go in peace.

Father felt in control of Ur. He slowly but surely made slight amendments to his caregiver's records when no other Nazi paid attention. This meant his efforts to save others in such a way were nil.

He also replaced pills so as to exacerbate his situation.

Again, no one cared the least.

His anger increased. Other prisoners ridiculed him while, at the same time, fearing his actions. To what extent did he exercise control over Das Kommandant?

Father explained that *his* Nazi was a mere artifact, that his power over prisoners, his capacity to make decisions, was insignificant. But people didn't trust his argument. For them it was a subterfuge.

"In Ur I kept my little secret."

His day of revenge came as the Nazi, alone in his bed, suffered from severe migraine. No medicine seemed to help. Father offered him a home remedy: "A drink from Sighet, my hometown in Romania." Eager to try anything, Father was asked to bring a glass.

He responded that he needed to wait at least a day, perhaps more. There was another prisoner knowledgeable of the recipe that he offered to talk to.

That night, Father returned to the barracks. He peed on a container and supplemented it with a bit of sugar from a sack kept by someone under a rotten pillow.

Next, Das Kommandant drank it. He felt temporary relief.

THE FOLLOWING NIGHT Father repeated his endeavor, and then the next, and the next. . . . For almost a month the Nazi unknowingly drank urine. It was medicine to him, and a collective ritual to the camp prisoners, since Father invited others—those who initially repudiated his association with the enemy—to urinate into the container. Every night somebody else contributed his share, after which a spoonful of sugar was added.

As years went by, his silences became more prolonged. Indeed, his use of words was rare: Father was a ghost, at home and anywhere else. He was around us, among us, but not *with* us. By then he was already gravely ill and had exhausted every possible medical option.

Hope, nonetheless, was still in him, and so he sought alternative cures to his sickness from Mother's side of the family.

Eventually he built an altar in his bedroom and prayed to the Mixtec idols by reciting the Mesoamerican poetry of Humberto Ak'abal. Then he returned to silence. He also inhaled steamed aromatic herbs.

Not too long before his death, he was brought a liquid cure in a greenish bottle. I looked at him. He seemed ready to ask about its contents but stopped himself.

He said to me: "Ah, it comes from the land of Ur . . ." And added: "In Ur there is no place for atonement."

Father drank the liquid without resistance.

Petition

BY MIHÁLY KORNIS

Translated from the Hungarian by Judith Sollosy

To Whom It May Concern,

With reference to your latest query, sent to me before making your final decision concerning my petition (Ref. no. 1909-1970, clerk in charge Mrs. Szalkai), enclosed please find my Claim Form along with a Supplementary Statement.

CLAIM FORM

(Issued in compliance with Official Decree #40, 1957 B.C.)

I. WHAT IS THE NATURE OF YOUR PETITION?

(a) I would like to be born in Budapest, Hungary, on December 9, 1909.

(b) I would like homemaker Regina Fekete for my mother and traveling salesman Miksa Tábori for my father.

(If for any reason my request re. the above-named individuals cannot be granted, I am open to further suggestions, provided my beloved parents will be identical with the people I will call Mother and Father.)

(c) I further request that my wife be the timekeeper Edit Kovács, and my son be the student Pál Tábori (see parenthetical remark under Section I/b, except that in this case the words "Mother" and "Father" should be understood to mean "Wife" and "Son" respectively).

(d) In view of the date on which I request to die (see Section II), I hereby renounce the joys of grandparenthood now and for ever.

II. HOW LONG DO YOU WISH TO LIVE?

61 years, 6 months, 3 days, 2 minutes and 17 seconds.

Please note: I have submitted similar requests to the authorities in the past (see my petitions # 80 B.C., A.D. 1241, 1514, 1526, 1711 and 1849).*

However, due to overcrowding on said dates, my petitions were rejected. This being my seventh petition in this matter, may I respectfully point out that 61 years is not such a long time to live, and if you should decide in my favor, I promise to make the most of it.

III. WHAT ON EARTH FOR?

(a) Because I would like to complete six years of elementary school and four years of secondary school, followed by the School for Commerce. After graduation, I wouldn't mind being a cashier at Haas & Son, then in 1939, with your kind approval, I plan to open a small notions shop in Király, later Mayakovsky utca. In 1940 I would also like to realize a cherished dream, and purchase a two-seater Topolino motorcar.

---

* The dates refer to major turning points in Hungarian history, none of which ended favorably for Hungary.

(When considering my request, kindly take into consideration that with said motorcar I hope to surprise Mother by driving her to the market.) Total time requested for shop, car, foodstuffs, soap, etc.: 3 years.

(b) Following the above, I have in mind a second world war including Nazism, the persecution of the Jews, and a yellow star on my chest. I am also planning to hand my automobile over to the Hungarian Army and my shop to the Department of de-Judaification of the Ministry of Commerce and Industry.

(*Please note:* You need not bother arranging my parents' transport by cattle car to Mauthausen, as I can probably have them stay at the Dohány utca ghetto.) Personally, I wouldn't mind joining a forced labor battalion, slaps in the face and duck walks included, after which I sincerely hope that the liberating Red Army will still find me and my family among the living (see Sections I & II). If you will kindly arrange this, I will immediately set about finding a bride for myself and fathering children, and will even join the Hungarian Communist Party.

(c) Between 1945 and 1948 I will be happy.

Total time requested for new shop, new automobile, foodstuffs, soap, etc.: 3 years.

(d) In 1949 I wish to make my son's acquaintance. I would also like you to kindly deprive me, once and for all, of my car, my shop, and my Party membership.

(e) And while you're at it, kindly expel my wife from the Party, as well. (In view of the fact that my wife will have precious little to do with private enterprise except through me, which might give rise to certain logistical difficulties, permit me to call your attention to a certain Mrs. József Csizmadia, better known as Babi who, I believe, could be persuaded to write an anonymous letter to the authorities informing them that my wife had attended the Vörösmarty utca grammar school, run by a Scottish mission. Furthermore, perhaps she could also point out that my wife maintains what could be construed as close ties with the United States through a certain Rose Kun, i.e., she receives, sends, writes and reads letters, etc.)

(f) As for my son, kindly deny him admission to kindergarten.

(g) I do not wish to participate in the 1956 (counter)revolution. On the contrary, my family and I will go on a hunger strike and eat nothing as a sign of protest against the upheaval. Though I will gladly go on four-hour guard duty shifts in our building every night in the company of one Dr. Aurél Kovács, dental clinic resident, I would nevertheless appreciate it if the above-mentioned Red Army could once again provide so-called friendly assistance to the country.

(h) From that point on, I wish to work first as an assistant buyer then a full-fledged buyer until the day I die.

Comment:

Except for what is specified above, kindly refrain from producing any further historical events of note.

Respectfully yours,
István Tábori

Appendix #1
Supplementary Declaration

Fully aware of my legal and civic responsibilities before the law, I the undersigned hereby solemnly declare that both as a retailer, truck driver, assistant buyer and full-fledged buyer, I will be a useful member of the Kingdom of Hungary, the Hungarian Republic of Councils, truncated post-Trianon Hungary, Greater Hungary, the Apostolic Regency and the Hungarian People's Republic.

I promise to honor and respect the governments of Emperor Francis Joseph I, Count Mihály Károlyi, Béla Kun, Miklós Horthy, Mátyás Rákosi, János Kádár, etc., etc., and to abide by their laws.

I shall stand at attention every time the Austrian, German, Soviet and Hungarian national anthems, as well as the *Gotterhalte, Giovinezza* and *Internationale* are played.

I shall duly respect the Austrian, German, and Soviet national flags, not to mention the red flag; I shall likewise respect the coats-of-arms of our nation, to wit: the apostolic cross, the crown of Saint Stephen; the hammer and sickle, wheatsheafs, etc., etc., etc.

I shall further respect my superiors Ödön and Pál Haas, forced labor brigade commander Vitéz Endre Garzó, Esq., general manager Kálmán Zsérczi, co-operative chairman Kálmán Zsérczi, Jr., etc., and shall obey them at all times. I shall do my duty both at work and outside of work—eating, sleeping, watching over progeny; visiting basements, polling booths and hospitals—to the best of my ability. I will help my wife with housework—washing dishes, vacuuming, wringing out the wash rag—without waiting to be asked.

As long as I live I promise not to importune the authorities with special requests—space travel, starring role in a big movie, freedom of speech; as for my death, I promise to resign myself with or without previous notice, and I shall worship no foreign gods, and shall bear no false witness against my neighbor; nor will I covet my neighbor's wife, his manservant nor his maidservant, nor his cattle, nor his ass, nor any thing else that shall one day be his.

Hoping that the above petition will meet with your kind approval, I am who I will continue to be,

István Tábori

Unus Multorum

BY PETER SINGER

January 14, 1997

A freezing fog hangs over Vienna, softening the light of the street lamps. There is snow on the ground and the bare branches of the trees are tipped with frost. I am walking down Porzellangasse, a broad street in Vienna's Ninth District. It is 7:00 P.M. A few cars are on their way home, but most people prefer not to drive in this weather, the roads are too slick. The street is lined with buildings four or five stories high. They have changed little since the great days, before the First World War, when Vienna was one of the great cities of the world, the capital of the Austro-Hungarian Empire, a European power that ruled over lands spreading east as far as what is now the Ukraine, and south along the Adriatic through present-day Croatia and Bosnia.

All of my grandparents lived in this city then. Of the four of them, I knew only my mother's mother, Amalie Oppenheim. She alone survived the catastrophe that overwhelmed Vienna's Jews. She came to live with my parents in Australia, where I was born just after the war. But tonight I will, in spite of Hitler and the passing of more than half a century since his death, begin to get to know another of my grandparents. In a backpack I am carrying a stack of papers—they must weigh at least five kilos—by and about my mother's father, David Oppenheim, including more than a hundred letters written to my parents and my aunt after they left for Australia in 1938.

This treasure trove of family history I have just collected from Dr. Adolf Gaisbauer, director of the Library of the State Archives of Austria. Last year Gaisbauer published a book called *David Ernst Oppenheim:Von Eurem Treuen Vater David.* The subtitle means "From Your Faithful Father David," and is the way in which my grandfather used to close his letters to his daughters. The book consists of a short biography of Oppenheim, and selections from the letters. I had known for many years of the existence of the letters, which my mother, Cora, and her sister, Doris, had carefully preserved. I had never read them. I can read German, but even people used to reading German handwriting found my grandfather's handwriting difficult. The problem was made worse because the letters were often written on both sides of very thin paper. My mother and Doris had read one or two letters to me, many years ago, but then I was busy writing and teaching about the ethics of our treatment of animals, and about the new revolution in reproduction that had created the first "test-tube babies." I did not ask them to read more.

I learned more about my grandparents ten years ago, when Doris retired from her position as a social worker and wrote a Master of Arts thesis about her father. I read the thesis, and returned it to Doris with a scribbled note:

Doris,
I read this with great interest. Congratulations on making your father live again. Now I'd like one day to read his works myself, to see what parallels (if any) there are with my own views,

despite our rather different fields, and intellectual backgrounds. (The sentence at the bottom of p. 90 especially struck a chord!)

That sentence is a paraphrase of an essay my grandfather wrote on the Roman philosopher Seneca. It reads:

> Oppenheim outlines, by way of example, the difference between the "genuine philosopher"—who aims to integrate teaching and life—and the "theoretical professor" who is concerned only with his professional standing and personal reputation.

Despite that spur, my work in bioethics took priority over delving further into my grandparents' life. So when I read the selected letters in Dr. Gaisbauer's book, I was reading them for the first time. They reached across nearly sixty years, and opened up a world that was at once closely linked with mine, and yet at the same time utterly removed from it. They also gave further glimpses of possible connections with my own work. David Oppenheim wrote about civilization, values, and what it is to be human. My father had been a businessman, and my mother a doctor. Both were educated people, and my father read widely, especially in history, but neither was a scholar, and neither spent a lot of time thinking about the big questions—about understanding human nature, or how we ought to live. Would I, in my grandfather, find someone whose overriding interests were close to mine? Was my own life echoing that of a grandparent I had never known? My career seemed, in some ways, surprising—my cousin once told me that of all the people he had known at university, I was the only one who had followed a path that he could not have predicted. By that he meant, I think, that he had expected me to go into my father's business, or perhaps to practice law. Instead, I had taken up philosophy. Was I following a bent that I had somehow inherited from David Oppenheim? It was a strange thought, but one that I could not let go.

AT THE END of Porzellangasse, I cross Berggasse, just a few doors from where, at No. 19, Freud had his home and his consulting rooms. Seeking traces of my grandfather I had visited the rooms, now a museum, earlier in the day. Here, from 1902 until 1910, the meetings of the "Wednesday Group," later known more formally as the Vienna Psychoanalytical Society, took place. At Freud's invitation, my grandfather became a member of the group in January 1910, and attended its meetings regularly for nearly two years. He presented a paper on suicide among students that the society published, together with comments by Freud and other members of the group, as a pamphlet.* My grandfather did not, however, put his own name to his essay. Instead, perhaps to ensure that an association with the controversial figure of Freud would not impede his career as a teacher, it appears under the pseudonym "Unus multorum," Latin for "one of the multitude." The phrase comes from a passage in Horace that reads:

> *"Today is the thirtieth—the Sabbath, you know.*
> *Do you want to affront the circumcised Jews?"*
> *"I have no religious objections."*
> *"But I have. I'm a somewhat weaker brother—one of the multitude."*†

David also began working with Freud on a manuscript called "Dreams in Folklore." But just as their joint work was nearing completion,

---

Diskussionen des Wiener psychoanalytischen Vereins, I Heft, *Über den Selbstmord insbesondere den Schüler-Selbstmord* (Wiesbaden: Verlag von J. F. Bergmann, 1910).
†Horace, *The Satires,* Book 1, Satire 9, quoted from Kenneth Haynes and Donald Carne-Ross, eds, *Horace in English* (London: Penguin Books).

Freud decided he could no longer tolerate the dissident views of Alfred Adler, until then the most prominent member of the group after Freud himself. He forced Adler out, in a manner that my grandfather found unacceptable, so David Oppenheim went with Adler and his friends, and doubtless Freud never spoke to him again. The manuscript on which they were collaborating, however, remained in my grandfather's possession, somehow survived the war in the custody of a non-Jewish friend in Vienna, and was brought to Australia by my grandmother.

I AM STAYING in a small hotel on the far side of the city from Berggasse. I could take the underground, but I am in the mood for walking. I pass an army barracks, a bizarre nineteenth-century red-brick medieval castle. I come to the Ringstrasse, which follows the lines of the ramparts of old Vienna and still circles the First District, the historical heart of the city. I am retracing a route often taken by Freud, whose daily constitutional walk to, and sometimes right around, the Ringstrasse was so predictable that people wanting to speak to him would wait along the way. But instead of going around the Ringstrasse, I cross it and follow a more direct line through the center of the city, along narrow streets lined with the palaces of noble families of the eighteenth and nineteenth centuries. The shops are closing. I come to Michaelerplatz, one of Vienna's most beautiful small squares. In summer it would be busy with tourists and people trying to sell them things, but in winter it is very quiet. In front of me stands the Hofburg, the great palace of the Habsburg emperors. The street passes under an arch with an inscription saying that Franz Joseph I completed the building begun by his predecessors. I walk through the courtyards of the palace, and emerge in a vast open space, the Heldenplatz, or Heroes' Square. On my left rises the curving wing of the New Hofburg, built in the last flush of imperial grandeur at the beginning of the twentieth century. In the middle of the square are gigantic equestrian statues of two of Austria's military heroes, Prince Eugene of Savoy, who crushed the Turks in 1697, and Archduke Karl, victor, albeit very temporarily, over Napoleon in 1809. The square is snow-covered and empty apart from a couple of civil servants on their way home. In my head is a photograph I have seen, taken in this square in March 1938. It is filled with people, tens of thousands of them, filling the entire square and swarming over the statues to get a better view. It is the week after the *Anschluss,* after German tanks made Austria a part of the Third Reich, and the people have come to cheer Adolf Hitler, who makes a triumphal entry. My parents and grandparents were in Vienna on that day.

On the other side of the Heldenplatz I again cross the Ring, and emerge onto Mariahilferstrasse, a busy street lined with brightly lit department stores, trendy clothes shops, and the inevitable McDonald's. On the street, I am back at the end of the twentieth century, and a long way from the Vienna of Freud or Nazi rule. My hotel, though, takes me back to the past. It is at the end of the department store strip, in an old building with high ceilings. Inside, it is a mixture of periods, with some modern fittings but also many signs of its prewar origins. There is no elevator, and after walking up three flights of stairs, I am glad to get to my room and to take my grandfather's papers off my back.

I SORT THE PAPERS into several stacks. The largest consists of the letters written to my parents and my aunt, some originals, some photocopies, many—thankfully—with transcriptions. I have already read extracts of them in Dr. Gaisbauer's book, and I know roughly what I will find there. I am not in the mood for that now. Almost as large is the stack of published writings—photocopies of sections of my grandfather's book, and of his many published articles. I put them to one side as well, and pick up a document in my grandfather's handwriting. It bears a stamp, like a postage stamp, with the head of the Emperor Franz Joseph I on it. But it has not been posted. It is an official application to the dean of the Philosophical Faculty of the Imperial and Royal University of Vienna for admission to the final examination for the degree of doctor of philosophy, on the basis of work completed. The date is May 4, 1904. David was then twenty-three years old, which would be very young for getting a doctorate today, but then it was the basic university degree, so there was nothing unusual about getting it at that age. I turn the page and find another stamp, a smaller one this time, and the heading "Curriculum vitae." This must have been a requirement for admission to the final exam. In my grandfather's handwriting, small but perfectly legible, he set out, in very formal German and in the third person, his course of studies up to that point:

> David Ernst Oppenheim, born on 20 April 1881 in Brünn in Moravia as the son of Joachim Oppenheim, attended, in the city of his birth, first the five grades of the elementary school, then the First German Imperial and Royal City High School. Here after eight years study he obtained a Certificate of Matriculation with Distinction. He then attended the University in Vienna, with the intention of studying classics in its two principal branches of philology and archeology. In accordance with this plan, over nine semesters he attended lectures on . . .

There followed a list of the lectures and seminars David had attended. The course titles showed that he was using the term "philology" broadly, to refer to the study of literature in its social and historical context, with the aim of understanding and appreciating the learning and culture that it represents.

My grandfather studied Greek and Latin grammar, syntax and style, archeological methods, Homer, Greek philosophers like Plato and Aristotle, the Greek lyric poet Pindar, Cicero's orations and letters, the satires of Juvenal, the elegies of the Latin poet Tibullus, and the histories of Livy and Sallust. To round out his classical education he studied Greek and Roman culture, including the Greek temples, antique art, monuments and dress, mythology, numismatics, the buildings of the Acropolis, Roman cosmology, the Roman Forum, Pompeii, Roman law, and theater productions in Greek and Roman times. Along the way, he found time for occasional seminars on the history of German literature, of philosophy in medieval and modern times, on Nietzsche, on European folk tales, and on high school teaching and reform, as well as taking a basic English course and a course on "Foundations of Psychology."

My grandfather would have been disappointed at my ignorance of the classics. Of the vast body of Greek and Latin literature, my teachers at the University of Melbourne and at Oxford required me to read only Plato's *Republic* and Aristotle's *Nicomachean Ethics*. My interests led me to read also several of Plato's other dialogues, Aristotle's *Politics,* a little of Epicurus, Epictetus, Plutarch, Seneca, some Cicero, and the *Meditations* of Marcus Aurelius. All of this was in translation—I know no Greek or Latin. My knowledge of the content of Juvenal's satires came secondhand, through Robert Graves's much more readable *I, Claudius.* I have never read Pindar, Sallust, or Livy, and until I read my grandfather's curriculum vitae I had never even heard of Tibullus.

I continue to scan through the documents and find one typed in English. Headed "My Scientific Work," it is five pages long and looks like a draft, because it has added handwritten corrections to the English. Even with the corrections, the English is clearly that of a foreigner with a good vocabulary and knowledge of the grammar of the language, but a weak grasp of its nuances and idiom. I know about this document from my aunt's thesis and from Dr. Gaisbauer's book: my grandfather wrote it after the outbreak of the Second World War and sent it to people he knew in America, asking them to circulate it among academic circles there, apparently in the slim hope of improving his prospects of being able to obtain a visa to go there. If the 1904 curriculum vitae portrayed a young man setting out on his life of inquiry, this document, written under much grimmer circumstances, marked its close. Nevertheless the opening sentences confirmed my sense that, despite the differences in our

education and in the fields in which we worked, my grandfather and
I were interested in similar issues:

> As a teacher of the classic languages in a Vienna secondary school
> I was bound by profession to interest my pupils in classic antiq-
> uity. . . . However, in spite of cultivating a field belonging to his-
> tory, it was not the view of an historian that led me to my
> particular work, but rather that of a humanist, in the original
> meaning of the word. For retrospections of ages and peoples
> long past—though I was charmed by them—did not by far seem
> to me so vital as a thorough insight into what hardly ever
> changes, the essence of humanity. For this very reason, I pre-
> ferred to make this knowledge the very aim of my classic pursuits.

To gain this insight into "the essence of humanity," my grandfather
writes, we need "a new psychology"—which, he says, has been
developed by Alfred Adler, the founder of the Society for Individual
Psychology. He then describes how in his book, *Fiction and Knowledge
of Humanity,* he uses Adler's psychology to assist in understanding
characters in literature, and thus to enlarge and deepen our knowledge of our fellow humans, and ultimately, of ourselves.

I PUT DOWN my grandfather's account of his own work, and think
about my own. When I began to study philosophy at university, the
discipline defined itself more narrowly than it had for most of its history. In 1964, "philosophy" did not include anthropology, or history,
or sociology or cross-cultural studies. We studied the ancient Greek
philosophers, but we treated them like contemporaries, with whom
we could debate the nature of goodness, or the ideal constitution of
the state. We knew little or nothing of the culture of ancient Greece.
We focused on questions that are amenable to reason and argument.
Going out to gather facts about the world was not doing philosophy.
I chafed a little under this restricted view of the discipline, for my

underlying interest was always in questions broader than those then considered fitting for academic philosophers. When I eventually decided to write my master's thesis, it was on a very broad question indeed. I asked what reasons could be offered for acting ethically. This led me beyond the bounds of philosophy, as then conceived, to broader psychological questions about human nature, and whether ethics and self-interest are in conflict with each other or are in harmony with each other.

These were questions that David Oppenheim would have been familiar with, for they underlie many of the classical texts that he knew well—Plato's *Republic*, Aristotle's *Ethics,* and Seneca's writings too—and they link up with the theories of psychology that he had discussed with Freud and Adler. But I still don't know what my grandfather thought about these questions. Perhaps the texts in front of me will tell me.

Thinking about my own work makes me ask myself what I am doing in Vienna with my grandfather's papers. For the past thirty years I have been working on issues like the treatment of animals, our obligations of the rich to assist those in danger of starvation or malnutrition, new reproductive technology, and life and death decisions for patients who are terminally ill. Now I am planning to put all that aside to study the life and work of a minor, forgotten scholar who died half a century ago. Why? Because he was my grandfather? Why be so concerned about one's ancestors? What difference does that really make?

One thing that fascinates me about my grandfather's life is the era through which he lived. The Viennese Jewish writer Stefan Zweig, whose life span coincides exactly with that of my grandfather, once wrote:

> Against my will I have witnessed the most terrible defeat of reason and the wildest triumph of brutality in the chronicle of the ages. Never—and I say this without pride, but rather with shame—has any generation experienced such a moral retrogres-

sion from such a spiritual height as our generation has. [*The World of Yesterday*]

My grandfather's life epitomizes this moral retrogression, in which enlightened reason was defeated by visceral emotion and brute force. But my life too is premised on the possibility of reason playing a significant role in the world. Have I failed to learn from his fate, and from the history of the twentieth century? Is it rational to believe that we can all learn from the tragedy of the Holocaust, and avoid its repetition? I have to hope that it is, to act as if it is, because there is really no alternative. It was after all Hermann Goering who, impatient with arguments, said, "I think with my blood." Reason is not everything, but without it we are lost.

Something else drives me toward trying to learn more about my grandfather's life and work, something related to the fact that it wasn't just illness or accident that deprived me of the opportunity to grow up with my grandparents around me. If I am determined to get to know David Oppenheim as well as it is still possible for me to know him, that is because to do so is to undo, in some infinitely small but still quite palpable way, a wrong done by the Holocaust. If I don't do it for my grandfather now, it is unlikely that anyone else will. My children are further removed from that period than I am, and the handful of people still alive now who knew my grandfather will soon not be here to answer questions. My grandfather's thoughts and work will be brought back to life as fully as possible by me, or not at all.

It's getting late. I want to get some sleep, but before I do, I need some fresh air. I go to the window. It is a tall casement window set in a white-painted wooden frame, curved at the top, divided down the middle and held together with a brass handle. I turn the handle and the doors swing toward me, but I have forgotten about the double glazing. There is another window, with a similar handle.

That opens too, and now a blast of cold air hits me. I look out at the deserted streets. These buildings were here when the Nazis came to Vienna. Fifty-five years ago my grandparents were living in an apartment a few kilometers away, dismissed from their employment, forced to take other families into their apartment, made to wear the yellow star whenever they went out, not allowed to use public transport, or even to sit on park benches reserved for "Aryans," learning of friends and relatives being deported to "the East" and not knowing their fate. That is when they wrote the letters I now have in this hotel room. Fifty-five years is less than one lifetime. It scarcely seems possible. Has the world changed so much?

Looking at the streetlights, I can see snow falling gently. In Australian cities, it never snows.

The Gospel According
to My Father

BY DAVID ALBAHARI

Translated from the Serbian by Ellen Elias-Bursac

After interminable autumn flooding, the river receded overnight, leaving behind it a bare, gaping space of muddy shores, and when we—Father, Ruben Rubenovi′c, and I—taking advantage of the first sunny day, went out onto the quay, suddenly Father nearly sobbed, shut his eyes painfully, and leaned with his full weight on my arm. "What have they done," he gasped, "what have they done with the river?" And I could see his knees shaking.

"Let's sit down," said Ruben Rubenović, former textiles sales-man, but Father refused to turn. He took off his glasses and stood there: his feet askew, his head drooping, his shoulders rounded. He rubbed his eyes with his thumb and middle finger, then his forehead, cheeks, lips. "I don't understand," he said, "I really can't understand. Why anyone would want . . ."

"Let's sit down," repeated Ruben Rubenović and took Father under the arm.

"I don't understand," said Father, turning to me. "You are always down here, you're always coming. What have they done with all that water?"

"I don't know," I said.

"Come on," said Ruben Rubenović and touched Father's shoulder, "sit down."

Father relaxed, went limp, his eyes filled with tears, his eyeglasses slid between his fingers. "Who did this," he glared nearsightedly into Ruben Rubenović's face, "who did this?"

"What's with you?" asked the former textiles salesman.

"What's with nature?" replied Father.

"Yes," said Ruben Rubenović, "what's with nature?"

Behind us, in the immediate vicinity, workers had descended on a half-demolished factory hall. You could hear the blows of mallets and the crash of falling girders.

"What is that?" Father spun around. "Who's making that racket?"

"They are demolishing the chocolate factory," I said.

"Maybe it was them," Father clutched my knee, "maybe it was them who did this to the river . . . Why don't you go? Ask them! Maybe they've diverted the flow . . ."

Ruben Rubenović picked up Father's glasses: "What's with you?" he asked. "What are you talking about?"

"About the river," Father shouted. "What have they done to the river?"

"With the river?" said Ruben Rubenović and looked around. The river had withdrawn, hidden in itself, suddenly laying bare the silty expanses of both shores. Forgotten boats wallowed on their sides, and poking out from among the larger and smaller rocks were branches, broken bottles, faded newspapers, cans. In the afternoon haze across the quay was the figure of a lone man out walking, a man with a hat and a small dog. Clouds were piling up over Belgrade, but above us shone the miserly winter sun. "The river is fine," Ruben Rubenović answered Father's question. "But you tell me what's with you."

Father wiped away the tears, took his glasses from the former textiles salesman, and peered through them around him: a man who has unexpectedly found himself in a strange place. "I don't know," he said. "Sometimes I sit like that with the little woman. I say nothing and I think about how everything is changing. I listen to the harsh blows of diggers, carpenters," he pointed behind his back, "and I think: don't worry, it's good, progress is happening, man is trying to get somewhere . . . But in the morning, when I leave for work, I stand still for a long time outside our front door, I don't know where I am, where I'm headed . . . I'd just as soon go back in . . ."

"That will pass," said Ruben Rubenović.

"My life will pass," said Father.

"What did you expect?"

Father said nothing.

On the other shore, among the underbrush, a car appeared. There was shouting and a dog barking, then the chuckle of a woman. Next to us, a little short-haired dog stopped and pricked up its ears.

"Come, Arnold," said the man with the hat, and we turned. "Lovely day." He smiled at us.

"It is nice," said Ruben Rubenović.

"The sun," said the man, "eh?" The dog sniffed our feet; he growled at my father. "Come, Arnold!" shouted the man with the hat and whistled. Father shooed the dog away; it backed up a few steps and barked loudly. Barking resounded from the other shore.

"Nothing can help with that," said the former textiles salesman and gently smoothed my father's hand. "You're hoping in vain."

"I am not hoping," said Father. "What is there to place my hopes in?"

"I was wondering that myself," said Ruben Rubenović.

"In him?" said Father and glances at me.

"For one."

"And what else?"

"Your wife. Your daughter."

"And you?" said Father. "You have no one. What do you place your hopes in?"

Ruben Rubenović gestures unspecifically, but in the general direction of the skies. "In nothing." And then he added, at once: "In everything."

"In God?" I asked.

Ruben Rubenović studied the skies, the river; he pondered: "Maybe."

"Huh," said Father.

We sat there, quiet. Behind the island appeared a barge moving lugubriously, then tugboats lined up. People bustled around on deck, bells rang, whistles and sharp curses were heard.

"Isn't the water level a little low?" asked Father.

"They know," I said. "They have markers, lines, lanterns, everything they need."

"At night they navigate, too?"

"Yes," I confirmed.

"Courage," said my father.

"Yes."

"I hear," coughed Ruben Rubenović, "that you have been inquiring, of late, about Jesus. Is that correct?"

"Who told you that?"

"So it is correct."

"Who told you that?" I repeated.

"I heard," said the former textiles merchant. "It doesn't matter where."

"Do they take their wives with them?" asked my father.

"Who? Where?"

"The bargemen," said Father. "On their trips, when they navigate."

"It's time you started doubting," said Ruben Rubenović without looking at me, "but watch that your conscience doesn't get to you. Doubting won't hurt."

"Why would my conscience get to me?" I said. "History has proven . . ."

"If I hate something," said my father, "it's history."

"You are right," said Ruben Rubenović. "Until the time when it will be up to historians to establish some truth."

"Artificial," said Father.

"Precisely," agreed the former textiles salesman, "artificial, yes. Until such a time history means nothing. In the best case, it becomes a weapon, but a weapon . . ."

"History speaks for itself alone," I said.

"Like time," said my father.

"History *is* time."

"But time cannot be recorded."

"Why do you believe in it then?" Ruben Rubenović asked me.

I said nothing.

"Do your doubting without textbooks, follow the spirit."

"It seems to me that's the way he is doubting," Father said.

"How would you know?"

"I read what he writes. He gives it to me sometimes."

"Then don't talk about it," frowned Ruben Rubenović. "Doubt! How do you doubt!"

I shrugged.

"Would you rather become a Christian?"

Father looked at me.

"Well," I said.

"Yes or no?"

"Depends," I said, "on the situation."

"You're on the fence," said Father.

"You used to criticize the Spanish Marranos," Ruben Rubenović reminded me, "and now you are suggesting that, depending on the situation, you might change your faith? How come?"

"I am not much of a believer," I said.

"The soul, my son, the soul."

The man with the hat and the little dog walked back by us, and we stopped talking. The dog sniffed our feet again, and again, disgruntled by something, it barked at Father. "Arnold, come," called the man.

"Going home so soon?" asked Ruben Rubenović.

"Well," said the man, "plenty for now. A little stroll before dinner."

"Yes, indeed."

"Good-bye," said my father.

We stopped talking again, faced with the river. We didn't turn, but it seemed as if the clouds had caught up with the sun: it was getting gloomier and cooler, a chilly breeze began blowing. Behind us, the racket continued with unabated ferocity: the echoes of blows alternated with the dull thud of falling debris. The air smelled like dust.

"Those are hellish jobs," said Father. "Barges, explosives, forests, no family, forever on the move—I cannot imagine how those people survive!"

"Eh," said Ruben Rubenović and turned around. "Should we be getting back?"

"I'd rather not," I said.

"We'll stay," said Father. "After all, we don't even take the same ways back."

Ruben Rubenović got up; he started buttoning up his old winter coat. "By the waters of the Danube," he said, "we sat and we wept, but what was it we remembered?" And then he left, without a word in parting, thumping his cane dully around him.

"Will you be stopping by this afternoon?" Father called after him, but he didn't answer. "What's wrong with him?"

"Most likely he longs," I said, "to hear the harps."

"Is that from some psalm?"

"Yes."

"Are you being nasty?"

We exchanged glances.

"He threw you with that question about the Marranos," said Father. "Admit it."

"What can I say?"

Father sighed, stood up, pushed his hands into the pockets of his coat.

"You've been different recently," he said. He didn't look at me.

"I don't know," I said, "I really don't know."

"What do you think about when Mother lights the candles on the Sabbath?"

"What about you?"

"I pray."

"Me, too," I said.

Father took several steps, strode down the concrete stairs. "Someone has ruined this river," he said, "but I just don't know who." He kept going down, without turning, and rapidly disappeared below the edge of the sidewalk. A little later I caught sight of him as he was gingerly skirting the shallow puddles and slimy mud, approaching the water's edge. It occurred to me that I should warn him: after all, his age, his obvious clumsiness, and the riverbed so slippery! But he kept moving along, persistently, avoiding obstacles, and when I thought he'd already gotten his shoes, feet, and pants soaked, he began to walk upon the water. The river shivered under the weight, waves rippled the surface; Father spread out his hands like a tightrope walker and then proceeded more surely, more and more confident in his own sense of balance. In vain, horrified, I closed my eyes. He advanced over the agitated surface, serene, firm, going further and further, his face to the wind, through the storm, the sleet, until he got across to the other shore and collapsed, utterly exhausted, on the dirty surface of sand. And there he sat, leaning on his elbows, panting, but still, from time to time, he found the strength to wave to me and call in an unexpectedly clear voice.

"Cross over," he called. "Cross over already! Come on, cross the river!"

"The Protagonist Introduced"
from *The Imaginary Jew*

BY ALAIN FINKIELKRAUT

Translated from the French by Kevin O'Neill and David Suchoff

If I were to write my autobiography, I would call it "The Story of an Adjective." —Isaac Babel

The typical scene of humiliation is the courtyard of a parish or grammar school. In the background there sounds the continuous and confusing din of children shrieking, running, and jostling one another in order to release, in the few minutes allotted to recess, energies pent up during those all-too-long hours of class. Some, alone or still, wait silently to return to their room. Others talk excitedly. A boisterous group has made a soccer ball from knotted rags. As usual, two trees in the courtyard mark one goal while directly opposite several book bags heaped into two piles mark the other. Five against five, with an alternating goalie: the match begins under the watch of few but feverish fans. Because of the school schedule, the game must be played in bits and pieces—continued at the next break, it will be finished at lunch. The boys are charged up and unsparing. They are, as they say on television, physically into the game. And since there is no referee, every close call provokes end-

less bickering between the two teams. The match is constantly interrupted until, inevitably, the point is reached when the disputes turn
into a fight. Two players, enraged, threaten and insult one another.
With his store of slurs exhausted, one of them shouts: "Go to hell,
you dirty Jew!"

The other, dumbstruck, at first looks about in search of help.
Naturally he expects general indignation. But no one seems to react
to the force of the remark. As if this were only one insult among others—an outrageous epithet, to be sure, but hardly more so than the
"asshole" or "scum" the two opponents have already hurled at one
another during the game. Eyes welling with tears, the "dirty Jew"
confronts his classmate, whom, despite his indignation, he has not
yet had time to hate. He attacks with his fists but the blows are
weak, a response to the claims of conscience. A crowd of kids has
formed, egging on the fight, chanting, "Blood! Blood!" But the scuffle is cut short. The name-caller wants to get back to the game, for
soon the bell will sound, and the victim is so hard pressed to turn his
embarrassment into vengeance that he gives up the fight and quits
the match, secretly hoping that the others will call him back. But the
gesture has no effect. His departure is met with indifference,
regarded as whim or momentary sulking. And the game goes on.

Alone in his corner, the dazed child contemplates his wound. No
longer an equal among equals, he has been given the plainest proof
that he is a member of a despised tribe. Jew. His entire life and more
will not tame the violence of this revelation.

Of course the term isn't entirely unknown to him: he attended a
Bar Mitzvah a year before, which, incidentally, bored him to death,
and his parents have already told him of anti-Semitism and its history
of persecutions. His familiarity with the word *Jew* before the incident was vague—less, far less than a full-fledged identity, and, if
anything, just the purely negative impression of being neither
Catholic nor Protestant. Nothing, finally, that might prepare him for
the worst, that is to say, for exclusion. Now, suddenly, in the guise of
today's banal altercation, this child like any other has been informed

that he is not like others; for the first time he feels within himself the raging impotence of the pariah. For the first time he is excluded from the common circle because he is Jewish, disdained by peers and provided by them with a self-image that is both disgusting and bizarre. He is isolated, cut off, unable to find in his bodily features or inner being the cause of this banishment. The insult is an act of baptism: the persuasion of which he is still unsure has become his truth and his name. He was nothing but a succession of moods before, or perhaps he was defined by his class ranking—but on this day he is bestowed with an eternal identity that he can neither reject nor recast.

The match has started up again, the circle has closed without him, he is exiled from the world by an injustice that he is powerless to oppose. But of course the ostracism will not last. After the several days of solitude demanded by his sense of honor, he will return to the circle. The gang will welcome him as if nothing has happened, once again he will know glory as one of the great dribblers, and if his team ever wins, savor the sweet pleasures of communion. But the damage has been done to his innocence and cannot be repaired; one does not forget such an event. In the midst of the idyll, of such moments of bonding, he will have the uneasy feeling that a new expulsion is at hand. I am Jewish: this consciousness of a hidden uniqueness, of an invisible and ineffaceable difference will condition each move that he makes. Later, perhaps, he will choose to "pass," and invest all the skill at his disposal in blatantly dissimulating his identity to flee the Semitic malaise. Perhaps he will transform this cutting term—Jew—into an intransigent, determined, harsh word, one of self-affirmation and defiance. Perhaps he will search the treasure of Jewish wisdom for something to turn the infamous reproach that has been affixed to him, one day at recess, into a mark of value and worth. Whatever his future decisions might be, he will never recover from this trauma.

But you already know this episode. A multitude of writers have recited it to you in innumerable versions. It is the uplifting story of pathos in which a child is snatched from innocence and born into Judaism, the story of an injury, or better, a curse. I myself would like to address and meditate upon the opposite case: the case of a child, an adolescent who is not only proud but happy to be Jewish and who came to question, bit by bit, if there were not some bad faith in living jubilantly as an exception and an exile. Certainly a coming to moral consciousness is at work here as well, but a slow, imperceptible one far from the theatrical kind. The adventure I speak of cannot be grasped in narrative: it was a drama without a fateful event, without a discernible rupture between before and after. It was a lengthy awakening that never took the form of a fall or a "rebirth." No mythic moment can capture the progressive malaise that taught me to give up my cozy domicile in the Jewish condition.

This is not to say that I have been miraculously preserved from anti-Semitism. I too have my collection of outrages, which I still exhibit on special occasions. Untouched by time, in the back of my mind are all sorts of insults I've managed to receive—from the catechism student, dripping with a bit too much zeal, who wanted to drag me to church in order to restore me to the straight and narrow, and perhaps, who knows, to receive congratulations from the chaplain for this superb feat of conversion, to a friend on vacation, a nice guy, cool and all that, who at a turn in the conversation remarked with peremptory calmness that six million Jews killed during the war had not been enough . . . Like any Jewish child I have known the straightforward racism of camp or gym classes. It was not in books that I first encountered the word *kike,* and yet it would call for either complacency or blindness on my part to have my story begin with the tragedy of a schoolboy, surrounded by proof of his sameness, suddenly finding himself completely different. Convinced, on the contrary, that fate had made me a completely different individual, unconsciously I realized that I was almost the same, and that *I did not deserve* the sense of historical preeminence that had inebriated my adolescence. The paradise from which I have been expelled is not one of concord, harmony and homogeneity but a region inaccessible to common mortals, an aristocratic Eden where dissidence held pride of place and which only outlaws and rebels might enter.

Think of it then: the Judaism I had received was the most beautiful present a post-genocidal child could imagine. I inherited a suffering to which I had not been subjected, for without having to endure oppression, the identity of the victim was mine. I could savor an exceptional destiny while remaining completely at ease. Without exposure to real danger, I had heroic stature: to be Jewish was enough to escape the anonymity of an identity indistinguishable from others and the dullness of an uneventful life. I was not immune to depression, of course, but I possessed a considerable advantage over the other children of my generation: the power to dramatize my biography. Only in an illusory sense were we cast together into the same misty and monotonous stretch of time; between their mediocrity and mine was an uncrossable barrier. They knew the torpor of untroubled waters; the tranquility I lived was always contradicted from within by the inherent precariousness of my condition. Judaism for me was a way of redeeming the quotidian. My life insignificant? The banality of my gestures was but an illusion: a docile student, a homebody, but within I was a nomad, a wandering Jew. A yellow-bellied petit bourgeois, in my dreams I was ready to strike back in violence against the fury of the pogroms. I projected the more profound truth of exile onto my sedentary existence; in every moment of peaceful times I sensed the coming thunder of the apocalypse. In short, I was safe, but I had a remedy for the anguish that arises from excessive security: I was Jewish. The calvary of my people gave my life a prestige and a beauty that I would have been unable to discover in its own unfolding. I resolved to search my origins for the memorable stories I was denied by the uninterrupted flow of the wise and studious existence I led.

No more than the next person was I spared the metaphysical assaults of the question, "Who am I?" Psychologically indecisive, lacking any clearly distinguishing personal traits, a pronounced tendency to imitate, with multiple and contradictory role models, none of which had enough authority to ensure it would prevail, prey to a constant worry of being nothing—I was well aware of the self-indulgent torments of a sheltered life. But at the moment of greatest crisis, when conscious certainty of my identity hung in the balance, I mobilized this magical fact: I am a Jew, that is, interesting, mysterious, unique; I have a history and countenance molded by twenty centuries of suffering. I can easily, when feeling low, curse my absence of personality, my inconsistencies and my hesitations— there is in me a deeper truth than that of character. Jew: in the worst moments of doubt this simple word kept me afloat. I was singled out, individualized: I escaped the vertiginous feeling of a dissolving self.

Me against them, faced off against Others. This is the romance and narrative in which I have spent the greater part of my life. Raised by indefeasible decree above the crowd and common destiny, set apart from peers without their becoming aware, I was the outsider, skinned alive, the survivor, and I couldn't savor the image enough.

Let those unfortunate members of the overwhelming majority, let those pathetic, average people, learn the ways of revolt. Me, I had been born recalcitrant. Just as they say of the son of a good family that he is well-born—not a blue blood but red-blooded—I had a rebellious pedigree. Without effort I was freed from the charge of prejudice, since for society I was its scandalous emblem. I was, if I might put it this way, offered a dispensation from every stupidity, exempted from any conformity by a privilege called Judaism. With it understood once and for all that the world was divided into torturers and victims, I belonged to the camp of the oppressed. I had no need of consciousness raising or of a dose of reality: from Spartacus to Black Power, an instinctive and unconditional solidarity united me with all the earth's damned. Was I not myself the living reproach that suffering humanity aimed at its executioners? From Judaism I drew neither religion nor a way of life, but the certainty of superior sensitivity.

Since I was an admirer of Sartre at the time, with what glut-
tonous pleasure did I avail myself of the vocabulary he bestowed
upon my existence. This inspired philosopher, without hesitation I
put him at my service and made him my tailor, and the outfit he created for me was luxurious, a true mantle of enlightenment . . . His
language carried my sense of conviction all the better, transforming
my complacent sense of well-being into courage and confidence.
With unimpeachable rigor he told me that I was an *authentic* Jew,
that I *assumed* my condition and that courage, even heroism were
required for me to claim so loudly and so strongly my ties to a people in disgrace. The preferred terms of Sartre literally intoxicated
me: in their sublime style I read an inscription of my life, and my
pronouncements of fidelity appeared to me as so many noble deeds.
Who could have resisted such a subtly persuasive form of flattery?
The enchantment of Sartre's prose filled the gap between what I
imagined myself to be and the existence I actually led. I was a nice
Jewish boy, indulging myself in nomadic fantasies and a revolt without risk, subject to none of their malaise. Sartre gave me a way to
feel worthwhile, whispered to me words of self-celebration. Without having earned it, I assumed possession of an extraordinary history and had the right to find it difficult to boot! Under the spell of
my own image, I immersed myself in a dream to which *Reflections on
the Jewish Question* gave the harsh and virile cast of reality: the authority on authenticity served as a caution to my blusters, the master at
puncturing ploys of bad faith offered, for a good while, validation of
my most infatuated and histrionic airs. The expert had given his verdict: my megalomania proved itself well founded, for my gestures
were in fact actions and my acting-out a form of commitment.

It's true, from as far back as I can remember, Jewishness has never
been a bother or a burden for me. It was not with lowered voice or
frightened or fearful murmur that I used to confess my origins.
Where others made discreet mention of their ancestry (vaguely, as if
it were an obscure fault, a biological blemish or social handicap), I
would broadcast my own, I was its herald. Some in my circle mar-

veled at such nerve. Instead of cowering like a cornered cat, following what they believed to be an age-old rabbinic reflex, I did an about-face and provoked the enemy. Big deal! Such a hero! Has there ever been a gentleman who blushed in shame at his coat of arms? How could I ever be embarrassed again by this Judaism, an honor, to my mind, a thousand times more worthy than a title of nobility? I was much too proud of my genealogy to think for a minute of hiding it. What was taken for my valor was, when all is said and done, simply the result of my immodesty.

Except for my parents and two or three uncles and aunts, I have no family. And it was by miracle alone that these few close relatives survived the general massacre of Polish Jews. I lived (and still live) surrounded by the vanished, whose disappearance increased my worth without managing to make me suffer. The interminable list of all these dead I've never known created my nobility. No doubt, when my parents recounted their nightmare journey through five years of war, and related what had become of their group, I was more than moved. I would cry in anguish and in anger. But I did so in vain, for the sorrow born of their story vanished with it, just as we forget the plot once the book is closed. The terror left no traces. Beyond the representation made me, its existence could not be sustained. It slipped with all its baggage into the nothingness that had gone before. In short, despite my efforts, I didn't carry the burden of mourning my exterminated family, but I did carry its banner. I, too, would recount family stories of the final solution, and my interlocutor, seized by a mixture of stupefaction, shame and respect, would see in me something other than myself: the faces of those tortured to death. Medusa-like, I petrified my public. Others had suffered and I, because I was their descendant, harvested all the moral advantage. The allotment was inescapable: for them, utter abandonment and anonymous death, and for their spokesperson, sympathy and honor. Since the actors had been annihilated, it was left to their narrator, their heir, their offspring to appropriate the reaction of their audience. At the end of the play, he alone came front-stage to bow before the applause. The effect produced wasn't intentional. I did not deliberately turn the catastrophe to the shallow ends of self-aggrandizement. I did not set out like a cynical and sordid swindler to embezzle what they possessed. But it isn't only intention that matters: while I was quite capable of assuming a sober tone and forcing myself to disappear into the story, in fact I showed off, amazed the gallery, commanded the admiration of the spectators. A part of myself had perished in Auschwitz, in a Polish forest or in the Lwów ghetto; I owed to the bond of blood this intoxicating power to confuse myself with the martyrs.

Lineage made me genocide's huckster, its witness and practically its victim. Before telling the story of my origins, I was simply an individual; afterward, there appeared an unheard-of character like someone miraculously healed, or a ghost. With this sort of investiture, any other title seemed wretched or ridiculous to me. Hence my remarkable lack of complexes. Most children, they say, like to invent an illustrious birth. They devote their secret dreams to changing parentage, to imagining an adventurous or princely family background for themselves. What need had I of such mythologies? What great lord, what bohemian artist could rival my ancestry? No more hyperbolic world existed than the one into which I had been born. My narcissism found its sustenance on the spot, and the fiction of my family romance always unfolded at the heart of my own family.

Thus, there was no virtue in my ostentation: I forged a tragic spectacle from the tragedy of my people, and I was its hero. In short, I played at being persecuted, and did so in the mode of pantomime or the purely ceremonious gesture that I carried off without actually compromising myself. I was a swashbuckler of the concentration camps—but why accuse myself? My date of birth alone explains this propensity to bombast. I was born too close to the Holocaust to be able to keep it from view, and at the same time I was protected by all the horror of this event from a renewal of anti-Semitism, at least in its organized and violent form. In a sense, I was *overjoyed*: the war's proximity at once magnified and preserved me; it invited me to identify with the victims while giving me the all but certain assurance that I would never be one. I had all the profit but none of the risk. I could, knowing my immunity, revolt against torture and racism. History—in irony or generosity—had made me a superfluous rebel in a peaceful era. Expatriate de luxe, a deportee for the fun of it, I lived in the security of anachronism.

Does this mean that anti-Semitism is an outmoded relic, best relegated to the museum of horror and superstitions between the fear of witches, the practice of magic and devil worship? Nothing permits such optimism. And above all not what one calls the lessons of experience. Each time, in history, that anti-Jewish violence has seen a lull, we have wanted to read this fleeting break as an ineluctable decline. Finally, we'd sigh, the world was leaving the Middle Ages behind. Each time, we were mistaken. It would require a heavy dose of ignorance or presumption to certify, on the basis of today's relative tranquility, that our epoch is any different.

The future of the Jews cannot be foreseen. In this matter only provisional truths are justified. Our contemporary truth is that the Jews are rather popular in Western Europe, and that they owe this rehabilitation in large part to the barbarism of the Nazis and its trauma. If there had not been death camps, Judeophobic prejudice would remain not only widespread (as it perhaps still is) but offensive and blatant. Let us imagine that in 1939, a fit of German conscience had driven Hitler from power and reestablished democracy. The insult "dirty kike" would still be part of our daily experience. It is only taboo now because forty years ago it was carried out to the letter by the regime of the Reich. The very goal of Hitlerism was, in effect, destruction of the barrier traditionally raised between hate speech and the murderous act. The classic slogans of anti-Semitism have been so effectively transformed into reality that they have lost, in a single stroke, all ritualistic or symbolic force. Today one can no longer say, "Death to the Jews," because this death has taken place. The waning of rhetorical anti-Semitism follows active measures of political anti-Semitism. Silence becomes the norm, because it is no longer possible to fashion a release or a verbal exorcism out of an effective program of annihilation. The call for murder, which, during the Dreyfus affair, was made without reference to any specific situation and constituted an end in itself, has in the meantime been burdened with history and is no longer anything but an advocacy of Auschwitz. The artistic haziness of unanchored words is over; the convenient distinction of words from acts doesn't hold in this domain; anti-Semitic opinion can scarcely be dissociated from the image of charnelhouses. This is what discourages, understandably, many anti-Jewish candidates for office (though not all, and it's this minority that perseveres in hatred that is truly unbelievable). In any case, as long as genocide survives in European memory, only a small number of people will devote themselves to this activity so common before the war: the suppression of the Jews in word or dream.

Thus I lived in a veritable cocoon. Nothing to fear, my two bodyguards warded off problems and prevented unpleasant surprises: history, kind enough to exempt me from its convulsions, and my mother, seized by a devouring and protective passion for me, dedicated body and soul to my personal bliss, as if she wanted to make amends, at every moment, for the initial risk to which she had exposed me by giving birth to a Jewish child. Tradition and psychology work together here: whether one is a Jew, in our time, is more than ever determined by the mother. She's the one who overfeeds us because she has known privation and who idolizes us because she was orphaned. One does not recover from such adoration. Egocentric and infantile, the children of a "Jewish Mother" are easily recognizable. These members of the brotherhood of Portnoys could not pass unnoticed even if they wished. As adults, they have the vulnerability and the look of children who've been loved too much. What there is of the Jew in them is not, as they would like to believe, the wisdom of wandering and the sorrow of persecution, but the impotence of an overgrown baby who is pampered, adorned, cuddled and powdered until old age. Identifying characteristic: mama.

These cherubic, overnourished, potbellied men fancy themselves to be Isrolik, little Tom Thumb of the Ghetto, the waif of the streets. They mask their inborn softness with the outcast's courage. But the bravado is false. For these mama's boys, Jewish history is a lullaby, the song that peoples their sleep with heroic dreams and permits them vicarious experience of the horror. Cowards in life, martyred in dream—they love historical self-deception, confusing the sheltered world in which they live with the cataclysm their parents endured. Among Jews they constitute a strange but widespread category, one that has not yet found a name. They are not religious, at least most of them; in vain they cherish Jewish culture, possessing only its sorry relics. They have not performed their apprenticeship to Judaism under the gaze of the Other. Neither ethnic nor denominational definition nor the Sartrian scheme could suit them. They are unwavering Jews, but armchair Jews, since, after the Catastrophe, Judaism cannot offer them any content but suffering, and they themselves do not suffer. In order to deny this contradiction, they have chosen to pass their time in a novelistic space full of sound and fury that offers them the best role. Like fanatics of the printed word who flee, by reading, the provincial boredom in which they languish, like spectators who project their desires, their frustrations into a panting plot they will never live—spellbound, these young people live in borrowed identities. They have taken up residence in fiction. The Judaism they invoke enraptures and transports them magically to a setting in which they are exalted and sanctified. For these habitués of unreality, more numerous than one might suppose, I propose the name "imaginary Jews."

The Library of Moloch

BY MELVIN JULES BUKIET

Three hundred faces stared, blinked, squinted, and otherwise engaged the camera while recounting the most awful moments of the century.

"Smoke, that is the first thing I remember, that and the body of my little sister."

"Yes, they hung the village elders by their beards."

"Oh, the experiments. I had forgotten. Of course, the experiments. What was it you wanted to know? What was it *they* wanted to know?"

The library was a four-room suite of offices in the base of a gothic dormitory in which aspiring lawyers lived, ignorant of the stories that the folks with branded arms told underneath them.

One room of the suite contained a receptionist's desk, a couch, and coffee table where academic journals gathered dust. The second room was a dustless repository of videotape disks set upon rows of sleek metal shelving, along with two monitors for viewing them. Never had both monitors been used at the same time, but the initial grants to establish the library were generous.

Then there was the director's office, and the testimony room where they actually produced the videotapes. This room had the air of a dental chamber where the patient reclined in a large padded chair, the videotape machine directed at the face like an X-ray tube, aiming to penetrate the skin to the soul. There was always a cool young technician fiddling with the dials on an imposing black console with blinking red lights and fluctuating meters. These interns from the university's School of Communication Arts were more interested in the quality of sound reproduction than the meanings of the sounds reproduced. Attending the meaning, however, was a doctor, whose gentle probing elicited the words, although here it was a doctor of letters who conducted the procedure. Delicate as he was, there was also the occasional wince and cry of pain.

Other libraries have taken lesser tasks upon themselves, to contain and construe the physical properties of nature or the intellectual produce of man. The Library of Moloch sought no less than a moral explication of the universe.

Fortunately, it had excellent source material. All that remains from the Crusades, for example, are a few moldy documents. Likewise, the other episodes of vast and imponderable iniquity, the Reign of Terror or the Conquest of Mexico, have faded from human memory, and hence perished in all but legend. There may be articles about Tamerlane or Gilles de Rais in the yellowing journals on the coffee table, but their ravages no longer have the pulse of life. The contemporary library has one invaluable resource that researchers into the more distant past do not, the victims. That was its avowed purpose, to find the victims of Moloch, to record them, to preserve their suffering, to remit immortality in return for the chronicle of their woe.

They had three hundred faces on file, nearly a thousand hours, tens of thousands of deaths described in ferocious detail. The library was a mausoleum; its librarians gravediggers. As for the individuals whose lives and memories were condensed onto half-inch tape, wound onto spools, stacked onto shelves—the hell with them.

～

DR. ARTHUR RICARDO, English born, American bred, headed the project. He was a highly civilized gentleman, with many diverse interests. He enjoyed chamber music, Oriental rugs, and nineteenth-century economic theory. The latter was a family hobby, because he was a nonlineal descendant of David Ricardo, the eminent mercantile essayist and apostate. In addition to his rarified pursuits, Dr. Ricardo was an avid moviegoer who regaled his intellectual friends with tawdry tales of Hollywood excess. How he found his life's calling in the Library of Moloch is a tale in itself. His specialty was medieval literature, but he realized that his students were more interested in iron maidens and autos-da-fé than they were the quest for the grail. Only if the grail was hidden within an iron maiden had they any chance of finding it.

At the moment when he was wrestling with his charges' gruesome misreadings of Ariosto, there was a scandal at his institution, the academy that housed the library. An elderly professor who was respected by all in his field (thermodynamics) was determined to have been a wartime collaborator. Nobody accused him of any personal wrongdoing, but he had signed a loyalty oath and he withheld knowledge of this when he sought to enter America. Clearly the man needed to be punished. Equally clearly, he had lived an honorable life since his youthful indiscretions. He was, in fact, a leader of the physicians for nuclear responsibility movement. Ricardo's sympathies were with the professor, but a squat little man appeared unbidden at the provost's inquiry. He demanded to be heard. "I worked at the mountain," he said, meaning the underground silos where the rockets the venerable professor had designed fifty years ago were produced, where scientists labored in isolation while slaves died to prove the learned men's theories.

Ricardo was not present when the man spoke, but a video recording of the speech circulated, at first covertly and then, by mass demand, at public screenings. The tape exerted a bizarre fascination. The professor was hounded into retirement.

"Imagine," Ricardo said to his class, "what we could do with the personal testimonies of the prisoners of the Inquisition, what that would tell us about the nature of faith in that era."

But one student said, "Can't we extrapolate backward from this witness? Does human nature change?"

At first, Ricardo wanted to dismiss the query. The first tenet of his life was progress, implying the perfectability of man. But the question bothered him. He had to admit that if human nature did change, it most certainly did so for the worse to just the degree that his generation's atrocities superseded those of the Middle Ages. Compared to the artifacts of the twentieth century, iron maidens were couture and racks no more than chiropractic devices. The stories of that one man who "worked at the mountain" were sufficient proof.

And there were many more stories. The man who gave evidence was the tip of the iceberg. There were others who worked the mines and others who stoked the fires. Who knew how many of these refugees from the land of brimstone were walking the streets, and each time one clutched his heart and collapsed to the pavement another storehouse of history died with him. Ricardo spoke to the videotaper, and together they conceived of the library. The university was eager to balance the scales of public opinion that had been tipped by the scandal. A board of prestigious names lined up to support the project. Grants were expedited, space allocated. Funding flowed.

Ricardo placed advertisements in ethnic newspapers, and contacted organizations that aided survivors. They tended to stick together. It was difficult to overcome their distrust of strangers at first, but their very cohesiveness made further testimonies easier. One by one, the men and women who lived through the war came to him. And he listened.

"Fire, a column of fire into the sky. It was night. The column must have been a hundred feet high. Maybe two hundred. I don't know. I'm no Galileo."

"Food, the lack of food. Hunger so great we would eat anything, grass, poison ivy, we would suck the juices from pieces of wormy wood. And you know what, Junior's cheesecake never tasted so good."

"The diseases, the scabs, the sores. We used to urinate on our wounds to anesthetize them. No, that's the wrong word. Anesthesia is what you do to the brain. My nephew's an anesthesiologist in Boston. Antibiotic? Antihistamine? Anti-something."

The more he heard, the more Ricardo needed. He grew insatiable. As the killers were driven to kill more and more, he wished to hear more and more of those they had been unable to kill. There were fifty thousand some of them, many more if one included those who hid in the woods, escaped eastward, or merely toiled away the war years in the brutal and often deadly labor camps scattered throughout the continent. Oh, he would tape them too, but it was the fifty thousand who had inhabited the capitols of death that he hunted, begged, cajoled, and, if necessary, bribed into telling their stories. He was like a collector who must attain not merely one of each species, but each and every one of the particular species he collects. To miss just one would mean an elemental loss.

"We arrived, and these men were beating us as soon as we arrived. With bayonets or gun barrels, screaming, *Heraus! Heraus!* That means 'Move quickly!' There were dogs, tearing at people, and everyone was filing past this desk and most everyone was going to the left except for a few big guys who were going to the right. So I shouted, 'Healthy. Twenty. Carpenter,' and I started to the right. I was puny, sixteen, and a student, but I started to the right, and a soldier knocked me down. I got up, and started that way again, and he knocked me down again. Well, I got up and started that way again, and the soldier started after me when the officer in charge said, 'Let him be. He'll die anyway.'" The man looked into the camera and snorted, "Hah!"

It was interesting, despite their experience they were optimistic. Or was it because of their past that they were optimists, because they were able to conquer adversity, because ultimately they had triumphed. They had homes now, and businesses and children, and were able to follow the course of their lives like ordinary human beings, yet those who listened to them were devastated and came to believe in the inevitable doom of a species capable of such enormity.

Dr. Ricardo in particular suffered since his work at the library commenced. Yet the more he suffered, the greater his passion for his self-appointed mission. He ignored his students as he expanded his collection. One hundred, two hundred, three hundred tapes on the wall, a thousand hours of horror, and he knew them all by heart. His wife was eager to have children, but he would not breed. The tapes were his children.

Ricardo's eyes widened at the stories of misery, at the rivers of blood which ran from the tongues of the witnesses, at the mountains of ashes heaped up beneath the videotape camera, mountains to obscure the eye of the camera, to bury the Library of Moloch.

MOST WITNESSES TOLD their stories voluntarily. These stories were equivalent to their souls yet they were willing to donate them to the Library of Moloch because they believed that to tell was to verify a past that had become dreamlike even to themselves. And after all, they were people of the book. Of course, the form was strange, but they had faith that this "tape" was a newfangled kind of a book, and they were willing to move with the times.

Yet some were suspicious. They had been convinced to go to the library by their children or coaxed by Dr. Ricardo, who had obtained their home phone numbers.

One old lady arrived wearing a large rhinestone brooch on a highly textured brocade dress. Her hair was cut short in a golden helmet. She could have been a dentist's receptionist, or a dentist's mother. When the tape started to roll, and Ricardo began by asking her to tell him "a little about yourself," she said, "Pardon me, but why do you wish to know?"

"Isn't that self-explanatory?"

"I never did understand the obvious. It usually hurt too much."

Ricardo was taken aback; he was forced to define the library's purpose. "To prevent such a thing from ever happening again."

"Ah, so you believe that my warning will keep armies from crossing borders, railroads from chugging down the tracks, fires from burning. I was not aware that I had such power."

"Well, not just your warning."

"Everybody's. Mine and Max Adelstein's and Dora Schwartz's. Poor Dora. What a responsibility. And her with pleurisy."

"Well, don't you think it is important"—and he called up a phrase from the survivors' own organizations, a deliberate redundancy that struck them as biblical in its admonition—"to remember. Never to forget."

"Ah," she nodded understandingly. "Never to forget, you say. To remember, you say. Did you ever think that we might prefer to forget?"

"But as a survivor, you have an obligation to—"

"You know, I never liked the word 'survivor,' it suggests too much personal ability. There was no ability. There was luck. We are not survivors, but merely remainders, or the remains. And you are jackals, feasting on the last tasty flesh that sticks to our bones. Tell me, is it good?"

"That is terribly unfair. I am sympathetic."

"Leeches. Vampires. You cannot get more blood from our loved ones, so you're sinking your teeth into us. I do not think you are unsympathetic. I think you are jealous, Herr Doktor Professor."

Ricardo said, "I wish you would not call me that," his clipped words emphasizing the last of the British accent he had shed as a child.

"And what charmed world do you inhabit where wishes are granted, Herr Doktor Professor?"

"Enough! I will not be insulted. If you insist, we will stop this session."

"Oh, so you will judge the validity of my story on whether I have the proper respect for you, Herr Doktor Professor?" The tiny lady squirmed delicately in her comfortable chair, her grandmother's eyes gleaming as she removed her glasses and rubbed them on her sleeve.

Ricardo surrendered. "You are right. We cannot judge. We are not here to judge."

The old lady made a gesture, a hand floating horizontally across an empty channel. It was the rod of the shepherd who winnows his flock by determining which pass beneath it and which do not. In the Yom Kippur prayer, the U-nisaneh Tokef, that image is a symbol of God's judgment for the upcoming year, who shall live and who shall die. It was also used as a deliberate parody in the land of evil, only instead of a gnarled shepherd's rod, a sleek leather riding crop was used, and the little ones, too little to reach that glistening leather while standing on their toes so as to make their topmost curls quiver, never had the chance to be whipped with it. Their slaughter was immediate.

"So, what occurred after you were deported?"

She answered this and the other questions he posed with brisk efficiency. But then, after she described the American soldier who "liberated" the eighty pounds that were left of her, she said, "And where were you during the war, Herr Dok—"

"I was young."

"So was I," she said. "I was young and in love and in Europe."

"Bala Cynwyd."

"What?"

"It's a suburb of Philadelphia."

"A suburb? Of Philadelphia?" Her voice was so skeptically inflected that she might as well have said, "A cathedral? In Vatican City?"

He bowed his head. "They call it the Main Line."

"How nice."

Her tone angered him. "It was. It was very nice. And I feel fortunate, but I do not feel ashamed. All right?"

"Fine by me." She lifted both her palms.

He said, "I don't have a gun."

"You don't need one. You have a camera."

"And what is that supposed to mean?"

"Nothing. Ignore me."

He wished he could. He had gotten what he wanted, another tape on the shelf, another cache of horror. The interview was over, but he could not leave it alone. "Jealous of what? Jealous of suffering? Jealous of death?" He tried to imitate the scornful laugh of one of his previous subjects. "Hah."

For the first time, Ricardo entered onto the record as more than an interlocutor from behind the camera, and the operator looked at the old lady as if for instruction or authorization to swivel the camera to view the professor's distress. She merely gazed into the lens with complete equanimity. Then she said, "There are two separate, inviolate realms. One is memory."

Ricardo answered as if in a trance, "And the other?"

She didn't answer, and it drove the doctor crazy. What was it that she wasn't telling him? What was it that none of them had told him? What was missing from his library? He mentally reviewed the names on the shelves. They were arranged alphabetically although they were also cross-categorized by age, sex, the nature of the torture endured, and the kind of response—from sorrow to anger to hatred to mystical contemplativeness. Yet something was missing.

And then it struck him. What bound and limited the library was that all of its subjects were victims. Where were their victimizers?

Amidst all of the workings of the man-made Hades, its transportation and extermination systems, recounted in detail for the librarians who spurred the informants to unearth even the tiniest additional tidbit concerning the kingdom of darkness, there was plenty about, but nothing from the lords of the infernal regions.

Of course, there was the legitimate desire to deny these men or their female counterparts credence. We do not want to hear their stories; we may find out how similar to ourselves they are. Besides which, the evildoers were hardly forthcoming. Though they pursued their crimes with vigor and pleasure, they were nonetheless aware that their actions were heinous. One arch villain even said that theirs was an episode which would remain hidden. But he was wrong. The library was intent on proving that. Maybe society had failed the victims. And politicians had failed them. The clergy had failed them. But the librarians would not.

Dr. Ricardo was sure that his register of martyrs hallowed them, and that his recordings of their lives saved them. Unfortunately, the beneficiary of his largesse was not convinced. The old lady not only refused to recognize his charity, she dared to question his role. "Watch out," she said. "There is only one sentence for those who tamper with forbidden mysteries."

"Do not threaten me."

"That's not a threat. It's a prophecy."

"Well, like it or not, we are in the archival era. This library does not exist in order to examine experience. Here experience exists in order to be examined."

The old lady stood as he ranted, and tottered away on the heels that brought her height to five feet shy, but the man who held the technological rod that measured her value in the new world did not notice.

❧

WHEN HE WAS finished, Dr. Ricardo was alone with his roomful of gray cylinders. The camera was off, and the lady was gone. He sat in her chair, still warm, and stared at the empty lens of the videotape machine. Looking down, he noticed that the arm of the chair had been scratched clear through to the stuffing, a mixture of straw and compressed fibers. Obviously one of the interviewees had been so tormented, his or her fingernails punctured the supple leather surface.

The library had money enough to repair the damage or replace the chair. But Dr. Ricardo was curious whose memories evoked such a reaction. He supposed he would never know. The cameras focused on the subjects' faces while he focused on the words.

He reached into his breast pocket and removed the pack of cigarettes he had purchased earlier in the day. He had smoked for years, stopped for years, and recommenced when he started his series of interviews.

"The fences were electrified. This was a blessing. One could always kill oneself when the pain grew too tremendous. Many people availed themselves of the facility."

Dr. Ricardo lit a cigarette and inhaled. The very process was soporific. So he fell asleep, and twisted in the soft contours of the chair, his head filled with images of his parents' home in Bala Cynwyd, outside of Philadelphia, ringed with barbed wire, on fire. Ashes from his cigarette dropped to the exposed stuffing.

Soon Dr. Ricardo wore a crown of flames, yet still he slept.

The flames spread. They rode across the seam of the carpeting on the floor and caught at the papers on his desk.

The fire passed into the storage room, and climbed the shelves. There the cylinders buckled under the heat, and they popped open, the tapes writhing like snakes in a burning cave, and the words of the witnesses escaped, and the pictures created by their words escaped. The guard towers, the barbed wire, the fires blackening the sky, escaped into the air along with the smoke.

Throughout the dormitory, the young law students woke with shrieks of terror. Their dreams were tainted; their beds turned to pyres. They staggered outside in their pajamas, clutching their seared case books.

Finally, Dr. Ricardo also woke, coughing up burned gray phlegm, sputtering. His precious tapes, the wall of evil that he wished to preserve, was being consumed before his eyes. He tamped out what he could, but he could not extinguish the blaze.

The librarian might have been able to save himself, but there was one more question he had yet to ask. He grabbed at the last tape on the shelf, the one that served as a bookend because the secretary had not had time to file it. His fingers blistered from the touch, but he jammed the cassette into the monitor whose cord was a glowing copper filament. Nevertheless, the machine worked.

The lady appeared on television against a background of flames. "Pardon me," she said, "but why do you wish to know?"

He punched the device's fast-forward mechanism. There was a blur, and when he lifted his finger, the lady seemed to smile as she said, "I do not think you are unsympathetic. I think you are jealous, Herr Dok—"

He hit the button again, and left his finger there for what seemed like an eternity. He lifted it to see her silence and hear his own voice from off-screen, "Jealous of what? Jealous of suffering? Jealous of death?" But where he expected to hear himself give a last, resounding, "Hah!" there was only continued silence. The machine may have been damaged by the flames, which rose up the curtains. He could hear sirens.

Suddenly the lady answered, "Yes, jealous."

In his delirium, he wondered if fire was the fate of all libraries. First there was the Library of Alexandria with the wisdom of the ancient world, and now, the Library of Moloch containing what its keeper truly believed was the wisdom of the modern world. Perhaps, he thought crazily amid the mounting flames, this fate was not inappropriate, for Moloch was the fire god to whom children were routinely sacrificed. Moloch, the Lord of Gehenna, lived outside of Jerusalem in what was truly the valley of the damned, forever exiled in sight of the heavenly city.

He started to answer the flickering screen, but she would not allow him an opening.

"Jealous of having a reason to hate. Jealous of tragedy, because your life is no Charleston. Jealous of a people who refuse to submit to the impurities that surround them. Jealous of those who adhere to a broken covenant. Jealous of the sacred. So here you have it, Herr Doktor, so enjoy!"

"I do not understand."

"My poor professor. You know, the killers never understood us either. 'How,' they asked themselves, 'can these people meet our eyes? How can they persevere no matter the punishment we inflict?' Mind you, they were sophisticated; they knew that it was not merely the scourging of the body of the community, but the anguish of being compelled to acknowledge that animals like them shared the same cruel flesh we did, breathed the same vile air. But that was the part that made it easy. We knew we were looking at God."

"How could you tell?"

"Because God is made in the image of man. We met Him a long time ago, in Spain and Rome and Egypt, and more genteel spots. We saw Him in a topcoat and derby ducking into Whitehall. And we saw Him in Washington, too. The truth is, He is everywhere, but only we can recognize Him, because we are old friends. We know His story."

"Can . . ."

"Of course I can introduce Him to you. And now, my good fellow, prepare to meet your maker, for those who enter the Holy of Holies are condemned to burn. I told you. I told you, there are two inviolate realms."

That was it, that was what he had turned the videotape on in order to hear. That was the lesson for which he risked his own immolation in order to learn. "What are they?" he screamed at the tape, as the flames kissed his feet, and cracked his knees that were as immovable as if they were lashed to a stake.

Although the screen itself had begun to melt with the intensity of the heat, the image was calm. "I told you. One is memory."

"And the other—the other, please! The other!"

The lady answered, "Theology."

Contributors' Notes

LEA AINI was born in 1962 in Tel Aviv. She worked as an editor for a daily newspaper for four years, until 1991. Since then, she has published four novels, including *Sand Tide, Someone Must Be Here,* and *Ashtoret;* two collections of stories, *Summer Heroes* and *Oleanders;* two poetry books for adults; and several books for children. She has received the Prime Minister's Prize for Literature and other awards.

DAVID ALBAHARI (1948), a writer and translator from Yugoslavia, has published seven collections of short stories and seven novels in Serbian. His book *Opis smrti* (Description of Death) won the Ivo Andric Award for the best collection of short stories in Yugoslavia in 1982, and his novel *Mamac* (Bait), won the NIN Award for the best novel in Yugoslavia in 1996. His books have been translated into fourteen languages. A selection of his stories, *Words Are Something Else,* was published in 1996 by Northwestern University Press. The same publisher also published the novels *Tsing* (1997) and *Bait* (2001). David Albahari has translated many stories and novels by contemporary British, American, and Australian authors including S. Bellow, I. B. Singer, T. Pynchon, V. S. Naipaul, and V. Nabokov. He was a participant in the International Writing Program in Iowa (1986) and International Writer-in-Residence at the University of Calgary, under the auspices of Markin-Flanagan Distinguished Writers Program (1994–95). He lives in Calgary, Canada.

TAMMIE BOB writes fiction and nonfiction and has published in *TriQuarterly, New Writers, The Chicago Tribune Magazine,* and the now defunct *DuPage Magazine.* "The Fate of Great Love" is the fourth published "Ruthie" story. "A novel seems to be emerging from this material," writes Tamme Bob, "which often feels like a thickly tangled cocoon, its embryonic moth slug- gish and hesitant to bite its way through. I return to the stories because I've become attached to Ruthie as she navigates separate planets: her insecure, cynical survivor family, and the insular culture of American suburban childhood."

LILY BRETT was born in Germany and moved to Melbourne with her parents in 1948. Her first book, *The Auschwitz Poems,* won the 1987 Victorian Premier's Award for poetry, and both her fiction and poetry have won other major prizes, including the 1995 NSW Premier's Award for fiction for *Just Like That.* Lily Brett is married to the Australian painter David Rankin. They live in New York.

MELVIN JULES BUKIET's most recent novels are *After, Signs and Wonders,* and *Strange Fire.* He teaches at Sarah Lawrence College and lives in New York City.

LEON DE WINTER was born in 1954 in Den Bosch in Dutch Brabant. In addition to writing ten novels and four collections of short stories (many of which have been translated into many languages), he has directed and produced numerous feature films and documentaries. In 1995, he received the prestigious Dutch National Book Gift. He is a political columnist for the *Algemeen Dagblad* and lives in Bloemendaal with his wife and two children.

ESTHER DISCHEREIT was born in 1952 in Germany. She studied in Frankfurt and was trained as a teacher, though she also worked in the metal industry and later became a typesetter. Poet, novelist, essayist, children's book author, and stage and radio dramatist, her works include *Joemi's Table, Merryn,When My Golem Opened the Door, Lessons in Being Jewish,* and *With Eichmann on the Bourse.* She was a fellow at the Moses Mendelssohn Center for European and Jewish Studies and has lectured widely in the United States. She has won stipends from the Hessian Ministry for Science and Art, the Stiftung Preussiche Seehandlung in Berlin, and the Berlin Senate. In the 1990s she founded the Word/Music Group.

ALICINA LUBITCH DOMECQ, born in Guatemala in 1953, is the author of the novel *El espejo en el espejo: o, la noble sonisa del perro* (The Mirror's Mirror: or, The Noble Smile of the Dog, 1983) and the collection of stories *Intoxicada* (Intoxicated, 1984). Her minimalist work has been influenced by Borges and Calvino. Her stories have been widely anthologized in Europe, Latin America, the United States, and Israel.

BARBARA FINKELSTEIN is the author of *Summer-Long-a-Coming,* a novel (Harper and Row, 1987), and "Return to Poland," an essay to be published in *Lost on the Map of the World,* Phillipa Kafka, editor (Peter Lang, 2001).

ALAIN FINKIELKRAUT is one of the most prominent of the new genertion of French intellectuals. He is the author of *The Undoing of Thought, The Imaginary Jew, The Defeat of the Mind, The Future of a Negation, The Wisdom of Love,* and *Remembering in Vain: The Klaus Barbie Trial and Crimes against Humanity,* among other books. He has edited the journal *Le Messager Europeen* and written frequently for *Le Monde, Liberation,* and other publications.

CARL FRIEDMAN was born in 1952. She is the author of *Nightfather, The Shovel and the Loom,* and *The Gray Lover.* Ms. Friedman lives in Amsterdam and is working on a new collection of short stories.

EVA HOFFMAN is the author of *Lost in Translation, Exit into History: A Journey through the New Eastern Europe,* and *Shtetl.* Born in Cracow, Poland, she lived in Canada and the United States for many years and now resides in London.

HELENA JANECZEK was born in 1964 in Munich to Polish-Jewish parents. She moved to Italy in 1983. Her published works include a collection of poetry in German (*Ins Freie,* Frankfurt: Suhrkamp, 1989) and her debut as a narrator in Italian, *Lezioni di tenebra* (Milano: Mondadori, 1997), winner of several prizes (Premio Bagutta Opera Prima, Premio Berto) and translated into German (not by her). Her new novel, also in Italian, is due to be published next year. She lives with her husband and son in the outskirts of Milan.

ANNE KARPF is a columnist and writer. She has been a contributing editor to *Cosmopolitan,* a lecturer in medical sociology, and she reviews books for the *London Times.* She is currently writing her third book.

ALAN KAUFMAN is the award-winning editor of the anthologies *The Outlaw Bible of American Poetry* (Thunder's Mouth Press) and *The New Generation: Fiction for Our Time from American's Writing Programs* (Anchor/Doubleday). Author of the poetry collection *Who Are We?,* he has performed widely as a spoken-word poet. He is the founder and editor of the controversial magazine *DAVKA: Jewish Cultural Revolution* and the Web zine www. tattoojew.com. *Jew Boy,* a memoir, first appeared in the United States in September 2000, published by Fromm International, and has since been published in the United Kingdom by Constable and Robinson. The American paperback edition is due to be released in Fall 2001 by Foxrock, the publishing imprint of Barney Rosset.

MIHÁLY KORNIS, born in 1949 in Budapest, is one of Hungary's best-selling playwrights and novelists. His first short story appeared in 1976 in the literary journal *Kortárs.* In 1975 he became involved with the democratic opposition, and in 1977 published *Napló* (Dairy), the first samisdat publication in Hungary. His play *Hallelujah* (1979), produced in 1981, turned him into a cult figure. His collections of short stories, *Alive at Last!* (Végre élsz!, 1980, uncensored version, 1992), from which this story is taken, and *In Praise of Fear* (A félelem dícsérete, 1989) were followed by *Daybook* (Napkönyv, 1994), which has been translated into several European languages to great acclaim. Mr. Kornis is presently working on the next volume of his *Napkönyv* trilogy. His works have also appeared in various prestigious journals and anthologies, including *Transit, Lower East Side Review,* and *Common Knowledge.*

Savyon Liebrecht was born in Germany in 1948 and immigrated to Israel as an infant. The author of three collections of short stories, *Apples from the Desert, Horses on the Highway,* and *It's All Greek to You, She Said to Him,* all published by Keter, her work has been translated into several languages. She writes television scripts and some of her stories have been adapted for television. She received the Prime Minister's Prize for Literature.

Gila Lustiger was born in Frankfurt, Germany, in 1963 and educated at Hebrew University in Jerusalem. Since 1987 she has lived in Paris with her husband, the French poet Emmanuel Moses, and their two children. She is the author of *The Inventory.*

Sonia Pilcer's latest work, *The Holocaust Kid* (Persea Books), is a collection of autobiographical stories. She has published four other books: *Teen Angel, Maiden Rites, Little Darlings,* and *I-LAND: Manhattan in Monologue,* which she adapted as a theatrical play. It had productions in Los Angeles, and ran for six years Off-Broadway. Her journalism and essays have appeared in *Forward, 7 Days, Village Voice, Los Angeles Times,* and elsewhere. Pilcer teaches at the Writers Voice and Berkshire Community College. She lives in Hillsdale, New York, with her husband and son.

Doron Rabinovici was born in 1961 in Tel Aviv and has lived in Vienna since 1964. He writes fiction, essays, and history. His books include *Authorities of Powerlessness: The Path to the Judenrat, 1938–1945, Austria* (essays), *Papirnik* (stories), and *The Search for M* (a novel). His works have won multiple awards, including the Ingeborg Bachmann Prize, the Ernst Robert Curtius Prize, and the Prize of the City of Vienna. He is the founder of the Friends of Peace Now in Austria. Since 1986, he has been an executive member of the Republican club New Austria.

Henri Raczymov was born in 1948 in Paris to a Jewish-Polish family. He is the prize-winning author of numerous novels as well as works of nonfiction including the essay "Memory Shot Through with Holes," published in *Yale French Studies.* His essay "Proust's Swan" is forthcoming from Northwestern University Press. He is married and has one daughter.

VICTORIA REDEL is the author of three books, *Loverboy, Where the Road Bottoms Out,* and *Already the World.* Her novel *Loverboy* won the S. Mariella Gable Award, was selected as a Borders Original Voice book, and was a featured selection from Quality Paperback Books. *Already the World* won the Tom and Stan Wick prize. Redel has been a recipient of fellowships from the National Endowment of the Arts and the Fine Arts Work Center. She has taught fiction and poetry at Sarah Lawrence College, Columbia University, and Vermont College.

THANE ROSENBAUM is the author of *The Golems of Gotham, Second Hand Smoke,* and *Elijah Visible,* which received the Edward Lewis Wallant Book Award in 1996 for the best book of Jewish-American fiction. His articles, reviews, and essays appear frequently in *The New York Times, Los Angeles Times,* and *The Wall Street Journal.* He is the literary editor of *Tikkun.* He teaches human rights and law and literature at Fordham Law School, where he also directs the program in Morality, Humanities and the Law for the Stein Center for Law and Ethics.

GÖRAN ROSENBERG is a well-known Swedish writer and journalist, born in 1948 to Polish-Jewish survivors of the Holocaust. Among his books are *Friare kan ingen vara,* an essay on the American idea (Norstedts, 1991); and *Det förlorade landet,* a personal history of Israel (Bonniers, 1996), also in Norwegian, Danish, Dutch, and German (*Das verlorene Land,* Suhrkamp Verlag, 1998), and forthcoming in French (*Denoël*). His essays have been translated and published in, among others, *Neue Zürcher Zeitung, Lettre Internationale, Daedalus,* and *New Perspectives Quarterly.* His latest book is *Tankar om journalistik* (Reflections on Journalism, Prisma, 2000).

RUTH KNAFO SETTON's first novel, *The Road to Fez,* was published by Counterpoint Press in 2001. Born in Morocco and raised in the United States, she is the recipient of literary fellowships from the NEA, PEN, Pennsylvania Council on the Arts, Sewanee Writers' Conference, Great River Arts Institute, Wesleyan Writers Conference, and Yaddo. Her fiction, poetry, and creative nonfiction have appeared in many journals and anthologies, including *Tikkun, Lilith, Another Chicago Magazine, The Jewish Quarterly, With Signs and Wonders: An International Anthology of Jewish Fabulist*

Fiction, and *Sephardic-American Voices: Two Hundred Years of a Literary Legacy.* She is the Writer-in-Residence for the Berman Center for Jewish Studies and the English Department at Lehigh University, and is presently working on a new novel, as well as a collection of poetry and tales.

PETER SINGER is Ira W. DeCamp Professor of Bioethics at Princeton University. His books include *Animal Liberation, Practical Ethics, Rethinking Life and Death,* and *Writing as an Ethical Life.*

JOSEPH SKIBELL, author of the novel *A Blessing on the Moon,* was born "inexplicaby" in Lubbock, Texas, in 1959. His stories have appeared in several literary journals, including *Story* magazine, and many of his plays have been produced nationally. He has received numerous literary honors, including a Helene Wurlitzer Foundation grant, a New Mexico Creative Arts Division/NEA grant, the Joel Climenhaga Creative Writing Award, James Michener Fellowships, and the Jay C. and Ruth Hall Fellowship in Fiction. He currently teaches creative writing at the University of Wisconsin and lives in Madison with his wife, Barbara, and their daughter, Arianna.

ART SPIEGELMAN is the author of *Maus, A Survivor's Tale,* for which he received a special Pulitzer Prize in 1992. He was cofounder and editor of *Raw,* the acclaimed magazine of avant-garde comics, and is currently a staff artist for *The New Yorker.* He lives in New York City with his wife, Francoise Mouly, and their two children, Madja and Dashiell.

J. J. STEINFELD lives in Charlottetown, Prince Edward Island, Canada, where he writes full time. He has published a novel, *Our Hero in the Cradle of Confederation,* and five short story collections. His writing has appeared in numerous magazines and anthologies.

VAL VINOKUROV is a writer, translator, and scholar of comparative literature living in New York City. His work on Patrick Chamoiseau's novel *Texaco* was awarded the American Translators Association Lewis Galatière Prize for Best Book in 1998. He is Director of the Undergraduate Program in Religious Studies at the New School.

Credits